TWENTIETH-CENTURY CZECHOSLOVAKIA

Josef Korbel

TWENTIETH-CENTURY

CZECHOSLOVAKIA

The Meanings of Its History

Columbia University Press - New York

Library of Congress Cataloging in Publication Data

Korbel, Josef.
  Twentieth-century Czechoslovakia.

  Bibliography: p.
  Includes index.
  1. Czechoslovak Republic—History.   I. Title.
DB215.K588   943.7'03   76-54250
ISBN 0-231-03724-4

Columbia University Press
New York   Guildford, Surrey
Copyright © 1977 Columbia University Press
All rights reserved
Printed in the United States of America
c 10 9 8 7 6 5 4 3 2

To
Mandula
and
Madeleine and Joe, Kathy and
Gene, and John and Pamela

Preface

In 1968, the world watched with wonder and disbelief developments in Czechoslovakia where many people, among them the top leadership of the Communist Party, were engaged in the fascinating experiment of transforming a rigid Communist rule into a "socialism with a human face." The experiment will go down in history as the "Czechoslovak Spring." History will also note, however, its consequences in the "winter" that followed: the Soviet invasion of the country and the capitulation of the architects of the Spring to brutal force.

The two experiences—of forging a concept of democratic socialism and of submission to outside intervention—were not new in Czechoslovak history. They only intensified my search for the answer to a question that has haunted me for many years: what can explain the puzzling phenomenon, so conspicuous in the nation's history, of a unique zeal for social advancement coupled with an equally unique record of defeat and failure?

In the modern history of Czechoslovakia, two themes appear which are, at first glance, mutually exclusive. One is the continuing quest, under ever-changing political and social circumstances, for personal freedom and social justice. This is the Czechoslovakia of the humane ideal. The other is one of recurring abdication, indeed, on occasion, renunciation, if not of these same values, then certainly of the commitment to defend them at any price. The result is a checkered history, with great progress followed by dismal retrogression. How does one reconcile in one people the bright efforts of 1918–38, of 1945–48, and of a few months in 1968, with the dark reversals of 1938–45, of 1948–68, and again, the dreariness since the death of "The Spring?"

Were there within the people themselves conflicting political and social forces working at cross-purposes, at one moment moving the nation toward remarkable achievements, at another drawing it to the brink of a moral abyss? Or was it the leadership, which at one time paved the people's way to progress, and at another, failed to inspire them to its defense? Or do the causes of this ambivalence lie in the nation's deep philosophical roots? In the words of André Sigfried, no nation can "disassociate itself from its past." Is it possible to trace Czechoslovakia's contemporary behavior to her traditions, both positive and negative?

If certain national attitudes do, indeed, reflect persistent philosophical beliefs, are these molded by intellectual leadership or, conversely, do national leaders merely interpret and refine the voice of the people? This is an excruciating question, and its mental and intellectual torment is only intensified by analogical experiences in the nation's centuries-old history. Every nation passes over high peaks and through deep valleys on its road through history. Each faces many tests of its basic ethical and national fiber; each must examine, in changing times, its ultimate purpose; each must seek, in moments of supreme national or international crisis, the guidance of its history and its philosophical conscience. It is a nation's response to that sense of its historical values, the firmness of its purpose to persist, that determines whether in any given moment it will move one way or another. It is the response of the Czechs and Slovaks to such moments that is the subject of this study.

The conceptual treatment of *Twentieth-Century Czechoslovakia* is historical only to the extent to which the nation's history is related to the principal theme of the study (hence, such topics as the Carpathian Ukraine, for example, or the country's foreign policy, are not treated here in separate chapters; similarly, since I have synthesized much material in the text, and to preserve an uninterrupted narrative, footnotes are reduced to a minimum). Needless to say, one does not approach the effort to follow and analyze the theme without trepidation and humility, nor without full awareness of its controversial nature. To borrow from Ernest Denis, however, I attempted to respond and write "neither without love nor without anger," for, as Karl Marx put it, "Truth is not without passion and passion is not without truth."

Acknowledgments

I am grateful to several institutions and individuals for their assistance in the preparation of this manuscript.

The U.S. Office of Education, Department of Health, Education and Welfare (under the authority of Title VI, Section 602, NDEA) and the American Council of Learned Societies extended to me a generous financial assistance. Robert C. Good, former dean of the Graduate School of International Studies and now president of Denison University, facilitated the work by a favorable arrangement of my teaching assignments. Dr. Paul Horecky, Anita Navon, and Eva Polach of the Library of Congress, and Richard F. Staar, Milorad M. Drachkovitch, Wayne S. Vucinich, Ronald Bulatoff, and the librarians at the Hoover Institution gave me most valuable help.

My former students, John West, Enrico David, and Louis Ortmayer, as well as Vera Henzl, contributed as research assistants, and Shirley Taylor, while typing the first draft, improved my English and style.

The manuscript was read in full by Madeleine Albright, Julius Firt, and Jiri Valenta, and in part by Irene Bolen, Radomir Luza, and George Barany.

My warmest thanks go to my editor for this manuscript (and

four other of my books), R. Russell Porter, who not only worked with his usual professional flair, but also identified with the theme with unusual understanding and affection. Agnes B. McKirdy, editor, Columbia University Press, did meticulous work on the final text.

Needless to say, none of these institutions or individuals bear any responsibility for the content of the book.

J.K.

Denver, August 1976

Contents

TWENTIETH-
CENTURY
CZECHOSLOVAKIA

A Prologue

On October 28, 1918, as all Europe was in the bloody grasp of the last phases of a war that was to be called a world revolution, a group of men called on the Austrian governor in Prague. Their purpose was to inquire, as the illustrious journalist Ferdinand Peroutka later put it, "if perhaps, by chance, a revolution was not permitted." The governor, alas, had no instructions. In the absence of such guidance, he was politely advised by these "men of the 28th of October," as they were later to be known, that the Prague National Council was assuming authority and would conduct itself lawfully and avoid violence. Avoid violence it did. That evening, even as the Czechoslovak Republic was being proclaimed, the socialist leader, František Soukup, called not for revolution, but for "music in the streets."

The events that followed this bizarre moment in the state's birth were equally cautious, equally civilized, equally puzzling, equally examplary of what we will come to see as a characteristic of Czechoslovak behavior. As the Republic was announced, the Austrian military commander was asked to withdraw his soldiers from the streets. The general obliged, and an agreement was signed by the National Council and the Prague military command to maintain law and order. When, for a moment, the situation threatened to develop into a clash between the Austrian troops and the hastily recruited groups of Czechoslovak volunteers, two leading Austrian generals were promptly shipped out of the country, and the Austrian command "capitulated" before the National Council.

To "preserve the dignity" of the day, the National Council appealed to the people to avoid violence and shun any act that would tarnish the nation's name. "Everyone must, without reservation, respect everything that is sacred to any other person. Personal freedom and private property must not be touched," the Council's statement read. The popular daily, *Národní Politika*, exhorted its readers not to dishonor "these solemn moments" by even the least misconduct or the smallest flaw, sure that the "educated, cultured nation of high moral standards" [1] would respond to the events with the "dignity that ennobles and beautifies." And dignity was preserved, as Czechs and Slovaks expressed their enthusiasm over the newly won independence in mass gatherings, in the singing of patriotic songs, and in the planting of lindens of freedom.

After all the Austrian gendarmes in Bohemia had been concentrated in Prague, its officers asked their commander in chief for instructions in case of demonstrations; his order read, "Stay off the streets." In Brno, the second-largest city in the country, when the local National Council called on the Austrian representative to relieve him of his jurisdiction, the Austrian inquired whether his successor had been designated. When an affirmative answer pointed to the person of a Dr. Černý, the official immediately sent a telegram to Vienna asking for a promotion for Dr. Černý so that the transfer of power would carry the imprint of legality.

1. *Ke vzniku ČSR: Sborník statí k ohlasu Říjnové revoluce a ke vzniku ČSR* (Prague: Naše vojsko, 1958), p. 45.

The German consuls in Prague and Brno were most impressed with the developments. They sent messages to Berlin, reporting enthusiastically on the peaceful change and praising the *Sokol,* a patriotic organization which they had denounced in the past and which had taken a leading role in the takeover. The consul in Prague even sent to the *Sokol*'s chairman a present of 500 crowns from the Reich as a token of recognition. The gift was returned, with thanks.[2]

Events in Slovakia took a similar turn: After making their intentions clear on several occasions during the war, political representatives met on October 30 at Turčansky Sväty Martin, a lovely town in the foothills of the Tatra Mountains, and in a solemn ceremony proclaimed their wish to create a common state with the Czechs. They did not know that Prague had already officially announced the existence of the Republic two days earlier. The Slovaks had been suitably represented in Prague, however, by Vavro Šrobár, the most respected Slovak politician, who had maintained contacts with the Czechs throughout the war and who put his signature on the first Czechoslovak law. But even his presence in Prague was as commonplace and unheroic as everything else—he had journeyed there to participate in a wedding.[3] It turned out to be a truly historic "wedding," as, after centuries of enforced separation, the Czechs and Slovaks were joined once again.

Thus—and it could have happened nowhere else in Eastern Europe—on October 28, in the ancient rolling plains of old Bohemia and the rugged mountains of Slovakia, two peoples reemerged as one nation from centuries of serfdom into the full splendor of independence—without the firing of a shot, a revolution sui generis.

Can any humanitarian fail to be impressed by a revolutionary process which values human life and rejects the bloody barricades? Can he deny the Czechoslovak revolution an ethical dimension of unparalleled civility? Yet, a nagging question intrudes. If the history of mankind attests to the less-humane wisdom

2. Jiří Kořalka, "Cesta k 28 říjnu," *Reportér* 3, no. 41 (1968): 8, 9.
3. Karel Pichlík, "Cesta k 28 říjnu," *Reportér* 3, no. 37 (1968): 9.

that "freedom is born in blood" then the "negotiated" revolution in Prague in 1918 may have had the foreboding aspect of "easy come, easy go." But during the joyful, uplifting days of October 1918, no one could know that, after it had experienced twenty years of freedom and social justice, the Republic would be crushed by the perfidy of its allies and the onslaught of Nazi aggression, and that it would be dismembered as it had begun—without the firing of a shot.

Less then a decade after that dreary event, following a brief three years of resurrection and renewal, freedom would again be driven from the Czechoslovak lands, and again without the firing of a protesting shot. And yet another twenty years later, the promising and exhilarating Czechoslovak Spring of freedom and socialist democracy would lie dead beneath the Soviet guns—once more, without a single shot fired from Czechoslovak ranks.

Chapter One

The Roots

There is no scientific way to trace or test either the precise nature or the exact degree of the influence on a people of their history. The impact varies from one particular individual or group to another, as does the very reading of historical facts themselves. Even a scholar inescapably reads the historical record in much the same way as he would look at a mirror—what is most clear to him is the image of his own values, his sense of his own identity. Yet, there persists in history the concept of national identity, and the transmission of that identity from generation to generation transcends even biological inheritance. The son of a Swedish immigrant in America has no particular trouble regarding Thomas Jefferson as a "forefather." The moments and the memories and the events of a nation's history implant themselves in the consciousness of each generation, and each generation, living its own life and creating its own identity, subtly changes the composition of the continuing stream of history.

Even when the dominant themes of a nation's history can be perceived by the historian, a complex tangle of questions and implications remains to be unraveled and analyzed. The motivations of significant national movements, their origins and unique qualities, their lasting or ephemeral effects on a nation's history must be questioned. The consistency or inconsistency of a nation's attitudes toward the events that shape its destiny must be understood and the external forces that influence its decisions taken into account. Nor can the critical question of what constitutes the national will be ignored. Is it represented by mass movements? Is it authentically expressed in the statements of political leaders, in the theories of philosophers, in the words of poets? Or, can the national will, or the lack of it, be detected only in the combination of social and cultural forces that strengthen each other or cancel each other out? Perhaps, finally, national will is expressed in the harmony of all these voices as its absence is found in their cacophony.

When defining a national identity, the historian must avoid regarding symbols as the true reflections of national disposition. More than enough harm has been inflicted upon peoples by deceiving prophets of patriotism, hucksters of social equality, preachers of manifest destiny. Symbols are deceptive and dangerous. Also, the wish to define a persistent national identity must not be allowed to distort either the past or the present. If the political, cultural, and military conduct of a nation in a certain past era permits a general characterization considered rather unique—whether positive or negative—the question of whether it is historically and philosophically legitimate to span centuries and project old values onto the contemporary scene must be faced.

With these uncertainties in mind, it is nevertheless plausible to speak of meaning in national history. Certain phenomena that reappear periodically can be verified, even though they are propelled in different eras by different dynamics of history, and their upholders, whether political leaders, philosophers, men of letters, or poets, find identifiable roots in their origin. These phenomena may deserve, according to individual judgment, praise or condemnation. They may appear contradictory, but they produce, over the centuries, patterns which lead to reflections of national identity and interpretations of the meaning of national history.

It is with some misgivings, then, that the historian approaches the task of finding the roots of the Czechoslovak inheritance in order to determine their nature and to determine what exactly they draw from the past to define, nurture, or weaken the present. But the roots are there, and they are vital to the nation's sense of self-identity. Indeed, as the great scholar, sage, and founder of the Czechoslovak Republic, Thomas Garrigue Masaryk, put it, "States maintain themselves by the ideas that led to their existence." What he did not say directly, but many times implied, was that states also destroy themselves by the loss or contamination of those same ideas.

In what soil, then, did the independent Czechoslovakia that emerged in 1918 have its roots? What ideas led to its existence? What were the meanings in its history that would give it strength to endure ever-changing circumstances or would weaken its will in moments of great national crisis? There are no easy answers to these questions, but they have been discussed cogently and well for many years, and the varying arguments deserve further examination.

The 600 years of Czech history prior to 1918 create in themselves no great debate.

Hussitism

During the first part of the fourteenth century, the kingdom of Bohemia was the seat of seething controversy, with preachers vigorously condemning the laxity of the church and the general deterioration of religious devotion and public morality. Defying the specific orders of the Roman Catholic hierarchy, some of them exhorted their flocks in the vernacular, thereby adding an element of national identification to the religious upheaval. Their sermons were the precursors of the fiery, charismatic sermons delivered by the great Jan Hus (1369–1415) less than a century later.

Hus came to Prague in 1402. He was pastor of the recently founded Bethlehem Chapel, which was to function as a sacred place for services exclusively in the Czech language, and rector of Charles University. Both institutions became forums for criticism of the church and theological disputation. Significantly, they were also the sources of the first stirrings of national feeling. Hus was supported by the Czech king, Wenceslaus IV, who was also Holy Roman emperor, and by many noblemen, and his teachings ignited a popular reform movement. The conflicts within the Roman Curia only exacerbated the situation in Prague. Exiled from Prague in 1412, Hus continued to preach the Gospel and criticize the church and its social structures, followed now by the common people who demanded piety and morality.

When Hus was condemned to death at the Council of Constance and subsequently burned at the stake in 1415, popular indignation against the high Catholic hierarchy and the new Holy Roman emperor, Sigismund, assumed formidable proportions. The Taborites, a radical group led by the great warrior Jan Žižka, took up arms in defense of their creed and marched from victory to victory. The Hussite movement spread quickly throughout Bohemia, though the rise of various sects inescapably weakened it. The Unity of Czech Brethren was the most striking of these sects in that it preached that Christ's teachings should be practiced in unadulterated purity.

Petr Chelčický (c. 1390 – c. 1460), the sect's spiritual leader, was a pacifist, pleading for a return to the religion of Christ. His followers saw in his doctrine not only strictly religious tenets, but also economic and social implications and a definition of man's relationship to society. Glorifying the moral superiority of simple countrymen, the Brethren chose to live in poverty, though they did not condemn private property on principle. In the initial stage of the Hussite movement, the Taborites, expecting Christ's imminent return to earth, had proclaimed that this event would inaugurate "such love between people that all things will be held in common amongst them . . . when kings, princes, and prelates will cease . . . when extortion of the poor will cease . . . when nothing is mine or thine, but all have everything in common." Not all the Czech Brethren embraced these more radical visions of the Reformation, but profound social concern was common to all the reform groups.

The Habsburg emperors, exalted defenders of the Catholic faith, found themselves fighting not only foreign threats of invasion, but also the embattled Czech noblemen. Hence, after the tragic defeat of the Czechs in the Battle on the White Mountain (1620), the Habsburgs rid themselves of this annoyance, executing 27 members of the Czech aristocracy and exiling some 150,000 Protestants. In 1624, every non-Catholic priest was ordered to leave the country. Among them was Jan Amos Komenský (1592–1670), better known as Comenius, the last bishop of the Unity of Czech Brethren. Comenius saw the real meaning of spiritual life in social conscience and education as well as in piety. To him, education was the very *officina humanitatis.*

The common folk who remained in Bohemia endured poverty of body and outrage of spirit; they were forced to recant their Protestant faith and were subjected to the systematic germanization of their culture. Three-fourths of the Czech lands were confiscated and distributed among immigrating Germans. The Czech peasants were debased to a class of pariahs. A group of adventurous bankers and aristocrats withdrew the solid Czech currency and replaced it with another that was devalued by 85 percent. Of 150,000 land holdings, 80,000 were abandoned. Leading towns lay in ruins. The population of the kingdom of Bohemia dropped from 3 million to 800,000. Czech books were put on the Index of the Roman Catholic church, and Czech culture and tradition were rigorously suppressed. The process of impoverishment and denationalization lasted for 200 years, though the influence of the baroque, evident in Czech architecture and poetry of the period, kept the flame alive.

The Awakeners

In the eighteenth and nineteenth centuries, the spirit of the Enlightenment and the French Revolution stirred a responsive spirit in the

Czech lands and in Slovakia. The healthy restlessness sweeping Western Europe inspired such men as Josef Jungmann, Josef Dobrovský, Jan Kollár, Pavel Josef Šafárik, Karel Havlíček, and František Palacký. They spearheaded a national reawakening that combined religious tolerance, liberalism, rationalism, and romanticism in a strange new mixture. Some of these men were Catholics, others Protestants. Some sought the salvation of the nation (which continued to vegetate under the cyclical fluctuations of Habsburg oppression) in the revitalization of the Czech language; others sought it in a revival of Hussitism and linked the people's well-being to the spiritual demands of Christianity and its standards of morality; still others sought to capture in a romanticized, poetic way the unique qualities of Slavdom. All of them held an adoration of the ideals of humanity in common. Significantly, there was also vast agreement among them on the means for achieving these ideals—peaceful endurance, education, and work.

Because of their unique individual concepts, a few of these men deserve special attention. Jan Kollár (1793–1852), a Slovak poet, was clearly a proud defender of his people, the Slavs. His mystic vision of Slav greatness as well as his humaneness caused him to write, "Whenever you say Slav, may it ever mean man." Kollár perceived the dual aspect of freedom: "He who is worthy of freedom respects the freedom of every man," and conversely, "He who enchains slaves is himself a slave."

František Palacký (1798–1876), called "the father of the nation," inspired the Czechs to identify with their Hussite heritage and wrote a massive history of the Czech people. He exhorted them to aspire to high values of spirituality and ethics. "My last word," he wrote in 1872, "is a sincere and heartfelt wish that my compatriots in Bohemia and Moravia, in whatever situation they find themselves, never cease to be true to themselves, to truth and justice." He saw this truthfulness manifested in the spiritual superiority that was the essence of Czech history: "Whenever we were victorious, it was always due more to spiritual superiority than to physical might, and whenever we succumbed, a deficiency of spiritual activity and moral bravery was always to blame." Palacký maintained that the nation had survived disasterous experiences because it "represented justice and right." He asked for endurance, morality, education, cultivation of the language, and daily, conscious work. Nothing worthwhile could be accomplished by force, "for the sword is two-edged" and the nation could find its fulfillment only as part of mankind.

Palacký found proof of these principles in the age-old conflict between Czechs and Germans and between Catholicism and Protestantism. He romanticized the peace-loving Slavs, who presumably built their society on consensus, whereas the Germans, he believed, established a historical record of rule by power. As to the religious aspect of the conflict, Catholicism was based on authority, which encouraged obedience and passivity of mind, while Protestantism was founded on reason, aspiring activism, and independence of thought. Bohemia was a battleground of the two concepts, and the behavior of its populace reflected the irreconcilable differences between them.

Karel Havlíček (1821–56), a valiant journalist and epigrammatist, was also a defender of the superiority of principles over power, but his view was based not so much upon idealism as on what he termed "a philosophy of common sense." While vigorously opposing Austrian absolutism, he was against revolution, against radicals as well as reactionaries: "I am altogether a great enemy of revolution by way of arms and firmly believe in revolutions of minds and hearts. . . . Nothing precipitate, nothing extreme can have lasting value—only *moderata durant.*" Havlíček saw education as the principal weapon against oppression: "There is no power in this world, even if it were allied with the whole of hell, that could hold an educated, noble, and courageous nation in subjugation, in serfdom." On the other hand, "No nation can achieve final victory through other than its own strength." For that reason, he appealed to his people, "Be a tiger or a lion, but never be a dog." In contrast to Palacký, who was conservative in matters of economics Havlíček was a liberal, who nonetheless maintained that "man has the right to work as well as an obligation to work. This is an irreversible truth." The government, just as it defended the right of the entrepreneur, must defend the right of the worker, and foremost among his rights was "the right to human dignity."

The Meaning of History:
Masaryk

The most profound writer and thinker of the late nineteenth and early twentieth centuries was Thomas Garrique Masaryk (1850–1937), without whom there would have been no Czechoslovakia. A professor at Charles University, steeped in history, philosophy, sociology, political science, and literature—a Renaissance man—Masaryk was, above all, a humanist with profound ethical and religious convictions. To him, the synthesis of religion and social justice uniquely characterized both "Czech humanism" and the true meaning of Czech history. Both were incarnated in the teaching and practice of the Unity of Czech Brethren; both found expression, though in an obverse form, in the period of the Counter-Reformation; and both surfaced again in the modernizing conditions on the nineteenth century. In political terms, they created a synthesis of ethics and religion, and of individualism, nationalism, and socialism. To Masaryk, humanity and nationality were complementary, and socialism, like nationalism, was "an expression of the same ideal of humanity." A nation, he said, was an "ethical personality . . . expressing itself in social ethics," and to him, "the Czech mind will always be primarily social." Masaryk felt that the Hussite movement, the Revolution of 1848, and the Christian socialism of the 1850s, all had their roots in the Czech ideal of humanity.

Inescapably, the heart of Masaryk's thought was his concept of man. In man's very existence—his metaphysical relationships, his spiritual being, his natural right to freedom and social dignity—Masaryk saw the fulfillment of the ideals of humanity. Religious consciousness—not churches—was a concomitant and refinement of humanism, the very basis of morality. The two concepts were inextricably entwined: one's relationship to God implied respect for every person and the obligation to help others, to live reasonably and morally. Even though morality can exist without religion, it is not perfect and complete. Religion is a necessary climax to the spiritual and cultural life. "Life without faith," he said, "loses certainty and strength."

Masaryk's concept of the humanistic, religious meaning of Czech history found considerable (though not unequivocal) support among such prominent scholars as Jaroslav Werstadt, Jan Slavík, Albert Pražák, and Kamil Krofta (1876–1945). Since it illuminates Masaryk's philosophy, Krofta's position deserves special note. He gave qualified agreement to Masaryk's idea that religion was a specifically Czech factor in the nation's history. Religion defined as an effort toward spiritual and ethical perfection was certainly a driving historical force in many nations, but there were few to whom religion had meant so much as the Czech nation. No other nation had "filled with religious thought such a great and significant part of its history, lived it through so strongly and profoundly in all its strata, and sacrificed to it so much of its vital energy, its material well-being and secular advantage as the Czech nation." The Hussite movement "has in the Czech history a similar importance as the great French Revolution in the French history." When the nation began to awaken in the nineteenth century to a new life, it could not return to the ethical forms of its ancestors, but it did revive its spirit and renew its faith in the noble ideals of humanity, freedom, right, and justice, which, wrote Krofta, "became a substantial and permanent component of the world view of the Czechoslovak nation."

In so many respects, then, Masaryk was a descendant of the idealists of the Reformation, but he also descended from another great figure of those early days—Žižka, the leader of the Taborites who, as they fought, heard in their hearts their famous chorale, "You who are the warriors of God" and whose motto was "Slay the enemy—spare not a one!"

"Are we not a nation of Žižka?" Masaryk asked, and answered, "Yes, we are, but also a nation of Hus and Comenius." Even as he said this, he knew that Hus's progeny had all been pacifists. Masaryk wished to reconcile this apparent dichotomy within the common bond of humanism. He did so with a commanding argument that voiced, in a sense, the whole human dilemma of men of ideals living in a world of militant evil. "In Žižka and the Taborites," he wrote, "we have without doubt a Czech type. Žižka—that is blood of our blood and bone of our bone—

yes, Žižka, that is we. It is a special enthusiasm, but one which does not lose even for a moment an awareness of its blindness. . . . It is an unbreakable valiancy terrible to the foe, but also terrible to the all-crushing victor—terrible to him because in the depths of his soul, he is troubled by doubts and by consciousness of guilt." Thus Masaryk justified the use of force while recognizing in Hus, Comenius, and the Czech Brethren, another "Czech type, and a type which, as history teaches, is more enduring." This philosophical conflict he saw reflected, but unresolved, in the Czech people. The result was their "incomplete character, neither Taborites nor Brethren." He did not seek the solution in a "golden middle road," but in a strenuous effort to "fuse harmoniously both qualities into a higher spiritual unity. . . ."

He did so because he viewed with foreboding the continuing vacillation of the Czechs between the resignation of the Czech Brethren and the forceful action of the Taborites, between passivity and radicalism, eventually adhering to a "religion of the past or of the present, and both only with lip service." He was particularly critical of the nation's "singular cult of and even inclination toward martyrdom, in which a peculiar passivity of character is manifested. It is indeed significant that its most luminous history begins and ends with martyrs, St. Wenceslaus and Hus. . . . It is truly an enigma—why Hus must suffer death and Wycliffe not." Even worse, he believed, the tendency toward passivity "is so strong that we cultivate even a false martyrdom . . . exposing our small wounds and asking for admiration. . . . Life is a struggle, particularly for a small nation, but one can come out of it with honor, difficult as it is." It was a position he clung to until his death—his sense of the larger and more lasting good of the worlds of Hus and Comenius and yet of the moral necessity to resist evil, by force if necessary.

Masaryk was embroiled in a continuous controversy, carried on through visits and correspondence, with Lev Tolstoi, whose philosophy of not resisting evil he criticized sharply. While advocating the ideals of humanity, a program of peaceful daily work, and while condemning violence, Masaryk insisted, "If somebody attacks me in order to kill me, I will defend myself; and if there is no other way, I will kill the violator; if one of us two is to be killed, let it be the one with evil intentions." In contrast to Tolstoi's mystic pacificism, Masaryk believed that a real humanitarian doctrine required constant vigilance, which implied resistance to violence and evil—in extreme cases, "even by iron." In 1917, in the midst of World War I, he wrote that war was "something terrible, inhuman, particularly this war. However, war is not the greatest evil. To live dishonestly, to be a slave, to enslave, many other things, are much worse." Later, as president of the Republic, he stressed again that a humanitarian program did not mean a complacent weakness. "On the contrary," he wrote, "love of one's neighbor, of the nation, and of humanity imposes upon everyone the obligation to defend oneself and to resist evil consistently, everywhere, at all times, and in all things." When Masaryk was close to eighty, John Galsworthy, sipping tea with him on the terrace of his country residence, asked him if he still disagreed with Tolstoi. Masaryk replied, "Old as I am, if someone attacked me, I would seize a brick with these old hands and throw it at him."

"There has never been any contradiction between my humanism and my effort for the defense of the country," Masaryk said. In the light of the events that followed his death, in 1937, one is forced to speculate upon what the course of Czechoslovak history might have been had he lived to utter these words in the dark days following the Munich Pact. More important to him than the physical defense of the nation, however, was its fidelity to the cause of ethics, and his political goals were firmly imbedded in this concept.

To Masaryk, politics was "an instrument, but the goal was religious and moral." His chosen instrument was a democracy, based on "trust in man, in his values, his spirituality, and the immortality of his soul." "Jesus, not Caesar," he stated, "that is the meaning of our history and democracy." Nor did he conceive humanism and religion as being separate from practical life. "With me," he wrote, "the theory and practice are like the rhythm of breathing, inhaling and exhaling." Jaroslav Werstadt, a Czech historian, characterized Masaryk as an "old-new [staro-nový] man" because, for him, the forms and means were new, but the ethos and ideal were as old as Christianity. Masaryk linked the ethical heritage of Christianity with modern forms of political and social life, proclaiming democracy to be the "political form of humanity." To him, the question was how to resurrect the values of Christianity, divested of its mysticism, and practice them in the modern world.

If politics was an instrument to Masaryk, it was never a sword, always a scalpel to be used with sensitivity toward man. Politics must reflect man's reason and emotions: "The methods must be absolutely objective . . . but the goal, the entity, the concept—that is an eternal poetry." The science of politics is empirical, but must grow out of fundamental ethics. He summed up his concept in a sentence that modern social scientists might well contemplate, "All social sciences require philosophical foundations." It was this philosophical sense of the centrality of the individual that made him critical of nineteenth-century liberalism, with its altogether secular understanding of the rights and needs of man.

This same sense made him critical of collectivism, which he saw suppressing the all-important individual consciousness and replacing it with an artificial mass consciousness. Collectivism silenced what is noble in man and provoked attitudes that debased him. It put the state on a pedestal and degraded the individual and the human, relegating man to the role of working and serving the "higher interests" of a collectivity.

Masaryk subjected Marxism to a thorough critical analysis. To him, scientific socialism by definition denied people the right of choice because "objectivity" was considered the exclusive basis for analysis and decision. Historical materialism, based on the premise of an objective interpretation of history, excluded ethics from its philosophical consideration and regarded the individual's moral, intellectual, and psychological concerns as no more than reflections of economic values, of poverty or wealth. To Masaryk, religion, emotion, morality, artistic and philosophic creativity, had their own intrinsic values. How else could Dante's poetic force, Michelangelo's creative passion, Newton's scientific fervor, or Jesus sacrificial love be explained?

It logically follows that Masaryk also rejected Marx's ideas about the class struggle, his view of the role of the state and the uses of power, his mechanistic conception of the equality of men, and his justification of violence. Masaryk posed the question, "Can a genuinely human morality be raised from violence by violence?" And he answered, "I am convinced that there can be no adequate humanitarian ideal or socialism without a religious foundation. Man can be an ideal to man only *sub specie aeternitatis.* Man is not only body, but also soul. An immortal soul." To achieve the optimum, man must pass, not through a process of physical violence, but through a "revolution of mind and heart," for without a "genuine transformation of the intellect and the psyche, without a change in thought and manners, a revolution might exorcise the demon only to put Satan in his place." This critique was written in 1898, twenty years before Marx's theory became a practiced political, economic, and social creed.

Masaryk's resolute convictions about social justice were an inevitable outgrowth of his ethical and religious weltanschauung. He wrote, "I was always for the workingman, often for socialism, seldom for Marx," and warned, "Socialism will either be humanistic or it will not be at all."

These, then, were the ideas of Thomas G. Masaryk, ideas that "were to lead to the existence" of a new republic, the ideas by which that republic must live if "it was to maintain itself."

Two other concepts important to Masaryk's sense of the Czechoslovak heritage should be briefly considered. The first was his view of the inevitability of the Czech nation's close relationship to the West. Many of the powerful historical currents that swept Europe had inescapably affected Czechoslovakia, and, in like manner, Hus and Hussitism, the forerunners of Luther and Protestantism, had profoundly influenced Europe.

The other concept was a means of dealing with the fact that Czechoslovakia was a small nation. Masaryk's answer was two-fold: education and work. "A small nation must work and work and work," he said, "and more intensively than large nations. A humanitarian program does not teach us to be passive, but to defend ourselves by work." He had no patience with those who justified unacceptable behavior by pleading physical defenselessness. "A lion remains a lion, even in a cage," he wrote. "He does not become a donkey." He saw public life in Bohemia toward the end of the nineteenth century as a nest of self-serving intrigue, one of the bitter legacies of 200 years of Austrian subjugation. "Since the politicians are unable to be lions, they turn into foxes; since they are unable to be heroes, they turn into lackeys and help themselves with a servile shrewdness. They even try to find an excuse by pointing to the smallness of the nation, saying it cannot live except by begging or intriguing." Masaryk would have none of it, but he knew the tendency was there, and in the days that followed, as he planned for the new nation's future, he voiced repeatedly his grave concern over this heritage.

Perhaps the problem was that when Masaryk tried to infuse the new Czechoslovakia with the spirit of Hus, he sounded like a moralist who knew well what the nation ought to be but not what it really was, attempting to wish away the effects of the preceding centuries. As Ferdinand Peroutka later put it, Masaryk was a unique phenomenon, living in the spirit of the Protestant philosophy of the Reformation. Had the tradition of the Czech Brethren truly been still alive, the nation and Masaryk would have looked much more alike.

Pekař's Concept

There was, in fact, a group of prominent scholars who questioned Masaryk's interpretation of the meaning of Czechoslovak history, and a "great debate" on the issue developed at the turn of the century and again in the middle of the 1920s. Representative of this group was Josef Pekař, the finest Czechoslovak historian of the twentieth century. Extraordinarily erudite and intellectually disciplined, he brought to historiography strictly empirical methods and meticulous research. Politically, he was conservative; theologically, he was Catholic.

Pekař's analysis of Czechoslovak history does contain points that complement aspects of Masaryk's thought—indeed, some are identical—but most of their ideas conflict. Pekař was particularly critical of Masaryk's concept of the essentially religious nature of the nation's history and the meaning of Hussitism. He considered Masaryk's thought in this area to be ahistorical and unscientific, more philosophy (and wrong at that) than history. Most fundamentally, Pekař raised the question of whether one can truly speak of a "meaning" in any nation's history or accept the scholarly feasibility of extracting one idea, one tendency, and interpreting it as a creative and sustaining force. Empirical study, he believed, would never even venture into Masaryk's realm of mystical teleology and religious meaning.

Further, Pekař insisted, if one must talk about "meaning" in Czechoslovak history, one still could not consider it as an autonomous development, bringing to the surface some special and characteristic virtues. To him, the nation's history had to be viewed as a development "determined primarily by the influence, example, ethic, and spirit of Western Europe." He also rejected Palacký's idea (as did Masaryk) that the Czechs and other Slavs were the exponents of a higher culture than their Germanic neighbors, that their history was, in essence, a continuous struggle between two worlds—one of liberty, virtue, peace, and democracy, and another of domination, violence, oppression, and feudalism. This notion, he insisted, again ignores the influence of Western Europe, as if everything indigenous were good and everything foreign were harmful. Czech history was only partly a history of "conflicts" with Germandom; indeed, the most powerful and significant factor in Czech history was the acceptance and absorption of the life and thought of the more progressive nations of the Germanic and Roman worlds. The proximity of Germany had had some positive impacts: it sparked Czech nationalism, taught the Czechs to think on high levels of culture and industry, and generally revealed to them higher ways of life, both spiritual and social. If the Czechs were "more advanced" than other nations in the area in economy, administration, discipline, and culture, Pekař argued, it was due to their German education.

He maintained that the Czech people contributed to civilization over the centuries not by cultivating some specifically Czech spirit, independent of the rest of Europe, but rather by being a vital part of European culture. As the spiritual identity of Europe changed, as each period of history found its own "soul" and its own meaning, so the Czechs exhibited a different "mentality" in the Hussite era, in the following two centuries of repression, and in the twentieth-century world of big cities, fast transportation, sports, and democratic and socialist programs.

Nor is it correct, Pekař asserted, to see Hussitism as a democratic movement with a social content, or to consider it an unmitigated blessing. Hussitism must be viewed within its historical context—the Middle Ages—and in terms of its final defeat as a human act that could have saved Bohemia from further destruction. It intended to create in Bohemia "God's kingdom on this earth, but its final result was unchristian murdering, passionate fighting, and a doleful and lasting division of national will." As for the historical impact of Hus and his followers, Pekař saw principally the coincidence that the kingdom of Bohemia was governed by a king who encouraged the revolt, while similar rebellions in other countries were harshly repressed. Nevertheless, he conceded, the revolutions against the church did reach their peak in Bohemia, because of the Czechs' longing for freedom and religious purity and because of their unique determination to stand against the encroachment of Germandom.

If one can isolate any particular meaning in Czech history, Pekař declared, it would be national awareness—the one element which provides for the uninterrupted continuity of a people's will over centuries, which links all generations into one spiritual entity, and which inspires the hope that preserves, strengthens, and ennobles Czech individuality among nations. "Can we, therefore, say that the meaning of our history is the national idea? I answer, that is so, and more than that: it is the condition of our history, it is its reason, its blood, its beating, living heart."

Having thus found the quintessence of Czech history, Pekař reached a significant conclusion: whenever the fervor of patriotic love went forward and related to the educational and moral progress of Europe, the nation grew toward greatness; whenever the national spirit waned or withdrew from outward commitment, the nation declined, with the threat that it might perish.

Peroutka's Analysis

Ferdinand Peroutka, a talented, insightful journalist and writer, added still another dimension to the interpretation of Czechoslovak history. Endowed with the ability to cut through mazes of philosophical complexity, he could also present his material in a readable style, as in his book, The Way We Are [Jací jsme?]. Accepting the historical fact that the Czech people lived at the crossroads of cultural and political interests, Peroutka expressed the conviction that their national character was influenced by the small size and uncertain existence of the nation. Throughout modern history the nation adjusted both its tactics and character to the exigencies of its size and the times. Inescapably, the Czech people played a game of "catch up" with the rest of Europe, reaching out to the West with which they identified but which regarded them as insignificant. Even when they utilized the Czech language as a weapon of national identity in the nineteenth century, they looked for models outside their own culture, for something European, and had also imitated foreign painting and foreign schools.

Peroutka's treatment of the religious aspects of Czech history was tantalizing and disquieting. The roots of Czech tradition, he declared, were not in the Reformation, but in Catholicism. Had the values of the Reformation survived the Counter-Reformation, there would be greater tenacity and endurance in the nation's character, and its ethical consciousness would be fuller and firmer. Further, the nineteenth-century awakening had a national, not a religious, impetus. It resurrected the nation's political awareness—in a Catholic and, at the same time, liberal environment. In fact, Peroutka claimed, Czech thought was much closer to French rationalism than to religious mysticism, but wherever a religious spirit existed, it was Catholic. The Czech Brethren, with their austerity and their belief that the only worthwhile satisfaction was duty fulfilled, were strangers to the Czech people, who returned to Catholicism (even though it was forced on them) because it was a more joyful religion. He pointed out that Czech literature, music, and art were all permeated by Catholicism; the most obvious products of Catholicism were the baroque and rococo architecture found in Prague and in every village in the countryside.

Finally, Peroutka claimed, the Czech people did not exhibit any particular humanistic qualities. They are not a nation of heroes, he said, but rather "shrewd lovers of life," fully penetrated by civilization and a sense of realism. In the Irish and Polish struggles for freedom there was much flame, determination, desperation, pathos, and excitement, whereas the Czechs had chosen to negotiate for their rights in the chambers of the Vienna Parliament. While this act was humane and civilized (and facilitated by the Austrian sense of fundamental decency), Peroutka continued, it was due to the practical Czech sense of the limitations of the human nervous system rather than to a sense of the limitless capacity of humane thought. As a small nation, they sought refuge in humanity and justice as a practical matter. The Czechs did not even consider fighting the Germans—not because of humanitarian principles, but because it would have been silly. They used the armament of spirit because it was the only armament they had, and they were humanitarian because pragmatic reason dictated it. There is an air of skepticism about Peroutka, and certainly his generalizations are sweeping, more stylistically exciting than precise, but much of what he said must be remembered.

There is a kind of fascination in the facile reasoning of at least one other Czech writer and thinker, Emanuel Chalupný. A leading sociologist, he based his analysis of the national character on the Czech language, for as he said, "The language is a mirror of the fate of every nation and the product of its intellectual and cultural life."

The Czech language consistently accents the first syllable of a word, and this feature, Chalupný reasoned, explains almost every aspect of Czech behavior. It is anticipatory: the Czechs plunge into action with vehemence and remarkable initial success, but their determination soon slackens. "Give him a stimulus and he will strike the match into flame, but as for keeping it alight, for putting it to lasting use—others have to take care of that." By analogy, then, in their religious history, the Czechs ignited the torch of reform ahead of all other nations, but the flame lost its intensity in a half-hearted Utraquism and others completed the enduring work of the Reformation; in their political history, the Czechs repeatedly produced new and liberating ideas that were never realized; and in their military history, the Czechs were led from success to success by the fiery Žižka, only to collapse in darkness after his death. Chalupný observed the same curse of early flowering, followed by stagnation, in the nation's economic and literary history, and even in music, the other creative arts, and, more recently, in sports. He did not, however, consider this quality purely negative. The other side of the coin, he believed, was an intellectual agility that was typically Czech: a gift for systematic logic, learnedness, clear thinking, and reasonableness—characteristics which the nation turned into weapons for its preservation over a period of 1,000 years.

From his anticipatory theory Chalupný derived another Czech characteristic: a tendency to concentrate on details and to have difficulty thinking in complex, universal concepts. Since details are always simple, the national inclination is toward simplicity, and since details invite special attention, they also provoke satire, witticism, and mockery, which are characteristic of Czech humor. Further, a concentration on details points to the joy taken by Czechs in minute, quiet daily work. Another rather extraordinary and paradoxical characteristic also interested Chalupný—the combination of mysticism and realism which not only indicates intellectual breadth and richness, but also implies a sense of insecurity and uncertainty. The first element is evident in the nation's cultural achievements, particularly in fiction; the second is evident in Czech behavior in the real world. One quality inspires optimism and attainment; the other, pessimism and indifference. Related to this, in Chalupný's view, is a sense of national pride in an almost 300-year history of Hussitism and an acute sense of humiliation in another 300 years of subjugation. Pushing the argument further, he suggested that the epoch of degradation created a sense of inferiority in the Czechs which is often repugnantly manifested as contemptuous rudeness to those beneath them and fawning servility to those above them.

Where, then, do these learned but dichotomous voices lead us? There can be little doubt that the almost 300 years of the Hussite and pre-Hussite tradition, which is generally viewed as a period of national glory, cannot be erased from the minds of subsequent generations. They serve as a fountain of inspiration and as a compass to find direction for further achievement. If this were not true, no wisdom could derive from experience. Nor can one lightly dismiss the evident truth that such experiences instill a sense of justified national pride, as well as a spirit of commitment to a tradition of humanism, democracy, and social progress.

By the same token, however, 200 years of subjugation, followed by another 100 years of precarious struggle to reawaken the supine nation and its dormant spirit, cannot but infect the fountain of inspiration and derange the compass needle. In such a world, ethics and principles are constantly confronted by the exigencies of existence and sheer survival and a dismal choice is faced—to live in humiliation or to die with an upright shield in hand.

Thus, the Czech people were for many years both fighters and battlefield in the fierce struggle of these incongruent forces which at one time propelled them to the heights of humanistic ethics, at another dragged them down to the necessities of accommodation, and at still others, left them simply inert and exhausted. As a result, a pattern seems to have developed: in times of assured statehood the Czech people strove for the ideals of humanity; in times of peril, they lowered their heads to save the national body. This was the legacy of the past that the new Czechoslovak Republic inherited—a history with many meanings, many portents of the future. With the rebirth of the nation in 1918, historical opportunities were knocking at the door and the regained spirit of freedom flung it wide open. Would the nation make full use of them?

Chapter Two

Confrontation
with History

On July 6, 1915, 500 years to the day after the martyrdom of Jan Hus, Thomas Garrigue Masaryk spoke in Zurich (but, in fact, to the world) with a vision and sense of mission that were as prophetic as the date was appropriate. He spoke of the new values that would emerge from the war—a conflict that he saw as far more revolutionary in nature than traditional power struggles. He spoke of international ethics, of the equality of nations, and of the right of self-determination on the part of oppressed peoples. Although his voice would become influential in world affairs, it was, on that day, a lonely voice, for the vision of World War I in those terms (terms which involved the inescapable dissolution of the Austro-Hungarian Empire) was not to be found in the thinking of either the political leaders of the Allied powers or, indeed, in that of the Czechs and Slovaks themselves.

The Czechs and Slovaks were by no means prepared for a confrontation with history when the war engulfed the European continent in the summer of 1914. True, their sense of national identity had been awakened. Their aversion to the oppressive Habsburg dynasty and its government in Vienna and Budapest was profound, and their yearning for freedom was intense. Still, there was neither definition nor determination to their national goals, and there was no sense of urgency about their role in the future Europe.

With the general mobilization of the Austro-Hungarian armies, Czech and Slovak soldiers were called to the colors. They joined against their will, and some gave vent to their real feelings by deserting. Thousands who had been sent to the Russian front crossed the trenches or sought capture by the "enemy." If caught by the Austrians, they were executed. Others expressed their political sentiments by shouting antiwar, anti-Habsburg slogans and singing forbidden nationalist songs. The saying, "The Russian is with us and the Frenchman will sweep away anyone who is against us," typifies the general acceptance of the idea that the fate of the nation in a world conflagration would be determined by outside forces.

Thus, at the outbreak of the war no one even visualized an independent Czechoslovak state. Acts of rebellion in a country guarded by Austrian and Hungarian forces seemed suicidal folly— and prudence, not folly, was the governing feature of the Czech and Slovak temperament. A small group of schemers, known as the "Mafia," did some planning for action in the future, but initially they dared no further than to revive fifty-year-old demands for the transformation of the monarchy into a federation with equal rights among its national components. This state of mind was indicative. The yearning of the leaders was for the defeat of the monarchy, but their every expectation was for its preservation, albeit reformed.

A Remarkable Trio

While the nation and its leaders in the homelands remained cautious in their political attitudes, three men, who had found refuge from persecution in the West, worked to prepare the world for the emergence of Czechoslovakia as an independent republic. Thomas Masaryk, Edvard Beneš (1884–1948), and Milan Štefánik (1880–1919) constituted an extraordinary trio, the unique qualities of each man complementing those of the others.

Masaryk, sixty-four years old at the time of the outbreak of hostilities, was an intellectual and ethical giant. He was free to set forth in the democratic West a political program (based on the philosophical principles sketched earlier) for his country. However, he needed time for contemplation of its proper directions. When he left Prague toward the end of 1914, though he had stated in 1893 that his country would gain independence when it was ready to claim full historical and national rights, he had no fixed ideas about its constitutional form. Initially, he was prepared to agree to seating a king related to the Romanov dynasty on the throne of *Hradčany,* the ancient residence of the Czech monarchs. He assumed that his people wished a monarchy, but as time passed, he concluded that a republican form of government, reflecting the revolutionary political and social changes in Central Europe, was essential. Masaryk was also convinced that the liberating ideas of democracy would come from the West, not the East, and it was this conviction that led him to the West in 1914. These ends were articulated in his historic speech on the five-hundredth anniversary of the martyrdom of Hus.

Edvard Beneš was only about half the age of the "old man" when he joined him in West Europe in the spring of 1915. At various times Beneš had been a student, a reporter in Paris, and an assistant professor of sociology, and he was known as a man of progressive social thought. He had followed Masaryk's teaching in Prague, but upon meeting the older man he fell completely under the spell of his intellect and identified wholly with his political philosophy. The two men, vastly different in temperament, became and remained close political allies until Masaryk's death twenty-three years later.

Beneš's capacity for work was unparalleled. A devotee of the French rationalists, he produced countless flawless memoranda that were infused with cold, precise logic and also other papers whose persuasiveness affected the position of Allied chancelleries. "Without Beneš, we would have had no Republic," Masaryk affirmed after the war.

Milan Štefánik, the third member of the trio, resembled neither of his two compatriots. A young Slovak, he went to France before the war to study astronomy. He quickly excelled in the field, as well as in social relationships. Never wavering in his loyalty to the Czechoslovak cause, Štefánik nevertheless accepted French citizenship, and the government in Paris sent him on various missions to Italy, the Balkans, South America, and the Pacific area. With the coming of the war, he gave himself unsparingly to the cause of the Allies, seeing no disharmony between his service to present-day France and a future Czechoslovakia.

In Štefánik were combined attributes of the scholar and the bon vivant, both of which opened the doors of political and intellectual salons to Beneš and Masaryk. Pierre Janin, the French general who knew Štefánik intimately before and during the war, described him as a "real bundle of nerves . . . with a precious gift of brilliance, supersensitive, with a unique power of persuasion." Štefánik never fully recovered from wounds received flying over Serbia and also suffered from bleeding ulcers—perhaps the penalty of the pride and ambition which constantly drove him. He was, however, a noble man and absolutely honest.

Štefánik's views were basically antidemocratic. He was convinced that "government for the people cannot be government of the people," and once said, somewhat enigmatically, "There are cases when a real republican can only be a monarchist." He had profound respect and admiration for Masaryk—theirs was the relationship of a loving teacher and a respectful pupil—though his intuitive, nervous sensitivity contrasted with the quiet perceptiveness of the professor. Referring to the "old man's" oft-repeated religious concept of life with obvious tenderness, he once said to Janin, "All this is quite crazy, but it really seems to me that Masaryk sometimes sees things a little bit too much *sub specie aeternitatis.*" [1]

Beneš and Štefánik had entirely different personalities,

1. Pierre T. Janin, *Milan Rastislav Štefánik* (Prague: Orbis, 1932), pp. 13, 33, 35, 65.

and, toward the end of the war, serious controversies developed between them. Beneš led a life of Spartan simplicity, while Štefánik enjoyed luxury, and the coldly logical mind of the one could hardly relate to the intuitive sensitivity of the other. They were, however, closely related by ties of friendship in war, by mutual respect, and by patriotism. Tragically, Štefánik died in 1919 when his plane crashed on his native Slovak soil as he was returning to his beloved country, the new Czechoslovakia.

Actions Abroad

Viewed in retrospect, the audacity of this trio as it set out in the spring of 1915 to achieve an independent Czechoslovakia is manifest. There was no home front support. In Europe and America little was known about the Czech lands, and nothing at all was known of Slovakia. In addition to a few lonely, learned scholars, some French politicians probably remembered, the protest of the Czech leaders against the German annexation of Alsace-Lorraine in 1870; readers of Shakespeare "knew" that according to A Winter's Tale, Bohemia was on the shores of the Mediterranean Sea; lovers of music enjoyed the works of Smetana and Dvořák; and (most important of all!) Prague ham was internationally popular. In Russia, some political and literary circles looked with sympathy on their oppressed "little Slav" brothers, but the more conservatively Orthodox considered the Czechs Catholic infidels. Though perfectly willing to fight the Austro-Hungarian Empire, Czarist officials never grasped the idea that any people would dare to revolt against an emperor.

In the configuration of world politics, where expediency always gets more attention than justice, none of the Allied powers even considered dissolving the Austro-Hungarian Empire. After all, though it was the enemy, they thought of it as an area of stability that would one day be useful to their various political plans. In 1915 they did not yet view the war as an avalanche that was sweeping away their most precious values and triggering new and unthought of forces.

Masaryk, the professor, knew better. In addition to laying

down the ideological foundations of peace mentioned earlier, he and his associates began to prepare a specific Czechoslovak program for their Allied benefactors. In November 1915, a manifesto for Czechoslovakia's independence was issued in Paris. To give their endeavors an institutional framework, Masaryk and his associates established the Czechoslovak National Council. But their cause was difficult. Masaryk did find a helpful base among the people living in Czech and Slovak colonies scattered throughout the Allied countries; as they became part of the democratic life of their adopted countries (with the exception of Russia), the political thinking and national goals of these people became more attuned to the direction of the times than did those of the Czechs and Slovaks at home.

Masaryk had little respect for Czarist Russia and was openly critical of its primitive structure and antisocial, authoritarian regime. For understandable reasons, the government in Petrograd had no warm feelings for him, either. The Russians suspected him of socialist leanings and regarded him as an agent of the West. In fact, he was a Slavophile, indeed, a Russophile—but of a special sort. He journeyed to Russia on several occasions, maintained regular contact with such intellectual luminaries as Tolstoi, Miliukov, and Plekhanov, and wrote a voluminous scholarly work, *The Spirit of Russia,* which is still considered a penetrating sociological analysis of the country's nineteenth-century history. He shared his nation's traditional sentimental attachment to Mother Russia and valued her contribution to the intellectual achievements of Europe. Further, he saw her potential power as a counterpoise to German imperialism and Austro-Hungarian expansionism; he wanted Russia to emerge from the war as an influential factor in European politics—but democratic and progressive. He made this position known on a number of occasions, and, ironically, some government groups in the Allied countries viewed him as a Russian agent.

When he embarked on his historic mission to the West in 1914, the Czech professor was little known to men in positions of political power there. He had established contacts before the war with Henry Wickham Steed, the influential foreign editor of the London *Times,* and with the respected English scholar, Robert

Seton-Watson; and in France the historians Ernest Denis and Louis Eisenmann and the publicist Louise Weiss offered their assistance. In the United States, his associations were at first limited to university circles and leaders of the Czechoslovak colonies, though his remarkable American wife, Charlotte Garrigue, assisted him materially in understanding her country's culture and politics. Masaryk was thoroughly versed in the literature and history of all the Allied countries. In spite of this lonely start, however, by the end of his four years of effort, those in power—Woodrow Wilson, Georges Clemenceau, David Lloyd George, and Vittorio Emanuele Orlando—who had once known nothing of Czechoslovakia, knew Masaryk well, and their great decisions were influenced by his persuasive arguments concerning the fate of his people.

At the end of 1916 and again at the turn of 1917–18 Masaryk's vision of Czechoslovak independence was exposed to grave dangers. Austria was tired of war and sent out feelers to the Allied capitals about prospects for peace. The Allies, no less exhausted, were anxious to explore the idea of isolating Germany from her still-formidable accomplice, and President Wilson carefully examined the possible terms of a separate peace. Such a peace would have buried the case for an independent Czechoslovakia, since there was no question of Vienna conceding freedom or even autonomy to her Slav subjects, nor would the Allies have submitted such a demand to Austria at that time. Fortunately, however, the secret contacts between Vienna and the West aborted as Berlin's control over her political and military policy tightened, and Austria-Hungary stayed in the war to endure complete defeat.

On the other hand, the February Revolution in Russia in 1917 gave an accelerating, though delayed, impetus to the advancement of the Czechoslovak cause abroad. There were thousands of Czech and Slovak nationals in Russian prisoner-of-war camps and many of them were anxious to join their countrymen who had lived in Russia since before the war in forming what was to become the nucleus of a Czechoslovak army on Russian soil. They organized the famous Czechoslovak Legion. For as long as the Romanov dynasty ruled Russia, however, the Czechoslovak

Legionaries were given no opportunity to participate as an independent unit in any battle against the Central Powers except,
occasionally, as reconnaissance units. Though the Czar had expressed some support for the Czechoslovak cause, his statements
were vague and without formal commitment.

The situation changed dramatically as a result of the February Revolution. The new Russian government was democratic and
progressive, and Masaryk had good friends in its cabinet, among
them the well-known scholar, Paul Miliukov. In May 1917, Masaryk hurried to Petrograd where he visited many Czechoslovak
units and set out to recruit as many men as possible, motivated by
the conviction that in time of war guns were the best supporting
argument for his political goal. The Czechoslovak Legion, whose
numbers varied according to changing circumstances from 40,000
to 70,000 men, was the only organized, seasoned force in the
chaos of revolutionary Russia. After witnessing the engagement of
the Legionaries in the Battle of Zborov in July 1917, Alexander
Kerensky finally recognized them as an autonomous unit. However, this political and military success had no lasting effect. The
October Revolution dashed Masaryk's hope for Russia's democratic future, and the separate peace negotiated at Brest-Litovsk in
March 1918 frustrated the Legionaries' plans to fight the Germans
on the Eastern front. Expecting to join the French army on the
Western front, they embarked on an apparently fantastic action:
the transport of units from the Ukraine, across Siberia, to Vladi-
vostok, from which they would cross the Pacific Ocean, the conti-
nental United States, and the Atlantic Ocean to reach France.
Only a small number of Legionaries made the journey. Most
of them, however, were fighting against the Bolsheviks in the Russian civil war, an action which made them famous and popular in
all Allied capitals. They returned to their homeland some eighteen months after the armistice ending World War I was signed at
Compiègne.

The setback in Russia did not prevent developments which
were of direct concern to a future Czechoslovakia from reaching a
denouement. After the failure to negotiate a separate treaty with
Austria, and after the entry of the United States into the war in

April 1917, the Allies began to look at the Czechoslovak national claims with greater favor. In December 1917, Beneš's inexhaustible efforts in Paris resulted in the French government's approval of the organization of Czechs and Slovaks into an autonomous force. One of President Wilson's Fourteen Points (January 1918) proposed autonomy, not independence, for the nations of the Austro-Hungarian Empire; had Vienna accepted this condition, the hopes of the Czech and Slovak people for true liberation would have been destroyed. But Vienna declined Wilson's peace program, and events moved unrelentingly toward a complete Allied victory and Czechoslovak independence. During the spring and summer of 1918, the Allied governments committed themselves to support the program of the Czechoslovak National Council in Paris. On October 14, 1918, Beneš proclaimed its transformation into a provisional government. France recognized it on the following day; three days later, in Washington, Masaryk proclaimed the Czechoslovak Republic; and one week later, the British and Italian governments recognized the provisional government in Paris.

Masaryk's Washington Declaration was not only an official summation of the values for which the Allies had waged the war and which he himself had repeatedly advocated for four years, it was also a solemn pledge of new political and social programs for Czechoslovakia. He stated that the new Republic, accepting the principles of the American Declaration of Independence, would guarantee full freedom of conscience, religion, expression, press, and assembly. The church would be separated from the state; women would be politically, socially, and culturally equal to men; the rights of national minorities would be protected. The Czechoslovak nation would carry out far-reaching social and economic reforms; large land holdings would be expropriated, and the privileges of the aristocracy would be abolished.

So Masaryk's crusade which had begun in 1914—and had been viewed at that time (and to this day by some historians) as unbelievably quixotic—culminated four years later in events which even its principal protagonist, always a realist, saw as the happy ending of a fairy tale.

Actions at Home

The people for whom this "happy ending" was to establish "a new birth of freedom" reacted to events with characteristic ambivalence. Masaryk had struggled long and hard because he knew that, despite centuries of anonymity and oppression, the Czech and Slovak "nation" still lived. Yet, there continued to be baffling behavior that seemed to disassociate the sense of nationhood from overt, consistent action toward its accomplishment.

At the outset of the war, political and ideological disorientation was a phenomenon common to both sides. No one (except, perhaps, Lenin and a few other Marxists, whose influence at the time was more potential than actual) anticipated the shattering effects that the war would have on all traditional institutions and political arrangements. Certainly no one expected the end of the struggle to signal the destruction of the old Austro-Hungarian Empire. It is hardly surprising, then, that Czech and Slovak politicians aspired toward something less than independence. Such a hope did lie deep within the people's feelings. But there *were* the Austro-Hungarian police. The struggle between aspiration and reality at times produced more than a frightened silence: it prompted opportunistic declarations, under pressure, of loyalty to the Empire.

Audacious political figures such as Karel Kramář and Alois Rašín, who led the Young Czechs Party, Václav Klofáč, the leader of the Czech National Socialist Party, and Josef Scheiner, the leader of the patriotic *Sokol* organization, were arrested on suspicion of high treason. Some of them, their imaginations fired by the impressive initial advance of the Czarist army, expressed, in veiled terms, support for the idea of offering the historic Czech crown to a member of the Romanov family. After the spring of 1915, however, as the Russians went from one defeat to another and the struggle in the West turned into a prolonged war of attrition, Czechoslovak politicians assumed a posture of "wait and see," although the "Mafia" kept up its secret contacts with leaders abroad. Indeed, as late as January 1917, when the Entente included among its war aims the liberation of the Czechs and Slovaks, the Presidium of the Association of Czech Deputies, which represented all political parties, reacted, under pressure from Vienna, with a solemn affirmation that it saw the future of the nation within the Austro-Hungarian Empire. At that moment, Masaryk and his associates abroad must have felt discouraged about the progress of their struggle not only against the ignorance of the Entente leaders, but also against the opportunism of the people at home.

Political events on the world scene, however, could not but affect significantly the politicians and the general mood in the Czech lands and in Slovakia. The February Revolution was expected to change Russia into a democratic state. The entry of the United States into the war in April 1917 brought into the Allied camp a young and vigorous nation whose democratic model and power were idealized. In this context, public expressions of the true sentiments of the Czech and Slovak people were no longer delayed.

In May 1917, 222 men prominent in literature and the arts, appealed to the politicians to speak up and represent the nation's wishes. Events then began to unfold with accelerated momentum. Before May had ended, Czech deputies issued a declaration asking for federation of the monarchy, in which the Czechoslovak nation would be unified. At the same time, an impressive demonstration occurred in Prague, where the people shouted "Long live Masaryk!" Never before had his name been publicly acclaimed.

The October Revolution in Russia had a definite but complicated impact on further developments. It released in Czechoslovakia not only long-accumulated social forces, but also deeply embedded national energies. Broad masses saw the October Revolution as a continuation of the democratization of Russia, and the working class, lacking a revolutionary leadership, sought expression of its position more in national than in class manifestations. The Soviet government's original demand for national self-determination spurred the enthusiasm of the masses, an enthusiasm which was reflected in a declaration by all the Czech political representatives. In January 1918, they asked for independence, stating openly that the fate of Czechoslovakia would be decided at

an international conference. Such demands were in no sense related to Lenin's "class" interpretation of the principle of self-determination (they were not even acquainted with the argument), and
when, in March 1918, revolutionary Russia signed a separate
peace treaty, leaving the fate of the oppressed nations to the
mercy of Vienna, the Czechs and Slovaks were profoundly disappointed. Fortunately, Woodrow Wilson's recognition of the right of
national self-determination—with a connotation quite different
from Lenin's—became a part of the Entente's peace aims.

In January 1918, strikes occurred in many areas controlled
by the Central Powers. Workers protested against economic conditions, food shortages, and, in some places, against the war itself. In
the spring, another element contributed to Vienna's policy: by the
end of May, some 400,000 prisoners had been returned from Russia to the Empire and were being readied for the Italian front; they
protested against the war and, in some cases, mutinied. Rising nationalism added another dimension to the strikes and protests in
the Czech lands and Slovakia. By then, the achievements of the
Czechoslovak Legionaries in Russia and the engagement of small
Czechoslovak units on the French and Italian fronts were known
all over the country, inspiring the people to resist further. At this
point, the national leaders rejected Vienna's offers to accommodate the nation's demands. Its pledges to restructure the monarchy
into a federation came too late. In July, all political parties formed
a National Council which decided to organize a general strike. October 14, 1918 was the day designated, and the strike was principally intended to shut off food and coal supplies to the armies of
the Central Powers. The National Socialists and the Social Democrats were in charge of the strike. A proclamation, addressed to
"All working people in the Czechoslovak nation," rejected negotiation with the imposed representatives of a foreign power and
solemnly stated, "The time has come. We have thrown off the
chains of subjected slaves. We have risen to independence. With
our own unbreakable will and with the sanction of the whole democratic world, we declare that we are standing here today as exec-
utors of a new state sovereignty, as citizens of a free Czechoslovak
Republic."

The general strike was an impressive manifestation of national determination. Strangely enough, words of warning against premature action came from the Czechoslovak Council in Paris and words of criticism came from the Prague National Council. As late as September 1918, Beneš urged his associates at the home front "not to be provoked by the Germans or anyone else into a premature rebellion. Any revolution which must come and for which you must be prepared and organized must occur in agreement with us." In the expectation that a decisive Allied attack would not take place before spring, he asked again that they be prepared, urging them, however, not to start "any revolutionary, mass action without instruction from us." [2] (It is interesting to note that as president of the government in exile in London during World War II, Beneš sent similar messages of caution to the resistance leaders at home.) As to the Prague Council, its conservative members protested that the proclamation went too far in speaking of a "free Czechoslovak Republic." Beneš's concern proved unfounded. Despite some disturbances, the strike took place, and, with equal typicality, in an orderly fashion.

Two weeks later, the Republic of Czechoslovakia was solemnly proclaimed by the National Council. After centuries of oppression, right had prevailed over might—indeed, had prevailed without might. The principles of self-determination and the rights of the oppressed, planted, nurtured, and defended in the capitals of the Entente powers by the grizzled "old man," Thomas Masaryk had been accomplished without the firing of a single shot—a fascinating and humane achievement, but one that cast a long shadow over the future.

2. Edvard Beneš, *Světová válka a revoluce*, 3 vols. (Prague: Čin and Orbis, 1928), 3: 172–73.

Chapter Three

Laying the Foundations

Sailing from New York to Europe toward the end of November 1918, Thomas G. Masaryk, provisional president of the Republic of Czechoslovakia, was preoccupied with the future of his country. Czechoslovakia was free and independent. He had been elected unanimously, in absentia, to the presidency by a provisional National Assembly. The dream had turned into reality—and yet, "one worry after another" raced across his mind. "Are we able to govern ourselves?" he pondered. "Can we . . . maintain our independence, maintain it permanently? Do we have enough ability, enough brains, enough perspicacity, enough will, enough resolution, enough perseverance?" His tentative answers to these questions were in the affirmative, but the uneasy questions themselves would reoccur.

There were also other problems. Before the war, Masaryk had engaged in many political controversies and had become known for his biting criticism. Assuming that "basically, people change only rarely," would those Czech politicians who had been his victims forget past controversies? He was sure that he himself "would not concede to anyone in matters of principle," neither would he fan the embers of old fires; as to "strictly personal aversions," he said, "I crossed them out of my mind."

After stopping for official visits in London, Paris, and Rome, Masaryk reached his native land on December 20. He had not seen his country for four years. At the time of his departure for the West, politicians and intellectuals were familiar with his professional and moralistic admonitions, but the people knew little about him. Now, though the people were free, and though they were thrilled and moved by his achievements, Masaryk knew they still lacked a coherent conception of their nation's future. Nevertheless, if there was ever an occasion when a people was justified in expressing strong emotion, even to the point of sentimentality, it was the day of Masaryk's glorious return to his homeland.

The Reunion

Despite the emotion and acclaim, however, the "professor" remained aware of his problems and faithful to his tasks. As his special train stopped in the little towns of Bohemia, Masaryk responded to the welcomes of local dignitaries with sober and meaningful words. On each such occasion—ten times in all—he spoke quietly of the difficult times ahead and of the need for all men to work diligently and seriously in their country's service. When the journey brought him to Tábor, the cradle of Taborite Hussitism, a single sentence sufficed to rekindle the humanist sense of Czech history as Masaryk understood it: "Tábor is our program," he said, "and we will remain faithful to that program." On the other hand, he spoke with equal sincerity to two bishops who paid him their respects on behalf of the Catholic church: "I beg of you to give the people a living religion." Two days later, he expressed his personal satisfaction that women were represented in the National Assembly, since "women should devote themselves to public activity just as men."

Neither his themes nor his manner was calculated to enhance his popularity. Indeed, voices were heard whispering that he had hardly returned home when he had turned "professor"— exhorting and scolding a nation still drunk on the heady wine of freedom. Still, he had fought for the equality of women before the war; he had included his American wife's maiden name in his own name (a most unusual practice in Europe); and the Hussite movement had asked that women be equal partners with men in the struggle for ethical purification. The movement must go forward. Had not Havlíček urged his people to work hard for the benefit of the nation? Masaryk would urge them further. Had not the Taborites reconciled the gospel of Christianity with the necessity of arms in its defense? Masaryk too, would bridge that contradiction. And if the Catholic church had dogmatized religion, then let it revive a vital, "living" quality. The inevitable question that emerged from all this exhortation was clear, and it drove him: would the nation and its leaders be willing and capable of picking up the thread of history, of fulfilling the humanist ideals that were Masaryk's vision of his country's destiny? Or would they lapse into petty, provincial jealousy and intrigue, into the practices they had learned so well during the years of subjugation and humiliation?

When Masaryk's train reached Prague on December 21, 1918, a brisk, wintry day, a strange group of men greeted him on the platform of the station that later carried the name of Woodrow Wilson. Masaryk had repeatedly emphasized the fact that democracy requires responsible political leaders and administrators, drawn from the ranks of the common people as well as the intelligentsia. The men gathered at the station did, indeed, represent all strata of Czechoslovak society—peasants and workers, bourgeoisie and intellectuals, writers and politicians, Catholics and Protestants. They were, on the average, some fifteen years younger than the man they came to honor (though hardly youngsters, for Masaryk was then sixty-eight).

Four of them require special mention (certain Slovak leaders will be dealt with later in a different context), not only because of their striking personalities, but also because of the crucial roles they were to play during the first years of the Republic.

Karel Kramář (1860–1937), the prime minister, was the best-known of the welcoming delegates. A former member of the Viennese Parliament, but also a hero of the resistance (he had been sentenced to death by the Austrian authorities but granted amnesty in June 1917), Kramář had an impressive bearing and a solid political education. He was the only man in the group with a strong European orientation as well as rich contacts with Europe. A consummate politician, seasoned in many battles in the Parliament, he was an ardent nationalist and Slavophile who had sought protection and assistance for his country from Czarist Russia. When his conservative convictions propelled him into leadership of the middle class, he had engaged in extensive and sharp controversies with Masaryk. At the Prague station, he greeted his old antagonist warmly, and the two men embraced.

As time went on, this warmth chilled. Masaryk's social concerns, his contempt for cheap nationalistic slogans and Slavic sentimentality, and his policy of nonintervention in Russian affairs clashed with Kramář's conservatism, his patriotic rhetoric, and his desire to aid the conservative white Russian politicians and generals. Kramář's party, the National Democrats, soon represented industry and the interests of the upper middle classes and lost its prestige and influence among the masses of the people.

Alois Rašín (1867–1923) was similar to Kramář in social background, education, and political outlook, and also shared with him the wartime prison experience and its aftermath—initial popularity and respect. His patriotism and integrity aroused both admiration and antagonism. As minister of finance in the first Cabinet and again in the fall of 1922, he saw a rigorous financial policy as the fundamental prerequisite for a stable, healthy economy. Such a policy required strict controls, sacrifice, heavy taxation of individual wealth, and hard work without adequate compensation. His dictum, "One is not paid for service to his homeland" enraged the masses, and its echo reverberated around the country. In 1923, Rašín was shot and killed by a Communist fanatic. He was the only victim of political assassination during the first twenty years of the Republic.

Vlastimil Tusar (1880–1924) stood at the other end of the

political spectrum. A trade union organizer and journalist, he earned a popular following among the workers, was elected to the Vienna Parliament in 1911, and soon became a leader of the Czech Social Democratic Party. As had other Czech politicians during the war, Tusar at first pursued a cautious course, but toward the war's end, his influential voice helped to swing the party leadership, in opposition to Bohumír Šmeral, its chairman, toward an uncompromising Czechoslovak policy. In 1920, when the party was torn to pieces and the country thrown into a violent class struggle by the conflicts between moderates and radicals, Prime Minister Tusar's unostentatious but determined negotiations and masterful maneuvering saved his party from self-destruction and his country from disaster. Having long suffered from a fatal disease, Tusar resigned in 1920, and he died in 1924.

Tusar's statesmanship would have failed had it not been for the support of Antonín Švehla (1873–1933), the most fascinating personality in the first generation of Czechoslovak politicians. From a farming family and without higher education, Švehla had become, even before the war, the recognized leader of the Czech Agrarian Party. Representing the small landholders, he became a keen exponent of social equality; his opponents nicknamed him— mockingly but not wholly inaccurately—the "Red Agrarian." His identification with the soil embraced his dedication to the country. He was the soil itself, earthy and enduring. When Tusar, a socialist, was called by Masaryk to form a new government, Švehla, the Agrarian, did not hesitate to join him in what became known as the "Red-Green Coalition." It was not only an unusual combination of seemingly contradictory forces, but also a rare political phenomenon in a Europe split between nationalist, conservative peasants on one hand and internationally minded socialists on the other. It was a typically Czechoslovak political accommodation, and one that enabled the nation to endure the future years of social and national turmoil. Two years after Tusar's resignation, Švehla renewed the association of the Agrarians with the Social Democrats, a coalition which remained the backbone of the government for four years and permitted the nation to achieve twenty years of stability and progress.

Intellectually, Švehla stood poles apart from Masaryk, but the president valued his qualities and services highly and considered him the finest statesman in the country. This earthy farmer, a kind of early-day Harry Truman, had healthy instincts; he took joy in the art of governing without seeking publicity, and he negotiated lustily behind the scenes. Švehla's many talents dominated the formative years of the Republic.

These, then, were the men who greeted Masaryk—tall, bearded, elegant, wearing a pince-nez and black winter coat and hat—when he stepped from the train for the reunion with his people. From the distance of fity years, one can affirm without hesitation that most of the men who extended him their affectionate welcome were of high calibre, with a sense of responsibility and dedication to the principles of democracy.

Grim Realities

The dizzying intoxication induced by newly won independence could not last indefinitely. The nation and its government were soon confronted by some sobering realities. Theirs was a polity, governed, as yet, by provisional legislative and executive bodies, its boundaries not internationally recognized until the various peace treaties had been formally signed. The country itself was threatened by an invasion of Slovakia by Hungary and by the short-lived proclamation of an independent Slovak Soviet Republic. The Sudeten German minority refused allegiance to the new Republic and sought a solution of its grievances in an alignment with Austria. Finances were in chaos, due to the enormously inflated old Austrian crown. The war had all but derailed the economy; coal production had dropped drastically, and transportation was in disarray. Lack of food aggravated social unrest, and the working class, suffering most, was radicalized by Communist agitation. Peasants were hungry for land. Strikes spread like wildfire, and attempts to seize land erupted around the country. Prisoners of war and Legionaries, returning home after years, could find neither adequate housing nor employment. As anticlerical sentiment rose alarmingly, the Catholic hierarchy was confronted by hostile mobs.

Some foreign official analysts understandably predicted an early demise for the new Republic, and they did not conceal their antagonism. The American minister in Prague, for example, referred in his dispatches to the "pro-aristocratic and anti-Czech tendencies" of the British chargé d'affaires. On the other hand, it took the U.S. Department of State four years to learn how to spell the name of the country. A Mr. DuBois, reporting from the vantage point of the American legation in Vienna and signing his letters to Washington "special agent," did nothing to hide his unfriendly attitude toward the Czechoslovak government. According to him, the nation leaned toward Bolshevik Russia. He claimed that the Social Democrats in general, and Tusar in particular were close to the Bolsheviks. To DuBois developments were most discouraging: many Slovaks expected to rejoin Hungary; the Czechs were basically atheists and socialists; and the Czechoslovak Legionaries returning from Russia were leftists who demanded socialization. With its diverse nationalities, the new state resembled the old Empire, and its internal conflicts were certain to bring it down. From his Viennese post "special agent" DuBois seemed unable to differentiate between surface activities and enduring values.

Richard Crane, the first American minister to Prague, did not share DuBois's antagonistic view, though his reports include some droll stories about difficulties involving the new Czechoslovak bureaucracy. In one of his first dispatches, Mr. Crane gently complained of the lack of effective organization—in the absence of Beneš—in the Foreign Office in Prague, where, he said, there were only two competent persons and one of them was about to leave for an assignment abroad. His French colleague shared Mr. Crane's view, reporting that he had "addressed over one hundred notes to the Foreign Office to which he had received not a single reply." As a result, Crane continued, "the Foreign Office is now ignored by all the ministers, who whenever they have important matters to take up usually go directly to President Masaryk."

On the more amusing side, Mr. Crane reported that, on the occasion of an official dinner, his invitation and place card read

"Mrs. Dr. Crane Richards." More amusing and infinitely more embarrassing was the reception for the Polish premier, Ignace Jan Paderewski. President Masaryk, the Cabinet ministers, and the entire diplomatic corps were at the railroad station, where "a big military display took place, the Czechoslovak and Polish anthems were played, and all stood at salute." All that was missing was Paderewski! Someone had blundered, and when the premier did arrive some time later, there was no ceremony at all.

On another occasion, Mr. Crane himself became the victim of poor management in the Foreign Office. An opera performance was given in his honor, but since President Masaryk was ushered in ahead of him and he was conducted to a side box, "the President received most of the applause," and Mr. Crane was practically unnoticed. The well-intentioned minister understood the problem, of course, and, in general, his reports were positive, affirming that there was "the greatest goodwill, especially toward the United States. . . . My mere request as the American Minister is sufficient to obviate lengthy formalities." [1]

Whatever the observations of foreign officials, the Czechoslovak government had to address the hard problems of daily business. The heritage from the disintegrated Empire had both positive and negative aspects. The new Republic, with 13.6 million inhabitants, comprised 26 percent of the population of the old Empire and 22 percent of its territory. It took over a disproportionately large portion of the Empire's industry, however, between 70 and 90 percent of all sugar refining, brewing, malt manufacturing, glass, textile, leather, chemicals, ceramics, and paper industries, and the greater part of the construction and building trades and coal mining. Industry provided the livelihood of 35 percent of the Czechoslovak population. Before the war, these industries, concentrated in the Czech lands, had found easily accessible, duty-free markets within the Empire itself, but now the Republic had to find new outlets and trade channels, and the country's economy became decisively dependent on exports and, therefore, on general, worldwide economic development.

1. National Archives, Diplomatic Branch, Record Group 59, General Records of the Department of State, 860F .404; 860F .00/73A; 860F .00/45; 860F .00/14.

The banking system was quite another problem. Before the war, Vienna and Budapest had been the only financial centers of the Empire; there had been no banking business to speak of in Slovakia, and the banking in the Czech lands was concentrated mainly in German hands. The first Czech bank, Živnostenská, was founded in 1869; its assets and activities grew rapidly, along with those of other newly established banks, because of the frugality of the Czech people and their dedication to economic growth as an encouragement to the nation's self-confidence. After the war, the banking business was still controlled by Germans. The Czech banks, because of their modest origin and control by small shareholders, were still small, although a few, particularly Živnostenská, soon assumed typical big-capital functions. With much of the industrial and financial capital under Austrian, Hungarian, or German control, the new situation created not only serious economic problems, but also provoked vehement national and social reactions.

Conditions in agriculture were even more pressing. Nearly 40 percent of the Czechoslovak populace worked on farms. The antisocial aspect of land ownership under the monarchy was striking and intolerable: according to 1896 statistics, in the western parts of the territory that later comprised Czechoslovakia (Bohemia, Moravia, and Silesia), nearly 600,000 landholders shared less than 300,000 hectares (an average of about 1.25 acres per landholder). At the other end of the spectrum, 151 landlords owned individual holdings of over 2,000 hectares each, comprising altogether nearly 1.5 million hectares, or 28.31 percent of total land in the country. In Slovakia and Subcarpathian Russia, the situation was even worse: 935 estates of over 1,000 hectares each covered 35 percent of the total land area, while 281,000 peasants shared 4.5 percent of the land.

To add political and national insult to economic and social injury, most of the large estates were in the hands of foreign aristocrats or the monarchy-minded church. As the American legation in Prague noted in an exhaustive analysis in 1921, "Three German families, the Schwarzenbergs, the Colloredo-Mansfelds, and the Liechtensteins, held 313,524 hectares of Czech lands, or more than the combined holdings of 594,033 families of farmers, of whom none possessed more than two hectares." [2]

In the eastern part of the country, three aristocratic families, the Palfys, the Coburgs, and the Andrassys, owned 268,000 hectares of land. Peasants, though obligated under law to help extinguish fires, were otherwise forbidden to enter the forests. The chicanery of landlords went so far as to be ridiculous: "Painters were forbidden to enter the forests for the purpose of making sketches and paintings" or, if they received permission, they were "not to pick strawberries." Since only one person in eight owned any land at all, the hunger for land created severe social and political tensions, driving people to emigrate (some to the United States, but most to Vienna and the industrial German-inhabited areas of northern Bohemia) and adding nationalistic stresses to the economic pressures besetting the nation.

A religious element compounded the situation. The Prague archbishopric and the religious orders in the capital owned 42,975 hectares of land, while the city of Prague owned only 90 hectares of rural land and the whole kingdom of Bohemia possessed only 1,225 hectares. In Slovakia and Subcarpathian Russia, two archbishoprics owned 54,000 hectares. Indeed, the Catholic church controlled 3 percent of all land in the country. In addition, bishoprics and monasteries were endowed with vast industrial concerns.

The problem of the Catholic church was not limited to economics. Many Catholics turned against the high hierarchy of the church because of its identification with Habsburg interests and the German and Hungarian culture which symbolized the values of the nobility. The Slovaks, however, were devout Catholics, and did not question the spiritual bonds with their church.

Among the Czechs, the prewar slogan "Away from Rome!" was popular with the masses. Radical feelings were expressed in mass meetings and in ardent identification with the Free Thinkers, whose numbers increased from 13,000 before the war to 724,000 in 1921; during the same period, membership in the Catholic

2. Ibid., 860F .52.

church dropped by over 1 million. In November 1918, a crowd in Prague gave way to uncivilized passions, tearing down a column of the Virgin Mary as well as a statue of St. John Nepomuk, a four-teenth-century priest, who had been elevated to sainthood by the Catholic church principally to obscure the memory of a real Czech saint, Jan Hus. The mood in the Prague streets gave credence to the popular saying that "in every Czech Catholic there is a drop of Hussite blood." The papal Curia was not ignorant of the rising tide of Czech anticlericalism, and did not count the Czechs among its most beloved flocks.

Masaryk had advocated the separation of church and state since the 1890s, and in his Washington Declaration had enun-ciated that doctrine as one of the principal requirements of the Republic. As president, he plunged vigorously into a struggle for the fulfillment of this goal. In his message to the National Assembly on the first anniversary of the nation's independence, Masaryk in-dicated the need to establish the state on a firm moral basis. Refer-ring to the origins of the American republic, which had flourished "because of its great reverence for religion and morality," he pleaded that Czechoslovakia, too, "aim at the separation of state and church" and, like America, free the nation "from ecclesiastical authority" as it had been established by Austria. He insisted that this process did not imply a "loosening of moral bonds. On the contrary, it must mean a reinforcement of general morality . . . a strengthening of real religious authority."

Masaryk's appeal did not go unheeded. The Parliament was ready to act. Social Democrats and National Socialists, who held a majority of votes, led the fight when a bill on separation was debated at length and with passion on the floor of the Assembly. Even the Czech Catholic Party supported the idea of sequestering church property on a basis of equality with that of other large es-tates. This first radical step by the government ran into interna-tional as well as domestic difficulties, however, and the bill never passed.

Edvard Beneš, the minister of foreign affairs, who had orig-inally advocated a policy of separation, sought a solution through direct negotiation with the Vatican. Aware of the church's influence over the Slovak Catholics and the German and Hungarian minorities, as well as over Catholic circles in Western Europe, Beneš felt his primary effort should be directed toward ensuring the territorial integrity and domestic peace of his country. Out of his conversations, a number of agreements were reached: the prewar jurisdiction of foreign dioceses—always a strong card in the Vatican's hands—was to be suspended and adjusted to national boundaries; German and Hungarian bishops were to be recalled and the appointment of new bishops was to proceed with the concurrence of Czechoslovak government; an equitable arrangement was to be made concerning religious education in public schools and the maintenance of parochial schools; church property was to be regulated; political agitation in Slovakia against the Republic was to cease; and the repeated protests of the Vatican against the commemoration of Hus's death as a national holiday were to be discontinued.

By the end of 1920, the aim of a complete separation of church and state had been quietly abandoned by all political parties. All bishops were replaced by a clergy responsive to national and democratic feelings. As the American minister in Prague reported, the three bishoprics in Slovakia had "perhaps the first national Slovak bishops since Cyril and Methodius"—that is, since the year 863! Some concessions were made to Slovak sensitivity in the matter of Catholic schools; church property was subjected to the law of land reform, though churches received a subsidy in some form; and Jan Hus, still a heretic in the eyes of Rome, continued to be celebrated by the people.

Slowly, religious hatreds (which had never reached the violent intensity of those between, say, the Irish Catholics and Protestants, or the Serbian Orthodox and Croatian Catholics) gave way to mutual tolerance and respect. In 1928, a modus vivendi, signed by the Czechoslovak government and the Vatican, formally confirmed the factual situation and established an international basis for peaceful development. In 1935, Archbishop Karel Kašpar was elevated to the cardinalate—the first "native" prince of the church in Czechoslovak history.

Revolutionary Threats

The accumulated pressures of the economic, social, and political problems (present in all Europe) threatened to destroy the new Republic. The multifaceted revolutionary potential, triggered by the deprivation of the postwar years but aggravated by the heritage of the previous 300 years, had to be defused and its new, dynamic forces and hungers channeled constructively, if the destruction of independence and freedom was to be averted.

It was little consolation to the Czechoslovak people that the situation in all the neighboring countries was even worse. For many years Czechoslovak industrial workers had been exposed to Marxist teaching. They were highly politicized and well organized, represented mainly by the Social Democratic Party, the strongest party in the country, even before the war. Easily stirred by radicalism, some of its leaders and most of their followers demanded immediate and extreme solutions. Ringing voices in Moscow spoke of equality and of the victory of the proletariat, appealing to the European masses to rise in revolution and smash exploitive capitalism everywhere. In Berlin, in Hamburg, Communists manned barricades and for a while local Soviets controlled some East German towns; in Hungary, the Communist regime of Béla Kun controlled the government; in Bavaria, a quasi-Communist rule was established and held power for a few weeks; and in Poland, the Red Army reached the gates of Warsaw, with a ready-made Polish Communist government trailing in its wake.

Workers in Czechoslovakia could hardly remain insulated from this revolutionary fervor. Nor did they fail to recognize that the new Republic, while giving them political freedom, had not liberated them from social humiliation and economic deprivation. They organized strikes and hunger marches. According to Communist sources, in the period between 1919 and 1923, 15,489 enterprises were on strike at one time or another, with 12.7 million working shifts lost (more than at any time until 1938); obviously, these strikes severely aggravated the economic situation. On December 10, 1920, the violent mood reached alarming proportions when a general strike was called; it was organized by the radical

Left as a means of seizing power. In violent actions in three different localities, thirteen demonstrators were killed. However, the radical Left failed to seize the government. In Czechoslovakia, any such attempt was certain to encounter formidable obstacles.

First, there was a universal concern for the fate of the young Republic. All classes of people shared feelings of national pride and were fully aware of the grave consequences of violent upheavals. Second, the National Socialist Party and the moderate wing of the Social Democratic Party (which still had a considerable following) refused to support the general strike. The working class as a whole did not endorse the radicals' conviction that the situation could not be remedied by democratic means. Third, and equally important in the light of Communist strategy, the revolutionary leaders lacked the determined cadres, the highly organized vanguard of the proletarian masses, to carry out a revolution, nor did they possess (as Communist scholars subsequently analyzed the event) sufficient knowledge of Lenin's theory on the strategy of seizing power. After serious ideological differences and organizational problems had been smoothed over, the radical Left finally established the Communist Party of Czechoslovakia in October 1921, but by that time the revolutionary situation had been deflated by a number of resolute and constructive measures carried out by the government. The fourth factor in the defeat of the Communist plans was Masaryk himself.

Masaryk Intervenes

Even before the war Masaryk had the friendly ear of the workers. Unusual as it was for a professor to visit the factories, he had done so and discussed with workers social questions in general and Marxism in particular. Later, as president of the Republic, he disregarded the formalities of his high office and plunged into action, going once again to these same human resources.

Speaking to Prague factory workers in April 1919, he stated that during the war, while he was fighting for political independence, he had thought about "social and economic liberation" and that he stood firmly behind their claims. Stressing as always an evolutionary and democratic process of change, he urged the workers to think carefully about socialism, a complex concept that required the cooperation of workers, management, and the bureaucracy. If socialization of the means of production was to become the goal, then the workers must know that beyond that goal was the major goal of achieving an ideal of humanity. The practice, not accomplishment, of socialism was the crux of the problem, and if workers wished to participate in the administration of factories, they must be well informed and fully aware of their own responsibilities. Socialism, therefore, meant not just organization, but education. Accepting the facts that the "current capitalistic social system" was one-sided and that "every one-sidedness must sooner or later come to an end," Masaryk, on the first anniversary of the Republic, nevertheless warned that in the process of socialization "one must keep carefully in mind the special qualities of the individual and the nation." Such is "not only an economic task but also an ethical necessity."

When the Communist agitation and violence reached its peak at the turn of 1920, Masaryk resolutely rejected both its methods and its extreme goals, and urged the government to act unwaveringly within a democratic framework to develop positive programs capable of moving the country toward democratic socialism. Turning to the intellectuals, many of whom were attracted by the Soviet example, Masaryk wrote a series of seven articles in which he analyzed with the authority of a sociologist and as a recognized expert on Russia—but clearly as a humanist as well—the questions of Marxism, the situation in the Soviet Union, and the unique meaning of "social revolution" in Czechoslovakia. The articles were not only a telling attack on Communist practices, but also, more importantly, a blueprint for action that his nation would take.

Pointing to the traditional emotional attachment of the Czechoslovak people to Russia, Masaryk declared that it had been founded on ignorance among Slavophiles in the past and was founded on ignorance among socialists (as well as enemies of bolshevism) in the present. Russian Bolsheviks were a small minority, while Czechoslovak socialists represented half the popu-

lace; Russian Bolsheviks had a revolutionary tradition, while Czechoslovak socialists had a tradition of parliamentarianism; Russian
bolshevism had a world-messianic character, while Czechoslovak
socialism was a national, populist movement, devoted to an ideal
of small-scale, concentrated endeavor, of daily work. The Russian
masses neither read nor wrote, and they were followers, "belie-
vers." "Yesterday they believed in the priest; today they believe in
the socialist agitator." Czechs, on the other hand, were literate;
they thought for themselves and were critical.

Further, Masaryk argued, Russian bolshevism was totally
different from even Marx's vision of economic and cultural development. "It is a communism of misery and disintegration," he
said, and there was no trace of freedom in Russia. The iron grip of
the present government could not be distinguished from the rule
of the church and monarchy in the Middle Ages.

All peoples and nations have the same goals—liberty,
equality, and fraternity—and social democrats had always accepted the principles of the French Revolution as their moral base,
but the Bolsheviks betrayed these principles as well as the ethical
content of socialism. The revolution in Russia was political, not
social, and Lenin's policy failed to implement Marx's theory of
social revolution. Terror cannot educate a people in true socialism,
and 1,000 years of habit cannot be uprooted by violence but only
by evolution and education, the careful maturing of new habits of
mind. The Bolsheviks had succeeded in "ridding themselves of the
Czar, but they have not yet ridden themselves of Czarism," Masaryk declared. The Bolshevik revolution was actually a product of
Russian backwardness, and even Lenin recognized that the level
of revolutionary struggle would be different in individual countries,
depending on the education and experience of the people, on an
objective assessment of the circumstances by thoughtful, tested,
and skillful leaders of the proletariat in every country. How, then,
Masaryk asked, could a Lenin decide the proper "degree of development" for Czechoslovakia, and what sort of leaders would ask a
Russian to make decisions for them? Education, he continued to
insist, was the basic prerequisite for socialism, for "as long as
workers are not really educated, as long as they are unable to control the production process and exchange of goods . . . the dicta-

torship of the proletariat is nothing else than a state of servitude."
As an ignorant supervisor cannot control production, he cannot,
however politically reliable, control the complex accounting of an
enterprise.

Parliamentarianism has many weaknesses, Masaryk admitted, but no better way has been found to represent and respect
both the majority and the minority. There is no socialism without
democracy. An economic and social equality, mechanically applied, is unjust, "an equality of misery." There can be no socialism
without education of leaders as well as masses. "Social democracy," he emphasized, "will remain the goal of real socialism," but
it cannot be achieved by following the Russian recipe and example:
"First, we ruin capitalism; then, we socialize the ruins." Rather, a
compromise with capitalism is required. Socialized enterprises
must produce not less but rather more than nonsocialized ones.
"We must produce more than in the past, otherwise, there will be
nothing left to socialize, nothing to distribute." Finally, Masaryk
pleaded for a truly humane and social revolution that would be
parliamentary in form and socially reforming in substance. Only
the politically and economically blind could accept the facile and
destructive slogan, "The worse the better." A civil war would not
only ruin the economy of the country, it would also corrode its independence. Against violence aimed at the Republic, he warned,
"all democratic forces would unite and stand to defense."

This was Masaryk's defense against the menace of expand-
ing international communism, but it was also a clear call to his nation to provide within democratic institutions and through prudent,
thoughtful, and educated behavior, viable alternatives, to right the
injustices of past centuries and the incivility of present suffering.
The nation and its government responded to his leadership.

Agriculture: Solutions

One month after the proclamation of independence, the National
Assembly enacted a law sequestering all large agricultural properties to prevent the manipulation of their sale by private interests,

particularly by land speculators. Masaryk later commented, "The sequestration law pre-empted social upheaval because it gave the people the hope of acquiring land." Four months later, in April 1919, the National Assembly passed the Land Reform Law, which directly affected 40 percent of the population, and, in its social and economic consequence, indirectly affected the whole country.

The sequestered land comprised 20 percent of all land; of the sequestered land, 17 percent was agricultural and 42.2 percent other rural, primarily forest, land. To alleviate the critical hunger for land, 3.5 percent of the sequestered land was immediately rented by the government to 265,000 tenants, with a ceiling of 150 hectares of agricultural and 250 hectares of diversified holdings per owner. The land was distributed among landless peasants, holders of dwarf lots, dispossessed prisoners of war and Legionaries, municipalities, cooperatives, and research institutes. The new owner paid a compensation based on the average price of land during the years 1913–15, receiving generous credit from the government. About one-half of the sequestered land remained in the hands of the original owners, subject, of course, to the imposed ceiling.

The execution of the Land Reform Law and related legislation took ten years. The final disposition was that of the sequestered land; the state and local governments acquired 12.5 percent (3 percent agricultural); individuals gained 31.8 percent (63.2 percent agricultural); and 55.7 percent (33.8 percent agricultural) was released to the original owners or was granted to them for thirty years.

As in the case of all radical solutions to social problems, shortcomings and failings plagued the land reform program. To some extent, political deals and nepotism distorted the principal thrust of the laws. The land that remained undistributed, the so-called "estate remnants," was sold to political favorites in average amounts of 100 hectares each, and this practice generated considerable bitterness. On the other hand, in 1921, 32 percent of all agricultural units represented dwarf holdings—under 1 hectare—but this unproductive situation was partly corrected by a subsequent reform that reduced dwarf holdings to 28 percent of all units by

1930, while middle-sized holdings (between 1 and 100 hectares) rose to 71 percent. The arable land picture was brighter: dwarf farms constituted only 2.6 percent, large farms of over 100 hectares 9.7 percent, while middle-sized farms comprised 87.7 percent of all arable land.

Another problem arose when the farmers encountered severe financial difficulties due to the world depression of the 1930s and were unable to meet their payments for the acquired land, for which the government had extended over 3 billion crowns in credit. Unable to meet their debts, many farmers were compelled to abandon their farms. It must be recognized that this failure was not related to the original intent of the land reform. Taken together, the land laws were an impressive embodiment of a desire for social justice, entirely consonant with the philosophical underpinning of modern Czechoslovak thought. Of the twenty-one European countries that introduced land reforms after World War I, Czechoslovakia envisioned the most comprehensive policy and achieved the most equitable implementation of that policy. In 1927, President Masaryk could rightly say, "The land reform, along with our revolution, is the greatest act of the new Republic; it is the climax and realization of the revolution itself."

Concomitant with the land reform, the development of cooperatives assisted the farmer in some aspects of his financial, production, and marketing concerns. With roots going back to prewar times, the cooperatives grew rapidly after the war. During the twenty years after 1918, the number of cooperatives of various types and their membership doubled, their capital tripled, and the assets administered under their aegis sextupled. The cooperatives were associated in federations, and all were gathered under the national Centro-Cooperative. In spite of all these supporting measures, however, agriculture still reflected cyclic financial strains, price fluctuations on the domestic and international markets, and changing supplies of industrial goods.

Emigration, long a safety valve for economic pressures, provided only a minimal solution during the 1920s and 1930s. While in the period between 1900 and 1914 there had been some 600,000 emigrants to the United States, between 1922 and 1930, only 276,000 persons, mainly peasants, emigrated, and in the depression years of 1930s, the number dropped to 6,000 a year. Represented by the powerful Agrarian Party and vulnerable to the political and financial machinations of some of its leaders, the farmer often stood in an unhappy and incongruous position. In spite of these vicissitudes, largely caused by factors outside government control, the Czechoslovak farmer remained immune to radical agitation and stood steadfastly loyal to his democratic convictions. Attached to the soil and therefore essentially conservative and individualistic, he contributed his solid weight to the process of strengthening Czechoslovak democracy.

Industry: Problems

In the long run, however, the fate of Czechoslovakia's political system rested largely on the political and economic power of the organized working class. Over 30 percent of the population depended on industry. In turn, industry's production depended on the importation of basic raw materials (except for coal) and on the exportation of finished goods. In the general chaos of the postwar world, neither of these activities contributed to growth in industrial productivity. Inflation was rampant and consumer goods scarce; real wages dropped 60 percent below the prewar level; the value of savings was drastically reduced, while the prices of manufactured products skyrocketed, multiplying twenty times in four years; food was in short supply, and the black market flourished.

The spring of 1919 witnessed a brief interlude of revitalization in the world economy, but during the following summer, a crisis gripped the world markets, and it hit Czechoslovakia in the fall of 1921. Industrial production fell to 86 percent of the 1913 level and had reached its lowest point by the end of 1922. Housing was high priced, a particular hardship for the hundreds of thousands of returning prisoners of war and Legionaries. The number of people unemployed reached the threatening figure of 353,000 in 1919, and while it dropped to 71,500 in 1921, it rose again to 207,000 in 1923. The situation was explosive, threatening an uprising of major proportions. As in the case of the crisis in agri-culture, disaster was averted largely through the operation of a responsible government which, under the inspired leadership of Masaryk, rose to the demanding occasion by introducing a number of economic and social reforms.

Democratic Government
in Action

The first Czechoslovak government represented all political parties; it was a government of national unity, inspired by the urgent need of a revolutionary transition from foreign domination to self-rule. It did not, however, reflect the distribution of the parties' popular support. The government was led by the respected but conserva-tive Kramář, and when the population in the Czech lands was given the first opportunity to express its political preference at the local level, eight months after the end of the war, the results indi-cated a clear leaning toward the Left. (Slovaks did not vote be-cause that territory was in the midst of the Hungarian Communist intervention.)

Kramář's government resigned, and the new government, which was constituted in July 1919, reflected more accurately the relative strength of the political forces, with the Social Democrats in the lead. The trend was confirmed on the next occasion that tested the political mood of the nation. The first national elections, held in July 1920 and this time encompassing the entire territory, gave the Social Democrats (both Czechoslovak and German) 36.8 percent of the votes, the Czechoslovak National Socialists 8.1 per-cent, and only 23.1 percent to all the center parties—Agrarian, Catholic, and Tradesmen—combined. The right-wing National Democrats garnered only 6.3 percent. The election clearly demon-strated the left-wing orientation of the people, who remained, even in these tumultuous times, faithful to democratic processes.

While the critical conflict between the moderates and the radicals approached a climax in the fall of 1920, the democratic leaders found a temporary solution in a step that became a

Czechoslovak rarity: the president appointed a "government of experts" who were not responsible to individual political parties but were still under the vigilant scrutiny of Parliament. This shrewd political maneuver freed the Social Democrats in particular to compete with the Communists in an open arena. The interregnum of experts lasted for one year, until the revolutionary tide had abated.

In 1919 the government responded swiftly to the explosive economic situation with a number of financial and social measures. In February, it introduced a new currency, simply by stamping the old, grossly inflated Austrian crowns and turning them into Czechoslovak crowns; it then radically deflated the new currency by an enforced 50 percent state loan. The circulation of currency was reduced, and propertied persons were required to pay a steep tax on their holdings. The immediate effect of these actions was the arrestment of inflation, which meant short-term hardship for the population, but which rapidly increased the value of the crown on the international currency market and opened the way to all-important foreign credit. This initial benefit was somewhat lessened in 1920, when the crown again suffered losses, but by 1923, its international value had stabilized.

Another step, reaching to the roots of economic independence, was the nostrification of foreign enterprises and banks on the territory of Czechoslovakia. Most of these industries and financial houses were controlled by offices in Vienna or Budapest. A law passed at the end of 1919 required the transfer of control to Czechoslovak territory, and all boards of governors were required to have a majority of Czechoslovak citizens. The transactions included changes in ownership and effected a material strengthening of domestic capital, which before the war had represented only one-third of the industries and trade. This undertaking required ten years and affected 235 enterprises, but the procedures were orderly and based on international agreements with the Austrian and Hungarian governments. Simultaneous with the process of nostrification, Czechoslovak banks engaged in buying, for a favorable price, shares of the concerns in foreign hands, an action which helped to fortify the economic foundations of the country. For political and economic reasons, the state itself acquired considerable property at this time. Based on the structure that had prevailed under the Empire, the state owned all the railways, the telegraph and telephone systems, the postal service, a number of fisheries, waters, electric plants, and machine shops, as well as vast forests. Street communications, and electricity, gas, and water services were owned and operated by municipalities. Suffering as it did from a lack of administrative experience, the process of socialization of the economy may not have been economically sound, but it reflected the people's healthy and characteristic concern for social equity. Karel Engliš, a highly respected theorist in economics, captured the political mood of the country and perceived its possible consequences when, as a member of the government in the fall of 1920, he stated, "We will socialize the country together with the socialists, and we will do it gladly. The Russian bourgeoisie failed to understand this and was, therefore, swept away." His conservative colleague, Karel Kramář, also recognized that "mankind is, indeed, moving toward socialization."

The government proceeded with equally deliberate speed and intensity in the fields of social welfare and workers' education. During first five years of the Republic, the Ministry of Social Welfare prepared no less than 157 laws and decrees, one measure following another in quick succession. Two months after becoming independent, the government reduced the old eleven-hour working day to eight hours. While debating the bill the National Assembly zeroed in on the fundamental problem which industrial societies, including Czechoslovakia, had failed to solve when its speaker reported to the Parliament, "Let us help the individual to find joy in his labor." The law was passsed unanimously by all political parties in the Assembly.

Another set of laws produced a relatively progressive policy of insurance against sickness and accidents, and later provided for pensions and paid vacations. Workers' demands for active participation in management and for sharing in profits were partially satisfied by the legalization of workers' committees for all mines and, later, for industrial enterprises with thirty or more employees. These committees assisted management in supervising the enactment of related laws concerning protection of labor and health conditions, in presenting motions for improving production, in mediating disputes, in deciding questions about the dismissal of employees, and in auditing the books.

The government further alleviated distress by establishing an indemnity and pension plan for 705,400 persons classified as war victims—invalids, orphans, and widows—and the critical housing shortage was relieved by state subsidies to the building trades. Nearly 250,000 houses were constructed in the Czech lands during the first ten years of the Republic—as many as in forty years before the war. A social institute was founded to foster research in social welfare. Special attention was paid to the education of workers. The government established libraries and study centers offering a variety of courses, arranged theater performances, concerts, and choirs for the workers, and offered technical courses in different languages and in trades for the unemployed. Through the years ahead, the government continued to subsidize all such activities.

The problem of financial relief for the unemployed was quickly addressed by several laws designed to alleviate the immediate and pressing consequences of the economic crisis of the first postwar years. Although these measures were only partially satisfactory, it should be noted that by the end of 1922, unemployment compensation in Czechoslovakia amounted to 20.6 percent of the daily wage, while in England it was 18.7 percent; in Austria, 11.3; in Germany, 9.5; and in France, only 8 percent. It was not until 1925, however, that the policy of unemployment compensation was put on firm ground. The Ghent system, as it was called, assured the worker of two-thirds of his daily earnings, paid to him through trade unions and to which the state treasury contributed half. The plan's great weakness, however, was that it did not cover the nonunion workers who represented two-thirds of the work force. As union membership grew, the situation improved. In 1919, Czechoslovakia participated in the Washington International Labor Conference, and it was the first country to ratify some of the conference's seven resolutions. Indeed, in some respects, Czechoslovak labor policy was more advanced than were the resolutions themselves.

All in all, the social policy of the immediate postwar years was both decisive and advanced. Such countries as Austria and Germany had introduced similar laws, but their implementation was drowned in revolutionary disorders and financial chaos. In Czechoslovakia, the social legislation had served to reinstate order, the rule of law, and to preserve freedom.

By the end of 1923, the democratic structure of the policy was safe and, until the dark days of the late 1930s, was not again to be endangered. The questions that had plagued Masaryk as he sailed from New York some five years before seemed resolved. The future of the nation, in dignity and independence, seemed assured.

Chapter Four

Years of Progress, Years of Trial 1920-1938

In the early 1930s, a decade after the Constitution was passed Masaryk observed, "I think our Constitution is good, but the question has always been and continues to be, how do you make the words live?" It was a profound question. It was clear to Masaryk's piercing mind that, despite independence, despite the apparent progress of the society, and despite the presence of freedom, more than a decade after the adoption of the Constitution, something was still amiss in the Republic. Only a man of his perception could have sensed the subterranean problems that would surface when the nation faced disaster. To all outward appearances, the fruits of freedom, of national pride, of idealism, were ripening everywhere.

The Force of Culture

Palacký, Havlíček, Masaryk, and the other political and intellectual leaders had repeatedly impressed upon the people the necessity of a good education as the prerequisite of political maturity. Despite the hostile attitude of the Austrian government toward cultural development in this still largely illiterate area, education became almost an obsession to the Czechs. In 1822, there were less than 1,500 Czech elementary schools in all Bohemia; twenty-five years later, 300 had been added, and by 1868, another 300. By the birth of the Republic in 1918, there were nearly another 4,000, making a total of some 6,000 elementary schools in all. Twenty years after independence, the number of lower and higher elementary schools had grown by another 300 percent. At the secondary school level, the increase in the same period was 200 percent. As to higher education, the Czechs were limited before the war to one university, Charles University, in Prague. Founded in 1348 and one of the oldest universities in Europe, Charles had become more and more a German institution, and only in 1882 was it divided into German and Czech campuses. By 1937, however, Czechoslovakia had sixteen universities or the equivalent.

Adult education, supported by public funds, was widespread. In 1936, for example, 61,000 lectures were arranged and were attended by almost 6 million people, and 4,500 courses were taken by 160,000 adults. By 1930, illiteracy had dropped to 4.1 percent (including Subcarpathian Russia), considerably lower than in any other country of the area.

Local public libraries were required by law, and books were published in great numbers. Addiction to newspaper reading was apparent everywhere, noticed by such foreign observers as Sir Robert Bruce Lockhart. Most papers were affiliated with a political party—not an unusual practice in Europe—but two independent dailies, Lidové noviny and Prager Tagblatt, achieved standards comparable to those of any reputable Western newspaper. The press generally enjoyed freedom, until it was curtailed in 1933 by a law passed in reaction to unbridled Communist agitation and the growing fascist extremism of the Sudeten German minority.

One of the most telling phenomena of all was the particular care taken to preserve the purity of the language. Any nation that suffers prolonged foreign oppression seems to sense that its language is far more than an instrument for the transmission of thought. Rather, it is sensed as cradle of culture, as an essential condition of national survival. For this reason, the Czechs and Slovaks treated their language with tenderness and respect.

Dating back to the eleventh century, the Czech language grew in richness during the Middle Ages, when it was not only the vernacular but also the official language, used by chroniclers, statesmen, theologians, and poets. Jan Hus reformed it and brought it to higher levels of expression. In the fifteenth century, Viktorín Kornel ze Všehrd, the founder of Czech law, did not see "why all things could not be uttered in as eloquent, or ornate, as delectable a manner in the Czech tongue as in Greek or Latin." Published toward the end of the sixteenth century, the *Bible of Kralice,* the first translation of the Bible in Czech, is considered by experts to rival the poetic majesty of the English King James version.

Alas, the "enemy" knows, too, the power of the language. With the Counter-Reformation and the process of germanization, the Czech language was relegated to the colloquial speech of peasant folk and replaced by German in all official, cultural, and educational spheres. Books in Czech were burned by tens of thousands. Their possession was punished by hard labor and sometimes death. By the middle of the eighteenth century, Czech, as a literary language, was on the verge of extinction.

With the new spirit of intellectual hunger and national identity triggered by the Enlightenment and the French Revolution, the Czech language experienced a rebirth. At the turn of the nineteenth century, several Czech and Slovak scholars studied and revived the language, and soon it was being spoken by the growing intelligentsia and the rising middle class. The restoration of the language became an integral part of the national reawakening. As Palacký put it, "Cultivation of mind without cultivation of language is sheer nonsense, and cultivation of language is a condition of a more noble spiritual life." Kollár spoke of the "silky Czechoslovak language," and a Czech poet, František Čelakovský, commented that "a number of literary words first saw the light purely out of sheer love for the language."

This ardent sense of the language has persisted to the

present day. After World War II, Pavel Eisner, pointedly titling his monumental study of the Czech language *Cathedral and Fortress* [*Chrám i tvrz*], wrote, "I love the Czech language because it is through it that everything was said that is dear to me, what I believe in and what I hope for." In 1954, Roman Jacobson observed that it was "difficult to find another land where the whole history of the nation and the national literature so unceasingly pivot upon the struggle for the independence and sovereign rights of the native word," and commented further that the whole dramatic history of Czechoslovak literature was filled with inspired hymns to the native language.

The history of Czech literature was indeed dramatic. After its "golden age" in the Middle Ages, when humanism flowered, the literature was constrained for over 200 years. Then, inspired by the liberating spirit of the French Revolution and riding the wave of nineteenth-century romanticism (moving later into an ardent quest for realism), it blossomed once again. Numerous translations of the literary works of great Western and Russian authors appeared. A national tradition in drama and opera was established. The National Theatre in Prague, which had been destroyed by fire, was rebuilt in 1883 from contributions of pennies that had been collected from village to village; characteristically, the National Theatre was the scene of national demonstrations during World War I.

The cultural renaissance achieved full vigor only with the nation's independence. Then, there was great creative ferment, particularly in poetry, with forms and substance changing and proliferating as eager protagonists experimented with or absorbed new artistic trends. Books replete with proletarian themes, aesthetic purism, patriotic rhetoric, and surrealism were published, as were social novels and historical treatises, and they all found eager audiences. Always, the most frequently expressed themes were humanitarian themes.

Theater, music, and the fine arts flourished. Prague alone supported twenty-three professional theaters, some traditional, some avant-garde, and many of them enjoyed state assistance. A reasonable price for tickets opened theater doors to a wide audience. The Prague Philharmonic Orchestra was one of the best in Europe. In the Paris schools Czechoslovak painters found an inspiring wealth of new forms and concepts, and some of them gave their creations a unique national flavor. Translations of foreign literary works satisfied hungry readers, with French works the most popular, English and American literature gaining ground, and Russian works always in demand, while interest in German literature declined. Scholarship expanded and improved in quality. Significantly, intellectuals, scholars, and artists enjoyed professional esteem and social respect.

The names of a few great writers must be mentioned: Karel Čapek, whose novels and plays became known in many parts of the world; Jaroslav Hašek, whose *Good Soldier Schweik,* published in numerous translations, has been compared to *Gargantua and Pantagruel* and *Don Quixote;* and Bedřich Hrozný, whose scholarly work is familiar to a small audience of indologists. Other important figures were the scholars René Wellek, Francis Dvorník and Alex Hrdlička; the composers Leoš Janáček and Bohuslav Martinů; and the musicians Rafael Kubelík and Rudolf Firkušný. All these and many more found artistic or intellectual homes at universities and concert halls in the West. The literary and intellectual atmosphere of Prague during the interwar period is depicted in the charming work *Books and Destinies* [*Knihy a osudy*], by Julius Firt, who, as director of an important publishing house, was located at the center of the Czechoslovak cultural world of the time.

Politics

To all appearances, then, the country was vibrant with life, with intellectual vigor and cultural richness. Yet, ten years after the Constitution was established, Masaryk asked, "How do you make the words live?" What worried him? The political and economic development of the nation was surely not the cause of his concern. Thomas Jefferson himself would have approved of the Constitution of 1920. In it there were guarantees of liberty, equality, and a balanced distribution of powers. A fairly detailed document, it spelled out the basic tenets of universal suffrage, secret balloting, protection of minorities, an independent judiciary, the final supremacy of the legislative branch of government, the collective responsibility of the executive branch, and the rather limited powers of the president, whose acts required the cosignatures of the government. Foreign scholars and observers agree that the Constitution was respected throughout the twenty years of the interwar period; no questions were raised in any quarter concerning the freedom of elections; the system of justice worked remarkably well; the National Assembly's authority was not questioned. The Constitution had established a basis for democratic development, and its implementation was marked by continuity and a coherent institutionalization of political, economic, and social forces that emanated, in general, from the traditionally cherished values of the country.

Masaryk's strange discontent was spoken against a background of relative tranquility, which was unlike the situations in other countries in the area. Polish democracy, bordering frequently on anarchy, succumbed to Józef Piłsudski's coup in 1926; Aleksandr Stamboliski was assassinated in 1923, bringing an end to efforts toward progressive development in Bulgaria; through the intermittent squabbles of its two leading parties, Austria turned to the dictatorial methods of Engelbert Dolfuss in the early 1930s; Yugoslavia, perennially wrangling over the problem of Serbo-Croat relations, had a new constitution and royal dictatorship imposed upon it in 1929; Hungary stagnated under the pressures of Admiral Horthy's ultraconservative elite; and Rumania's political parties became impotent under the increasing authoritarianism of King Carol. The fates of the German and Italian democracies need not be mentioned. Czechoslovakia, on the other hand, withstood pressures from the Right and the Left, and moved slowly, cautiously along the path of democratic evolutionary progress.

It was true that the spirit, if not the letter, of the Constitution was sometimes besmirched by practices which provoked justifiable and often intense criticism. The electoral law, passed immediately after the Constitution had been approved, provided for proportional representation, with the votes distributed in such a way that even small political parties had a good chance of participating in the National Assembly. From the point of view of representative democracy, it appeared to be an advanced and equitable system, but it did have a serious flaw: it encouraged a process of splintering. In the national elections of April 1920, for example, no less than seventeen parties sent representatives to Parliament (six others failed to get even one deputy elected), and only three of the seventeen polled more than 10 percent of the vote, while ten could not muster even 5 percent. In later elections, there was some movement toward middle-sized parties, but at no time in any election did any party gain a plurality. In 1920, the highest percentage, 25.7, went to the Social Democrats. Even that percentage was not entirely representative because the Communist Party did not exist at the time. In 1935, when Nazi agitation had practically wiped out all democratic German parties, the second-highest percentage, 15.2, went to the Sudeten German Party.

The unhappy consequence of all this was that not even two parties could secure a plurality through coalition; thus most governments were composed of five or more parties. It is no wonder, then, that these governments' programs were a mixture of opposing concepts and mutual concessions, lacking the coherence and force of a single programmatic thrust. Perhaps this situation was one of the lesser causes of Masaryk's disquiet; it was indeed, frequently, a *Kuhhandel* (horse trading), a term with a familiar Austrian ring, or as a Czechoslovak statesman put it, "We agreed that we will agree." Still, if compromise characterized Czechoslovak politics, and if it frequently seemed to obliterate a sense of firm direction, it at least, for the moment, reconciled contrasting positions—a condition that is one of the essential ingredients of a working democracy.

Other election practices, too, cast a shadow on the intent of the Constitution. For one thing, voters had no opportunity to vote for independent candidates; names could be put on the ballot only by party machinery. Moreover, the parties insisted on strict discipline, demanding that their representatives vote in Parliament according to the party-line decisions of the leadership, no matter what their personal convictions might be. The locus of the decision-making process, therefore, was neither in the coalition government, nor in the National Assembly, but in the party caucuses. An outgrowth of this process that invites no admiration was the institution of "The Five [Pětka]." This had its origin in 1920, when a government of experts was appointed for a transitional period. The leaders of five political parties (hence the name), while not formally responsible for the government program, directed it de facto by advising the government and piloting its bills through Parliament. Since the practice apparently proved expedient, it developed into an informal institution and its activities continued in the subsequent period when the government was again politically representative.

No liberal can excuse these practices. It would be difficult to believe that they pleased Masaryk, but his disquiet would have arisen from more serious dissatisfactions. The practices themselves are not difficult to explain or understand. The country faced many internal problems, and with the exception of Austria and Rumania, its neighbors were eager to exploit its weaknesses and were not without hostile intentions. As the ideological conflict throughout Europe intensified, the Czechoslovak democracy, exercising its own influence on the people of the surrounding states, increasingly irritated their fascist-inclined governments. None of these factors were conducive to the encouragement of full-blown, individualistic competition between massively powerful political parties. Such is the meat of demagogues, and in that atmosphere there is far too often a lack of responsible discussion and orderly process, leading to consensus building. Facing the many outside pressures, Czechoslovak democratic leaders embarked on the path of collective responsibility, and while this practice would not pass any rigorous test of the fundamental tenets of democracy, "The Five" may conceivably have saved, for the time, at least, the structure of democracy and its principal ingredient, personal freedom. Although the political technique was not exactly in the spirit of Jeffersonian democracy, it nevertheless proved effective in the defense of fundamental democratic ethics and assured the country of progress in the face of serious internal and external pressures. The history of both the Communist and fascist movements in Czechoslovakia during these early years certainly validated the country's basically democratic spirit and strength.

The CPC

After its founding in 1921, the Communist Party of Czechoslovakia functioned without interruption during the interwar period, whereas Communist parties in Central and Eastern Europe and in the Balkans were outlawed. According to official Communist sources, at the time of the Party's establishment—when the economic crisis had reached its peak and the working class was responding to Marxist lures—it had 300,000 members. By 1923, when the Party participated in communal elections for the first time and made considerable inroads into the following of the Social Democrats, its membership had nevertheless dropped to 132,000. In the national elections of 1925, the Party gained 13.2 percent of the vote, becoming the second-largest party, with forty-one seats in Parliament, but by that time its membership was down to 93,000. Four years later, in the next election, the Party gained 10.2 percent of the vote and, with only thirty seats, had moved down to fourth place. Communist sources do not record Party membership for 1929, but two years before, they claimed a membership of 138,000, which by 1931 had declined to only 40,000. By 1936, Party membership was up again to 70,000, and in the last free elections in 1935, the Party again received only 10.3 percent of the vote and thirty seats. These figures reveal not only the nation's political temper, but also the government's responsible activities in a time of crushing depression and international distress.

The fluctuations in Party membership also reflected the changing and confusing ideological attitude of the Party itself toward the very existence of Czechoslovakia. The Party faced the dilemma of reconciling the nationalist impulses of the working class with Marxist internationalism, and it had to do so in the face of constantly changing directives from the Third International.

The problem had its origin in the different political goals presented by the radicals during the war. In Russia, a group of left-wing social democrats had to compete for the allegiance of the Czechoslovak Legionaries. To do so successfully, their leader, Alois Muna (disregarding a strictly class-oriented proletarian argument) embraced a "social patriotic" ideology and, just a few days before the October Revolution, appealed to his followers to fight for an independent Czechoslovak state and even pledged allegiance to Masaryk. Then, six months later, in May 1918, he quickly and conveniently adjusted his position to agree with Lenin's interpretation of the principle of self-determination and, rejecting the idea of a bourgeois Czechoslovak Republic, asked for "the right of self-determination of the Czech nation to a social revolution." [1]

What Muna did not know was that Bohumír Šmeral, his counterpart in Prague, was pursuing a different policy. Before the war, Šmeral had been a respected and popular leader of the Czech Social Democratic Party, and his goal was, as he called it, the Austro-Marxist solution, namely transforming the Austro-Hungarian Empire into a socialist federation. Until the last days before the end of hostilities, he rejected any idea of future Czechoslovak independence, and, in fact, professed his loyalty to the Empire. Ignoring the nationalist feelings of the Czech workers, he ordered a black flag to be hoisted at the Party's central office on the death of Emperor Franz Josef, in November 1916. In May 1917, at a meeting of the Dutch-Scandinavian socialist parties, he admitted that "the whole nation was filled with a mystical faith in independence," that "ninety-five percent of the whole Czech nation had treasonous thoughts" and, including the workers, followed T. G. Masaryk. He confessed that he himself belonged to the remaining 5 percent, who looked at the situation "differently, rationally, soberly, and politically realistically." As late as May 1,

1. Karel Pomaizl, *Vznik ČSR 1918: Problém marxistické vědecké interpretace* (Prague: Čs. akademie věd, 1965), p. 71, n. 74.

1918, he was organizing demonstrations under the slogan "May of Peace," which reflected the recently concluded separate peace treaty at Brest-Litovsk. Šmeral even visited the Austrian foreign minister, Count Czernin, seeking his consent to the nature and scope of the planned demonstrations, "so that state interests would not suffer harm." Czernin was, of course, highly gratified by Šmeral's loyalty and concluded the audience with words that were devastating from the point of view of Czechoslovak hopes and interests: "I repeat: without social democracy, we could not wage this war for even one week." [2]

When the end of the war turned his plans for an Austro-Marxist solution into a forgotten dream, Šmeral faced still another dilemma. The Third International had branded the newly founded Czechoslovak Republic an artificial state, a product of the capitalist Versailles Treaty, and a pawn of French imperialism, and had instructed left-wing radicals to disassociate themselves from the moderate social democrats, wage a revolutionary struggle, and unite with the revolutionaries of the German and Hungarian minorities. But Šmeral, a devout Marxist, still could not reconcile himself to the existence of an independent Czechoslovakia and looked now toward another solution, a "United Socialist Europe." He was also politically sensitive enough to the feelings of the workers, however, to resist the foundation of an internationalized party, and he believed—against all Lenin's teaching—in the prospect of socializing the country through victory in parliamentary elections. In the end, he succumbed to pressures both from Moscow and from within his own Party, and in October 1921, the Communist Party of Czechoslovakia was founded, embracing all national elements: Czechs, Slovaks, Germans, and Hungarians. It was, indeed, a conglomerate, both proletarian and international, but with its founding, the troubles concerning contradictions between ideology and pragmatic politics were intensified. At every session of the Comintern, the CPC was criticized for a lack of revolutionary fervor. Finally, in 1929, its leadership passed into the hands of Klement Gottwald, whose task was to "bolshevize" it. The effects were

2. Zdeněk Kámík, *Socialisté na rozcestí: Habsburk, Masaryk či Šmeral?* (Prague: Svoboda, 1968), pp. 28, 45, 58.

soon felt, both in increased revolutionary pronouncements and decreased followers. In various statements by Party leaders, Czechoslovakia was described as the "jail house of nations"; in fact, it was said, "the Czech nation cannot be free as long as Czechoslovakia exists."

Before long, the Party's revolutionary "Bolshevik" spirit gave way to another political strategy. Faced with the peril of expansionist Nazism and fascism, Moscow in 1935 ordered the members of the Third International to pursue a policy of promoting the Popular Front. Now the CPC readily accepted the existence, the unity, and the territorial integrity of Czechoslovakia, and called for the defense of the Republic.

As the years passed, the CPC continued this nimbleness on all major questions concerning the structure of the country, but throughout the 1930s, it seemed to be much more successful in dexterity than in popularity.

"A Pathological Scum": The Fascists

At the other end of the political spectrum, the fascist movement never had a chance among Czechs during the interwar period. In general, fascism fed on animosity toward established institutions, and stemmed from an environment of political and social discontent. Without a clear ideology, it attracted disgruntled, uprooted individuals, who were saddled with feelings of inferiority for which they tried to compensate with mass vulgarity, hysteria, and the profession of a monopoly on patriotism. A ready prey to demagogues, their chauvinist anger turned against anything foreign; anything sensitive irritated their fundamental coarseness, and moral scruples were beyond their understanding. Power was their single goal, and their drive for power was facilitated by vacillating democratic governments and pusillanimous political parties, which neither challenged their power nor designed programs, adequate to meet the discontents on which fascist movements feed.

Czechoslovakia offered no favorable climate for fascism.

There were demagogues on the scene, and feverish individuals eagerly listened and responded to their flood of innuendo and diatribe, but sober people, by far the majority, were distrustful of any extreme remedies for social ills and looked instead for constructive and orderly solutions. Even Masaryk was not spared the denunciations of the fascists, but Edvard Beneš, his foreign minister, became the permanent target for their attacks. In the middle of the 1920s, however, when the movement aspired to achieve a firm organizational framework so that it could move on to forceful action, its bluff was called, and the reality of fascist impotence surfaced.

The movement centered around a once-popular figure, General Rudolf Gajda. He had been a talented officer in the Czechoslovak Legion in Russia and, with daring strategy, had commanded his troops in several successful operations against the Red Army. Admiral Kolchak even appointed him chief commander of his White Army, where he served for a brief period. It was not commonly known that his unstable character had led him into a plot against Kolchak. For a while, the legend of his Siberian exploits glorified Gajda. He was sent to the prestigious École de Guerre in Paris and was subsequently appointed chief of staff. He was wooed by chauvinist circles, and he responded eagerly to their outbursts with demagogic statements. In the spring of 1926, newspapers carried sensational stories that, in July, Gajda would use the mass congress in Prague of Sokol, the national gymnastic organization, as a means of carrying out a fascist putsch. The government ordered Gajda to retire from the army, and on the "fateful" day of the Sokol congress—nothing happened. However, Gajda's retirement, and the publicity surrounding his activities, unleashed a veritable pandemonium of accusations and counteraccusations. As the American legation in Prague reported, understating the case, "A series of political scandals and bitter attacks on public men which have led to actions for libel and slander are filling the Czechoslovak press and contributing nothing to raising the tone of public life in this country." [3]

The "public men" the legation mentioned were, in particu-

3. National Archives, Diplomatic Branch, Record Group 59, General Records of the Department of State, 860F .00/253.

lar, Beneš and Masaryk. The right-wing newspapers, together with Jiří Stříbrný and Karel Kramář, two leading adversaries of these statesmen, drew Masaryk and Beneš into the center of the furor. Masaryk considered this poisoning of the political atmosphere serious enough to pick up the gauntlet, and he publicly branded the fascists "pathological scum." Looking always at the deeper causes of social disruptions, Masaryk, in a press interview at the height of the campaign, characterized fascism as an anonymous movement, without a program, an association of malcontents, and commented that it was not a serious problem for Czechoslovakia, "except that it indicates a decline in liberalism . . . a testimony to a political disarray which has seized the bourgeoisie." Masaryk also confirmed the allusions in the press to Gajda's involvement with a foreign power.

Although an investigating committee was established by the Ministry of National Defense, the campaign continued unabated, and in January 1927, Gajda formally founded the Fascist Party. To expose the opportunism of his ultranationalistic and now extremely anti-Communistic convictions, the government released a series of documents dating back to the autumn of 1920 (when Communist agitation had appeared to threaten Czechoslovakia's independence) which implicated Gajda in contacts with the Soviet government. He had secretly expressed a desire to go to Russia to offer his services to the Soviet army, with a Colonel Krakovski acting as his contact with Hillerson, a member of the Soviet commercial mission to Prague. Chicherin, the Soviet commissar for foreign affairs, telegraphed to Hillerson that it was "inopportune" to invite Gajda on behalf of the Soviet government and instructed him to "arrange it so that the initiative comes from him and not from us." If Gajda asks to come to Russia, the message continued, "we cannot object; the authorization is assured in advance." Chicherin was interested in what Gajda could offer, but made it clear that the Soviet government had "nothing to offer him." Nevertheless, he advised Hillerson that Moscow attached "great importance to relations with him" and urged Hillerson to "devote to these relations all your attention and to encourage them."

The affair was brought to an end in January 1928 when the

Council of Discipline of the Ministry of National Defense found Gajda guilty, deprived him of his military rank, and reduced his pension by 25 percent. Lewis Einstein, the American minister in Prague, concluded his series of reports to the Department of State with the sentence, "The fascists of course protested, but their influence is a waning one and the fascist movement appears to be rapidly dissolving." [4]

The dissolution of the "pathological scum" was not as rapid as Einstein had predicted. In the national elections of 1929, Gajda joined forces with Stříbrný, also a dubious political character, and, under the banner of the National League, won 0.9 percent of the vote and 3 seats out of 300 in the National Assembly. Then, in January 1933, a group of fascists under the command of Gajda's brother staged an attack on the military barracks in Brno, with the goal of seizing power in the country. The attempt turned into a farce, but still, as late as the 1935 elections, Gajda's party polled 2 percent of the vote and secured six seats in the National Assembly—the apex of fascist achievement in Czechoslovakia. Gajda offered his services to the Nazis after they occupied the country in March 1939, but even the Germans realized that he had been utterly compromised with the Czech people, and they declined his offer. Though only an episode, the history of the fascist movement demonstrated that the Czechs were not attracted to extremes; they disposed of the fascist threat in a democratic fashion even while, in many other European countries, fascism was on the rise.

The fascist agitation in the mid-1920s did have a lasting effect on two segments of the populace—the army and the police force. In order to depoliticize the military and the police, a law was approved in April 1927 which deprived them of the vote and prohibited political activity in their ranks. This law spared the nation the military intervention in political affairs so sadly familiar in other states of the area, but it also denied the officer corps, the police, and the army in general the opportunity for an education in democracy.

On the whole, the governments of Czechoslovakia were

4. Ibid., 860F .22/25.

able to attend to their economic and social tasks in an environment of political peace. Technically, their composition—always a coalition—experienced a rather high rate of turnover (eighteen) in the twenty years of the interwar period. Politically, however, only three of these periods signified a substantial change: 1920–26, the time of the "Red-Green Coalition," with a left-oriented policy; 1926–29, the era of the "Black-Green Coalition" (which the leftists contemptuously called the "Coalition of Squires"), with a centrist position and without the participation of the socialists; and 1929–38, a period of a broad coalition, again including the socialist parties.

The peaceful transitions from one coalition to another were assisted by President Masaryk, whose unquestioned prestige and popularity (and his own activist attitude) encouraged him to intervene in moments of crisis. By the time Beneš succeeded him as president, in December 1935, his own authority was widely recognized, making it possible for him to influence government policies, as he put it, "in a new tempo, but in the old spirit." The stability of the government in the years 1923–29, an unusual phenomenon in a Europe exposed to ideological pressures from the extreme Right and Left, rested largely on a favorable economic growth, and, in the later years of renewed economic crisis and political turbulence (the German minority), on an acute sense of the need for national unity.

Economic and Social
Development

In 1924, industrial production was back at the level of 1913. By 1929, the year of peak economic growth, it had surpassed the 1913 level by 41 percent. Unemployment dropped from 96,000 in 1924 (and from 353,000 in 1919) to 38,600 in 1929. Social tensions were greatly alleviated, and the revolutionary spirit of the early 1920s had evaporated. This period of economic prosperity proved only too brief; the world depression hit Czechoslovakia like a thunderstorm.

Agriculture, always a sensitive sector of the economy, had been protected by import tariffs since 1925, but in the face of the general slump in the world market, new measures had to be introduced to safeguard farmers against complete ruin. In 1934, the government established a grain monopoly which acquired the exclusive right to buy and sell all agricultural products, as well as to control their import and export.

Industrial production experienced a similar strain, though the effects were felt somewhat later. When the blow fell, however, its consequences affected the economy and the social situation even more severely than did the agricultural depression. In 1929, exports, always vital to the economy, represented 25 percent of the GNP; by 1933, they had declined to less than 40 percent of the 1929 level. Industrial production in 1933 amounted to only 85 percent of its 1913 volume. With a slow upsurge in the world economy, industry resumed growth, reaching 94 percent by 1934, and by 1937, 136 percent of the 1913 production level. The GNP, however, was slower to recover, dipping in 1935 to 80 percent and then swinging upward in 1937 to 95 percent of the 1929 level.

Though all segments of the population were severely afflicted by the depression, the working class suffered most. In 1933, unemployment reached the unprecedented figure of 738,000 (according to some sources, 920,000) and by 1937 had declined to a still relatively high figure of 408,900.

During the period of the "Coalition of Squires" (1926–29), there had been some setbacks in the process of social justice, but the subsequent economic crisis and the renewed participation of the socialist parties in the government accelerated the effort to meet the most pressing social needs. Unprepared for the crisis and, pressed by heavy financial strains when it came, the government was at first slow to enact laws to cushion the human hardships it inflicted. Step by step, however, it introduced a number of alleviating measures. Unemployment benefits to members of the trade unions were increased, and nonmembers received food coupons and Christmas bonuses. Labor-management relations and insurance practices were progressively im-

proved. By 1936, collective bargaining extended to 2,860 con-
tracts, covering 995,000 employees. A law passed in 1935 regulated the conditions under which factories could be closed or could
discharge more than 10 percent of their employees, and it also
required employers to give workers advance notice of their dismissal, according to length of employment. The same law stipulated that workers be granted paid vacations and specified holi-
days, and it established labor courts.

As to insurance, by 1938, out of 4.5 million workers in the
labor force, 3.3 million were insured against sickness and 2 million
against industrial accidents. If unable to work because of illness or
accident, employees received a daily allowance for a period of up
to fifty-two weeks. Pension policies, amounting to around one-half
their pay, were extended to all office employees, teachers, railroad
workers, and postal workers.

All of these measures, however, fell short of the basic needs
and expectations of the working class. Once again, social tensions
intensified, and a revolutionary situation appeared to be developing. In 1928, the Sixth Congress of the Third International issued
an appeal to all Communist parties and working masses to over-
throw their capitalist governments and seize power. In response,
the CPC set out to disrupt industry. Numerous strikes occurred;
mass public demonstrations were the order of the day; "hunger
marches" threatened orderly daily life; and the landless proletariat
attempted to seize land by force. The government had no choice
but to intervene, and the inevitable result was physical and violent
confrontation. According to Communist sources, 29 persons were
killed and 101 wounded in clashes that erupted during the critical
period between 1930 and 1933.

Yet, the tensions had begun to abate by 1934, and, as the
economic pinch slackened and the government's social reforms
began to succeed, the energy of the revolutionary impulse drained
away.

In retrospect, one can ascertain that, critical as those times
were, the "objective conditions" for a successful social revolution,
as Stalin had pictured them, did not exist in Czechoslovakia. The
working class failed to regard the social situation as "intolerable"

and was not, as it was supposed to be, electrified by the revolutionary vision. Privations rarely reached a point beyond human tolerance, and the workers' spirit, given to reasoning and compromise in the typical Czechoslovak way, was not ignited by a revolutionary spark. Further, the government, which the Communists expected to be unable to cope with the revolutionary situation, was never rendered impotent, and it succeeded in relieving the most serious exigencies while keeping a firm hand on the threats of disorder. According to Stalin's theory, the neutral masses, who were not actively engaged in the struggle between the proletariat and the bourgeoisie, the so-called "amorphous masses" who comprised the overwhelming majority of the population, were supposed to tip the scales in favor of the revolutionary forces by joining them at the last moment. Instead, they stayed calm and detached. As a final blow, Stalin himself failed to act on his own postulate and offered no aid to the Czechoslovak proletariat. Rather, he concentrated on industrializing the Soviet Union, a task for which he needed foreign credits, capital goods, and peace in general. His conditions for a successful revolution were met in only one respect: the capitalist countries were unable to help the Prague government; they had problems enough of their own. Thus Czechoslovak democracy survived another crucial test, and by 1937, life was almost back to the normal ways of peace, steady work, and economic and social progress.

Why, then, the melancholia of Thomas Masaryk's remark at the midpoint of the apparently healthy growth of the Republic? What was wanting? Education? The record was remarkable. A diverse and energetic cultural life? The evidence was clear. Political stability? The events demonstrated that Czechoslovak democracy, though by no means perfect, persisted in the defense of fundamental freedoms, far more than did its east European neighbors. Economic progress? The struggles had been enormous, but they were those, endured by all the world and, as the years progressed, greater and greater number of Czechs and Slovaks shared in the fruits of labor in field and factory.

It was not, then, any fault or failing in educational, economic, or political sectors of his country that caused Masaryk to fear that the "words" of the Constitution did not "really live" in the hearts of the people. Rather, as a deeply spiritual man, he knew that only through the restoration of his people's national self-confidence could the ultimate victory be won, and he wondered if the pressures of the age would permit that restoration to take place.

Deaustrianize!

Masaryk's perception cannot be expressed in statistics. It was, rather, a sense of intangible qualities. What he sought can grow only from years of tradition, from habits born of self-assurance in an environment of prolonged peace and security. These elements were still missing, he believed, and he summed up the problem and its solution in one word: *"odrakouštět"*—deaustrianize. Centuries of second-class citizenship, of political, economic, and social segregation from the mainstream of developments, tend to make a people acquire the habit of humiliation. To assure their material existence, they abdicate their dignity; to gain some slight advantage, they are willing to bargain away their self-respect. After 1918, their Constitution invited the Czechoslovak people to act as free men and women. The question Masaryk asked was whether they could truly free themselves from the character that 300 years had stamped upon them.

Masaryk spoke to the point unceasingly. "Democracy needs leaders, not masters," he said, and when pointing out weaknesses in the national character, he criticized the intelligentsia which had "its own share of the blame—priests, teachers, writers, bureaucrats, and the rest altogether who educate and lead the masses." The new democratic Republic demanded a "new man" who must get rid of old political habits. In his first message to the Parliament, Masaryk expressed concern about "a certain fear of responsibility" and, one year later, in October 1919, he specified the needs of the government in concrete terms: "We need a successful administration, a new type of official, a new bureaucracy . . . new in the sense of industrious, conscientious, honorable and honest, and, withal, thinking and thoughtful." He hoped for the "recognition and execution of the principles of equality of all people, recognition of freedom for all citizens, of humanitarian principles of brotherhood within and without—that is a novelty not only political but also ethical."

He had words of praise for peasants and workers, but described the urban and intellectual circles as "unfinished." "Talented we are, that is true," he admonished, "but we are . . . unstable, not wise enough, politically immature." The words of the Constitution that declared the Czechoslovak people to be free men were not enough. To Masaryk, the need was for a new spirit, a new style, an unostentatious pride in one's own achievements—and the phrase he used most often was "deaustrianize."

Apparently, the Czechoslovak people lacked the ability to stand erect and firm for their principles and rights. Individual and collective responsibility were submerged by selfish inclinations. Although social consciousness was embedded in the minds of the Czechoslovak people, their individual commitment to human relations was blurred. Pettiness tended to obscure large perspectives; envy and jealousy precluded acting in good faith. The motives and attitudes of those in high places were suspect. Common sense suffered from the onslaughts of demagoguery. Pedagogy, respectable in subject matter, was paralyzed by narrowness and rigidity, offering little encouragement to independent thought or education in citizenship.

There persisted, for example, a relationship between the authorities at various levels and individuals in all sectors of life that was a direct outgrowth of the Austrian *Obrigkeiten* treatment—a combination of fear and formal regard for official function, an acute consciousness of dependence on the good will of someone in a superior position. This situation was apparent in relations between worker and employer, and student and teacher, in the hierarchy of administrative structures, and in the stratification of economic enterprises. It discouraged freedom of opinion and expression, retarded the growth of constructive ideas, and corrupted mutual respect and dignity.

The bureaucracy, generally well educated and efficient, was

feared and despised. Underpaid, it found an outlet for its frustrations in condescension toward the people it was supposed to serve and not command. It was unthinkable that an official communication would end with a complimentary closing such as the American "sincerely yours" or "yours truly," much less with the English "your obedient servant." The Czechoslovak bureaucrat was neither "yours" nor "sincere" nor "true," and he most certainly was not an "obedient servant."

These attributes are typical of authoritarian societies, but Czechoslovakia was by no means an authoritarian country. Rather, these were the product of the past that Masaryk feared: the years fraught with repression, the evils inherent in a situation where servility is essential to survival. Unlike the old established societies of the West, whose long, evolutionary history had no experience of prolonged foreign domination, Czechoslovakia was not yet stable and the climate so essential to full growth in freedom was new and tenuous. Czechoslovakia belonged to the Western world by virtue of its religion, culture, and ethics, but it was still tied to the habits of a past generation in which survival was the principal value and freedom the luxury of the secure. The nation needed, as Masaryk knew, the time and the peace and the will to rediscover and cultivate its own self-confidence, to return to an awareness of the primacy of its own historic, humanistic values. "Often, maybe daily, I tell myself," Masaryk said in the early 1930s, "we need another thirty years of quiet, reasoned, and participatory development, and then our state is secure."

That was not to be. Masaryk's son, Jan, minister to the Court of St. James, visited the ailing president frequently to enliven his father's old age with his inimitable wit. On his last trip, in September, 1935, as tensions in Czechoslovakia increased and the international situation darkened, Jan reportedly greeted the old gentleman with, "Why, father, you'll outlive this Republic yet." This gentle raillery was not to become quite a fact: Thomas G. Masaryk died two years later; the Republic, which he had fathered and for which he lived, took one more year to die. The time Masaryk prayed for was not given; the sands ran out too fast, too soon.

Chapter Five

Relations between Czechs and Slovaks

Though in 1918 the Czechs and Slovaks were united into one indivisible state, their continuing relationship soon emerged as a serious problem. It is a problem familiar to all students of nationalism, and it always seems to exist at some level wherever a state lacks complete ethnic and national homogeneity. In the course of their history, most states have acquired variegated populations within their borders. As long as a society retained a feudal structure, the factor of national identity was submerged. After the American and French revolutions, however, nationalism rapidly began to develop as a political force, and it has now become the most decisive element in world politics. During the nineteenth century, it was the driving power in the liberation of smaller nations; it shaped the political map of Europe after World War I; it brought statehood to many nations in the Third World after World War II; and it has reemerged today, even in such old societies as Great Britain.

No ideology has ever been able to solve the problem of multiethnic or multinational states satisfactorily. The Nazis pursued a policy of suppression and, as a final "solution," planned to exterminate "inferior" peoples; the Soviet Communists advocated, in theory, the principle of equality of all nations, but failed to implement it in practice; the democratic governments though by definition committed to guaranteeing constitutional rights to all ethnic groups, have also been negligent in living up to their obligations.

Czechoslovakia is no exception to this rule. Whether in the period of the democratic regime between the two wars and for the short period after World War II, or during the Communist regime that has governed since 1948, conflicting political and economic purposes have afflicted the relations between the Czechs and Slovaks. A fierce controversy about the causes of these tensions, and about the policies for removing them, has spanned the entire existence of the state, but it has never resulted in an enduring solution. In this controversy, as in others, emotions and politics have prevailed over reason and obscured the fundamental issues.

An analysis of the events related to the problem reveals that the goal of Czechoslovak policy—to assure both the Czechs and Slovaks personal freedom and social justice—was admirable. It must be asserted at the outset that in matters of personal freedom and human rights, the Slovaks enjoyed the same experience as the Czechs. In the area of human progress, their achievements were even more remarkable in view of the low level of the base from which they started. Constitutionally and legally, there was no discrimination. Nevertheless, serious lapses did take place and in the process inhibited the consistent growth and interdependence of the two nations.

To reduce the problem to its fundamental terms, though Czechs and Slovaks had common ties through ethnic identity, closeness of language, cultural values, and the desire to form a united state, these attributes were adversely affected by a 1,000-year history of separation which had created two dissimilar societies. At the end of World War I, Slovakia was a backward country, without political rights, at an underdeveloped stage of economy, with an inadequate educational system, without indigenous administrative experience, without technological and industrial skills, and with a small intelligentsia. Conversely the Czech lands, in spite of many limitations imposed on them by Vienna, had achieved a respectable level of development in all these areas. The amalgamation of these two contrasting entities into one state was a formidable task. Despite great progress during the twenty years of the Republic, another thirty years of peace was needed to permit these dissimilar societies to grow together and resolve their problems.

The problem of unifying peoples of widely diverse levels of cultural, political, and social sophistication can also be found in the history of that small area which was to become first the easternmost territory of Czechoslovakia, and later a pawn on the chessboard of East European politics, Subcarpathian Russia.

Although its story is not directly related to the principal theme of this work, it vividly parallels Czech-Slovak experience and thus deserves a brief mention. For centuries, this area had shared the experience of Hungarian oppression with Slovakia. During World War I, the question of its future naturally arose. In the fall of 1918, a group of Ruthenian representatives in the United States, led by Gregory Zhatkovich, reached an agreement with Masaryk, according to which the area (the name differed according to the political and cultural orientations of the leaders) would form a part of Czechoslovakia. This agreement was approved by President Woodrow Wilson.

During the chaotic days and weeks following the end of hostilities, varied associations came into existence in Subcarpathian Russia, each proclaiming its intent that the territory should join either Hungary, or the Ukraine, or Czechoslovakia, or even that an independent state should be established. For one month in the spring of 1919, the government of Béla Kun proclaimed a Soviet Russian republic in one district. The episode was soon forgotten, however, and in May a representative Central Russian National Council confirmed in a formal declaration the decision of the American Ruthenians to join Czechoslovakia "on the basis of full autonomy."

Despite all this, the country was not granted autonomy,

even though autonomy was also constitutionally guaranteed. The reason was simple: Subcarpathian Russia lacked the political, cultural, and economic know-how to administer its own affairs. The centuries of Hungarian rule had left the country with a heritage of appalling poverty, of practically nonexistent education, and of divided cultural loyalties. In 1921, Subcarpathian Russia comprised only 3.45 percent of the populace of the whole of Czechoslovakia; its illiteracy rate was 57.6 percent. There was no choice but to administer its affairs from Prague. When the country did receive autonomy as one of the consequences of the Munich Pact, chaotic developments ensued, and finally, after the German occupation of the Czech lands and the proclamation of an independent Slovakia, the territory was annexed by Hungary. After World War II, Subcarpathian Russia was incorporated into the Soviet Union.

The Burdens
of the Past

After a short period of rather loose association with the Czechs in the Great Moravian Empire, the Slovaks were isolated from them by the beginning of the tenth century, due to the Magyar invasions which had culminated in the complete absorption of Slovakia into the kingdom of Hungary. A 1,000-year separation ensued. The feudal system relegated the Slovaks to serfdom; only a very few were admitted to even the lower nobility or to membership in free cities. Latin became, and until the beginning of the nineteenth century remained, the official language. Bratislava, today Slovakia's capital, was occasionally the seat of the Hungarian government and Parliament. With the abolition of serfdom in Hungary in 1785, however, economic and social structures began to change and, stirred by the French Revolution, sentiments of Slovak national identity began slowly to emerge. A new intelligentsia, small in number, began to speak for reform. As in the Czech lands, language was the first and principal weapon in the struggle for national revival. Because Czech, since the Reformation, had been used as a literary language (called *bibličtina,* after the *Bible of Kralice*), the first prominent Slovak awakeners, Jan Kollár and Pavel Šafárik, wrote in that language. As the patriotic struggle required a broader national base, however, two other reformers, Antonín Bernolák and Ludevít Štúr, advocated raising two different local dialects to the level of literary use. Štúr's position, in favor of central Slovakia's dialect, finally prevailed.

The process of awakening the national consciousness was encouraged throughout the nineteenth century by indigenous poets, mostly of a romantic bent, such as Andrej Sládkovič, Samo Chalúpka, Janko Král, Ján Botto, and Svetozar Hurban Vajanský. It is noteworthy that their writings not only reflected Slovak national sentiments, but also expressed concern with social questions. In addition, Slovak cultural associations were founded, and a few newspapers, some edited in Vienna and Budapest, appeared.

Parallel to these developments, political programs—rather timid in their goals—began to surface. Memoranda of demands were addressed to Vienna or Budapest, given additional weight by intermittent peasant rebellions and, toward the end of the century, by workers' strikes. The revolutionary year 1848 appeared to offer the Slovaks an opportunity to claim their rights in a convincing fashion. First, they looked toward Louis Kossuth, but when his fierce nationalism turned against them, they tried to achieve their aims by supporting Vienna. A few hundred Slovak (and Czech) soldiers joined the Austrian army in an attack on the Hungarian revolutionaries. The strategy of playing Vienna against Budapest failed, and a process of rapid political decline set in.

A policy of relentless magyarization was launched by Budapest in all sectors of Slovak life—educational, political, economic, and social—and Hungarian was increasingly used as the official language. The Austro-Hungarian *Ausgleich* in 1867 endowed the Budapest government with legal and political legitimacy in its indiscriminate suppression of the Slovak nation. It found a telling expression in a remark by the Hungarian prime minister, Koloman Tisza, who said that such a thing as a "Slovak nation" did not exist. The educational system was directed toward denationalization. There was no Slovak university; the three Slovak secondary schools were closed in 1874; and, five years later, Hungarian was made mandatory in all elementary schools. By 1918, according to Hungarian statistics, there were no more than 30,118 children of

Slovak origin attending the 276 schools that gave instruction in their mother tongue.

Another result of the policy of magyarization was that, in 1910, out of over 6,000 public officials and over 1,800 lawyers, only 150 in each category were Slovak. In the whole of Slovakia, only one judge declared himself a Slovak. During the period between 1867 and 1918, social and economic conditions drove 750,000 people to emigrate, mostly to the United States. An active national awareness was limited to some 1,000 members of the intelligentsia in Slovakia. Slovak cultural associations were dissolved and their meager funds confiscated. Newspapers appeared, only to be banned. As a national entity, the Slovaks were literally on the verge of extinction. In the Czech lands, however, education (as noted earlier) was markedly growing during the same period, so that only 2.5 percent of the population was illiterate.

Economic exploitation accompanied the cultural deprivation. After 1867, the mineral wealth and cheap labor of Slovakia began to attract Hungarian investors. Mines were opened and factories founded; in the years between 1900 and 1910, the number of industrial enterprises increased by 23.6 percent and the number of workers by 45.6 percent. The labor force consisted chiefly of Slovaks, and the small middle class enjoyed few of the benefits of industrial development; its participation in the financial investment amounted to only about 2 percent. Those who invested were mostly shareholders who had accepted Hungarian nationality—there was no other way to secure a decent livelihood. In contrast, Bohemia experienced a period of growth in the national economy.

Slovak political life was limited to largely ineffective, though courageous, interventions in the Parliament in Budapest, to secret meetings, and to occasional resolutions, signed by valiant individual leaders who had no substantial following. Budapest had also seriously curtailed the right of suffrage; in 1901, only 6.1 percent of the population of Hungary was allowed to vote. Slovakia sent 58 representatives to the Parliament, but they were mostly Hungarians. Ten elections were held between 1867 and 1918; in four of them, no Slovak national was elected to Parliament; in three, two Slovaks were elected; in two elections, 1901 and 1907, Slovak representation improved to four and seven members respectively; and in the last election in 1910, it dropped again to three. The three political parties—the Slovak National Party, the Slovak People's Party, and the Slovak Social Democratic Party—were relegated to the fringes of political life. In the Czech lands, in spite of Viennese pressures, the political parties were vigorous and rooted in the populace.

Common Values
from the Past

The burden of the past notwithstanding, the history of the relations between Slovaks and Czechs produced enduring links, a sense of unity that spanned centuries. Their cultural and spiritual values transcended the vicissitudes of separate political and economic development. Even the negative aspects of subjugation seemed to deepen their awareness of the need for communality.

During the Hussite period, the Czech army reached Slovakia, and many warriors remained there for years. With them came priests bringing Hus's teachings to the country. Czech was accepted as the literary language and remained in use among the majority of Protestants for centuries. Slovak students came to Charles University in Prague, and poets, scientists, and writers moved to Bohemia during the Reformation period, just as Czech intellectuals later found refuge from religious persecution in Slovakia, after the Battle on the White Mountain in 1620. In 1783, the first newspaper in Slovakia, *Prešpurské noviny* was printed in Czech, though discontinued four years later. In 1785, a literary paper, *Staré noviny literárního umění*, was written in *bibličtina*. A chair of Czechoslovak language and literature was established at the Evangelical Lyceum in Bratislava in 1803. In fact, the whole concept of Czechoslovak unity took root in the soil of Slovakia. Palacký himself received his education at the Lyceum, spent fourteen years of his youth in Slovakia and, from his studies and experience there, developed the conviction that one Czechoslovak nation and language existed. During his later years in Prague, when pleading with the Habsburg monarchy for the idea of federalization, he envisioned Czechs and Slovaks forming a single federal unit. His contemporary, Havlíček, shared Palacký's position on the Czechoslovak nation and advocated it in his writings.

With the accelerated magyarization that occurred after 1867, Czech and Slovak intellectual contacts and consciousness of unity intensified. Czech literature reached Slovakia, and the Czech public became, in turn, increasingly interested in Slovak development. A group of Slovak intellectuals, *Hlasisti* (deriving their name from that of their rallying focus, the newspaper *Hlas*), came to Prague and worked closely with their Czech counterparts; all were ardently devoted to the idea of Czechoslovakism. The working classes of both countries became generally aware of their common national and social interests through their respective Social Democratic parties. The Czech Social Democrats, strong and well organized, extended a helping hand to the struggling Slovak party, which was in danger of being absorbed by the Hungarian Social Democratic Party. At the beginning of the twentieth century, Czech capital penetrated the Slovak economy on a modest scale and encouraged some growth of the negligible Slovak capital. Masaryk was intensely active in Slovak matters and visited Slovakia frequently. After 1908, representatives of the Czechs and Slovaks met regularly at annual meetings. Abroad, particularly in the United States, associations of Czech and Slovak immigrant groups found varied forms of cooperation.

Since the contacts between intellectuals and politicians, and the centuries-old cultural and religious bonds had withstood political and economic adversities, World War I offered a special opportunity to test the solidity of these experiences and to translate them into a meaningful program of action.

The Wartime Aspirations

It is interesting to note that although the conviction of the "oneness" of Czechs and Slovaks had permeated the minds of Slovak leaders throughout the nineteenth century, when the war broke out, their circumspection concerning a future union with the

Czechs was matched only by that of the politicians in Prague. The propagation of a future Czechoslovak unity was left to Masaryk, Beneš, and the Slovak, Štefánik, who received powerful support from the Czech and Slovak groups abroad, particularly in the United States. As early as October 25, 1915, Slovak and Czech national organizations in Cleveland, Ohio, signed an agreement concerning the "independence of the Czech lands and Slovakia" and "a union of the Czech and Slovak nations in a federation." Another agreement, signed in Masaryk's presence on May 30, 1918, in Pittsburgh, Pennsylvania, confirmed the program of unification, but its wording later became a source of bitter controversy—a curious symbol of the growing discord. These political pronouncements were undergirded by a persuasive argument for unity that had originated on the battlefield. Some 5,000 Slovak soldiers joined the Czechoslovak Legion in Russia; 1,600 joined in France and 1,000 in Italy. At a congress in Kiev in August 1916, the Legionaries approved a "Memorandum on the Principles of the Czechoslovak Movement," in which they expressed a "desire to evolve into a united, politically individible and free nation. . . ."

Meanwhile, political spokesmen on the home front were not idle. Slovak representatives met with their Czech colleagues in Prague and Vienna, and by the spring of 1917, the Czechs in Vienna had begun to speak publicly, on behalf of the Slovaks, for future unity. Their activities found a corresponding resonance in Slovakia herself. A rally, organized on May 1, 1918, at Liptovsky Sv. Mikuláš, asked for the right of self-determination for the "Hungarian branch of the Czechoslovak stem." A secret meeting at Turčiansky Sv. Martin, on May 24, 1918, expressed itself in favor of "establishing a Czechoslovak state" and Father Andrej Hlinka (about whose political genesis more will be said later) stated, "Let us not beat around the bush; let us say openly that we are in favor of a Czechoslovak orientation. The thousand-year-old marriage with the Hungarians didn't work. We must part ways." [1] A resolution passed at the meeting claimed for the Slovak nation

1. *Za svobodu českého a slovenského národa: Sborník dokumentů k dějinám KSČ v 1938–1945* (Prague: Státní nakl. polit. literatury, 1956), p. 48; L. Holotík, "Vznik Československa a jeho význam pre slovenský národ," *Historický časopis* 6, no. 4 (1958): 494.

"the right to form an independent state together with Bohemia, Moravia, and Silesia." Slovak soldiers in Hungarian regiments mutinied, and strikes by Slovak workers multiplied.

The movement for unity culminated logically in the historical Declaration of Turčiansky Sv. Martin, on October 30, 1918, in which representatives of all the Slovak political parties, organized in the National Council of the Slovak Branch of the United Czechoslovak Nation, spoke on behalf of "the Czechoslovak nation" for the right of self-determination and complete independence, attesting that "the Slovak nation" was "linguistically, culturally, historically, a part of the united Czechoslovak nation." The terminology echoed, unknowingly, the wording of the Declaration of Independence, proclaimed two days earlier in Prague, and of the first law of the Republic, which also spoke of the "Czechoslovak nation." Indeed, when the united country was given a final legal framework in February 1920, the preamble of the Constitution opened solemnly with the words, "We, the Czechoslovak nation. . . ."

The term was used by politicians of all shades and in both parts of the country before and after the end of the war, testifying to the enthusiasm for unity. Little did they realize that the very phrase "Czechoslovak nation" would later turn into a symbol of discrimination against Slovaks and acquire a connotation which, instead of strengthening unity, would contribute to its erosion.

One Nation—
Two Nations?

Whether or not Czechoslovakia was the home of two nations—Czechs and Slovaks—or of one nation—Czechoslovaks—was not, of course, a question of semantics. It was a problem of sharing, or not sharing, common cultural values.

Scholars have wrestled with the issue for a long time in an effort to define the ingredients of "nationality." Such definable attributes as common heritage, common territory, and common language in recent times have been considered relevant only in the context of subjective criteria, all of which are the products of an emotional attachment or, as Hans Kohn defined it, "a state of mind." Ernest Renan defined nationality as "the wish to live together, for better or worse [*un plébiscite de tous les jours*]"—and it may generally be just that simple.

In Czechoslovakia, however, the "simple" definition was not applicable. Both sides were entirely sincere in their positions; both wished to "live together," but each viewed the political situation differently, and each sought different solutions. To the Czechs, Czechoslovakism came easily, since they had fraternal sentiments toward their oppressed brethren. They certainly had no ulterior designs to absorb or exploit them. Words of love for the Slovaks, offers of a helping hand, flooded the Provisional National Assembly in the first weeks after liberation. One resolution, for instance, stated, "We promise to all that we wish to substitute our unlimited love for Slovakia for what has been her enormous suffering. Full cultural and economic development of Slovakia will be one of our foremost, our most precious, and most grateful tasks."

To the Slovaks, too, Czechoslovakism offered prospects for freedom and progress in unity, but there were also forebodings concerning the future of their national identity. There were understandable reasons for their fears. One was the relative population in the two areas. According to the 1921 census, 73.50 percent of the population of Czechoslovakia lived in the Czech lands, while only 22.04 percent lived in Slovakia. Another reason was the concentration of economic and cultural power in the Czech lands and the corresponding lack of it in Slovakia. Czech protestations of love raised the fear that Slovakia might well be smothered by all this communion, might, indeed, disappear. In such a situation, the question of preserving the national identity transcended all other considerations. External appearances were carefully examined for hidden meanings and motives, and inadvertent actions took on a distorted significance.

All Slovak political parties were "all-Czechoslovak" in scope, and all did profess belief in the concept of one Czechoslovak nation. The Slovak Populist Party and the small Slovak National Party were exceptions, believing firmly in a distinct Slovak nation. However, at the peak of their popularity, they represented no more than 6.9 percent of the electorate in the whole country and 32 percent in Slovakia. In the four national elections, the political parties representing Czechoslovakism gained an average of 37.2 percent of the vote, while the Populist Party registered 5.8 percent. If one considers Slovakia alone, incomplete election information reveals that the two strongest parties, the Agrarians and the Social Democrats, received an average of 26.5 percent of the vote—a substantial showing of support, considering their Czechoslovakism.

Nevertheless, the election results did not accurately represent the feelings of the Slovaks concerning their national individuality. A voting majority may legitimize a situation, but it cannot obliterate the national diversity that emanates not only from deep-rooted national attitudes, but also from equally entrenched differences in the quality of life.

Some sense of the complexities of the "Czechoslovak" or "Czech-Slovak" identity question may be gained by a closer look at the protagonists of each. With one exception, all the prominent Slovak leaders believed profoundly in the oneness of the Czechoslovak nation. They had spent part of their lives in Prague before the war, and most of them were Protestants. Three are of particular importance to this study.

The most eloquent and stubborn Slovak advocate of Czechoslovakism was Vavro Šrobár. After he had been expelled from a Hungarian secondary school, he moved first to Moravia and then to Prague. Having absorbed Czech culture and believing in its Western character, he hoped that it might permeate and transform the amorphous, backward culture of Slovakia. During the war, he urged Czech politicians to speak out on behalf of Slovakia, and for a brief time he was interned by the Hungarian authorities. Šrobár was in Prague on October 28, 1918, and he signed the Declaration of Independence. He was appointed to the first government as minister with full powers for Slovakia. He put his Czechoslovakism, to him an article of faith, into immediate practice. When he returned to Slovakia, he took a number of Czechs to assist him in the enormous task of Czechoslovakizing his native land, which to him meant modernizing every sphere of life—political, administrative, economic, social, and cultural. Echoing Masaryk, he had stated before the war that the Slovak question was primarily a religious and ethical one. If he had in mind liberal ethics and an anticlerical approach to religion (which is very likely, though he himself was Catholic), he was obviously bound to run into intense opposition from Slovak Catholics, and he did. Šrobár was finally overwhelmed by the reality of the situation in Slovakia, and he was forced to admit it twenty-five years later, during World War II; by this time, a distinct Slovak national identity (though without Catholicism) had become the accepted premise of the Slovak nation and its representatives.

Milan Hodža (1878–1943), another prominent Slovak leader, was both intellectually and politically more complicated than his senior colleague, Šrobár. Czechoslovak by conviction, Hodža braved Hungarian persecution, writing articles in Hungary and delivering fiery speeches in the Budapest Parliament. He pleaded for universal suffrage and for Slovak equality. He found his way into the audience chambers of Archduke Francis Ferdinand, who was known for his dislike of Hungarians, and when his hopes for an improvement in the Slovak plight dimmed, he wrote (in a vein similar to Palacký's earlier prophetic statement), "We know that the Slovak nation existed when this Empire did not yet exist—and it will exist in the future, when this Empire has ceased to exit." He appealed to Slovaks to send their children to Czech schools, as they were deprived of their own educational institutions. This outrageous program earned him an eighteen-month prison sentence. He pleaded on behalf of impoverished peasants, of "the working people carrying the burden of life," and of people "nationally and socially oppressed." During World War I, in contrast to Šrobár, he kept his options open and, though in contact with Czech politicians, avoided speaking of the future union of Slovaks and Czechs. After the war, however, he represented Czechoslovakism, became the leader of the Slovak branch of the Agrarian Party, and slowly abandoned his populist, progressive past. He was a member of the government on several occasions and prime minister in the critical period before and during the Munich crisis. He was, above all, an ambitious man of action, capable of changing his political philosophy. Toward the end of his life, during World War II, his convictions about the unity of the Czechoslovak nation gave way (like Šrobár's, although for different reasons) to a pragmatic defense of the individuality of the Slovak nation.

Ivan Dérer exceeded both Šrobár and Hodža in his zeal for Czechoslovak unity. A prominent leader of the Social Democratic Party and therefore ideologically committed to progress for the working class, he saw Czechoslovakism as the only way to bring Slovakia social advancement, and he believed that Czechoslovak, rather than Slovak, national pride would free his country from the hated Hungarian heritage. Rigid in outlook and political practice, he remained faithful to his convictions, through changing emotions and circumstances.

Milan Štefánik (whose personality and political convictions have been described earlier) requires special mention here. Had he lived to enjoy the free Czechoslovakia for which he had labored and fought during the war, he would without a doubt have practiced what he had said, rather simplistically, in the past: to him, every Slovak was a Czech living in Slovakia, and every Czech was a Slovak living in the Czech lands.

The idea of one Czechoslovak nation found powerful support among the vast majority of Czechs. As mentioned before, all the political parties (including, for a while, the Communist Party) took the concept for granted as the one common element in their divergent programs. It was a basic tenet of the creeds of Masaryk and Beneš. Masaryk was born in Moravia, close to the Slovak border, and his father was a Slovak. To him, Czechoslovakism was not only a question of cultural and ethical unity, but also a political necessity. "There is no Slovak nation," he stated, somewhat categorically, "it is an invention of Hungarian propaganda." The statement was correct in the sense that Hungarian revisionist goals and irredentist activities tried to exploit the conflict between the concepts of one and two nations. However, it lacked historical justification, since before the war the Budapest government had denied the existence of a Slovak nation. Nor was the revisionist propaganda effective; the Slovaks' attitude toward the Hungarians remained unchanged; they felt nothing for them but hatred and hostility. Masaryk's conviction of the oneness of the Czechoslovak nation did not, however, imply political and administrative centralism. In September 1921, while traveling in Slovakia, he stated that it was a mistake if centralism prevailed over autonomism. He made it clear, though, that he did favor cultural autonomy. Such required the development of a rich cultural life, and a special Slovak character, he applauded. He also insisted firmly on the need for unity and solidarity in state affairs. It is strange that Masaryk, a man of extraordinary sensitivity, who defined politics as an art as well as a science (and with a strong emotional component), overlooked the potential danger of the emotional factor as he insisted on the oneness of the Czechoslovak nation. Death spared him the sorrow of witnessing the death of his vision when the Slovak leadership proclaimed Slovakia's independence in March 1939.

Beneš's position was identical to Masaryk's. However, he lived through the turbulent evolution of the entire one-or-two nations question. During the dark days following the Munich Pact, he observed the leaders of the Slovak Populist Party negotiating with the Sudeten German Nazis, and he experienced the shame of Slovakia's declaration of independence six months later. During World War II, he saw Slovakia, her national distinctiveness finding new expression in a sham, Berlin-created "statehood," fighting alongside the Nazi Germans. He participated in efforts to solve the postwar problem of relations between the Czechs and Slovaks, refusing to bow before irreversible emotional realities and drastically changed political circumstances. Under pressure, he did make a gesture when he conceded, toward the end of the war, that those people who wished to consider themselves Slovaks or Czechs were free to express their positions; he also stressed that nothing should prevent those who considered themselves Czechoslovaks from enjoying equal rights. Beneš, of course, thought of himself as a Czechoslovak, and the experience with Slovakia from Munich to the end of the war only served to deepen his belief in the unity of Czechs and Slovaks, a belief sternly reinforced by his unconcealed critical feelings toward the Slovaks as a whole.

Against this impressive array of statesmen and politicians stood one man who was passionately dedicated to the idea of the distinctive individuality of the Slovak nation. He was Andrej Hlinka (1864–1938), the founder and unquestioned leader of the Slovak Populist Party. A fiery orator who was fascinated by his own words, a courageous fighter for the rights of his people against Hungarian oppression, and a fanatic Catholic priest, he sought the salvation of Slovakia in union with the Czechs. However, he saw the Slovak national movement as one which had "its roots in social, natural, and psychological causes," and on one occasion in 1908, lecturing in the Czech lands, he stated, "Our relations with the Czechs must be brotherly and natural, stemming from the heart and the blood. . . . We must awaken the Czechs in matters of religion and the Czechs must resurrect us nationally, economically, and culturally." He continued, "I am not worried about the language, since each is almost the same as the other; it is [Czech] atheism which could destroy us." [2] These last words reveal a concern that became a fundamental cause of the controversy between the two nations.

Nevertheless, when liberation came, Hlinka enthusiastically signed the Martin Declaration, which included the words "the Czechoslovak nation." A few days later, he acknowledged that the Slovaks would not "have seen freedom if it were not for the Czechs," and pledged that his people would "stay with them, which does not mean, however, that we have stopped being Slovaks." Again, in January 1919, he expressed gratitude to the Czech people, saying, "We can thank our brethren, the Czechs, that we are today a free nation and that we can shake hands. Our wounds were great, our struggle was difficult, and if it were not for the brotherly Czech nation, our pain and Egyptian slavery would never have come to an end." Still, his gratitude to the Czechs in no way diminished the affection and pride he felt for his own peo-

2. Samo Fal'tan, *Slovenská otázka v Československu* (Bratislava: Vydav. politickej literatúry, 1968), p. 22.

ple, whose innate qualities he loved with a blind passion and trust, a quality that was missing from the minds of his Protestant Slovak antagonists. Just as others had no doubt about the essential unity and coherence of a Czechoslovak nation, Hlinka never questioned the concept of a unique Slovak identity. When facing a tribunal in 1920, he declared, "We have never been one nation with the Czechs; we have an entirely different mentality, a different temperament, different culture, different songs, different literature," [3] and he could have rightly added, for himself and his followers, a different political philosophy.

In spite of his irrepressible convictions, Hlinka emphasized his loyalty to the Republic and its integrity. The problem was that the logical consequence of his concept of Slovak individuality was an autonomy for which his Czechoslovak opponents believed Slovakia was not sufficiently mature. The sorrowful experience that followed, which to some extent justified the Czechoslovaks' objections, raises the question of whether political wisdom as well as respect for human emotions would not have justified a constitutional guarantee that within a specified time after the foundation of the Republic, Slovakia would be granted autonomy. Lacking such a hope, the Slovaks grew increasingly bitter, barbed words intensified, and demagoguery clouded the issue and removed it from the realm of thoughtful consideration. Noble goals on both sides were obscured by questionable means, and the official stand, expressed in laws concerning the indivisible oneness of the Czechoslovak nation, became an empty posture, invalidating the spirit, if not the letter, of the Constitution. As time wore on, more and more Slovaks identified themselves not only as Czechoslovak citizens, but also as Slovak nationals.

It is therefore apparent that in many ways the conflict between the Czechs and Slovaks stemmed from the differences that 1,000 years of history had produced in two heterogenous cultures. It is also apparent that the deeper, more meaningful effect of that millenium of separation was the one that eventually produced a collision of values: the spirit of liberalism, progress, and reform

3. Juraj Kramer, *Slovenské autonomistické hnutie v rokoch 1918–1929* (Bratislava: Slovenská akadémie vied, 1962), pp. 18, 81.

wrestling with forces that put high premium upon the values of authority and the obeisant mind.

Progressivism
versus Conservatism

In contrast to the orderly transfer of authority in the Czech lands during the months following the end of hostilities in 1918, Slovakia was in chaos. When Hungarian authority collapsed, there were no organizations to replace it and no skilled hands to construct such organizations. Dynamic political and social forces, suppressed for centuries and now without leadership, erupted in ugly acts of pillaging, in anti-Semitism, and in the occupation of industrial and business premises. In December 1918, the Provisional National Assembly in Prague passed a law enacting extraordinary temporary measures to control the situation in Slovakia and despatched Šrobár, the newly appointed minister, to restore order there. He collected a few scores of Legionaries and members of the gymnastic organization, *Sokol,* to pursue the assignment, but they were halted by Hungarian units which were in the process of reoccupying the country. The Allies ordered the Hungarians to withdraw, but a few months later, in May 1919, they returned once more on the orders of the new ruler in Budapest, the Communist leader, Béla Kun. Under his patronage, a Slovak Soviet republic was proclaimed, but as Kun's army was compelled to withdraw by an Allied ultimatum, the Soviet regime in Slovakia collapsed on June 23.

The mammoth task of resuscitating Slovakia began. Hungarian executives, administrators, land owners, judges, and magistrates had gone, and there was virtually no one to replace them. Šrobár moved swiftly and, endowed with full powers, demoted the Slovak Magyarons and promoted inexperienced persons he considered reliable to their vacated positions. Šrobár measured that reliability by the degree to which their liberalism, progressivism, Czechoslovakism, and to a considerable extent, Protestantism matched his own. Slovakia could not furnish even a minimum number of candidates who possessed such demanding qualifications.

Slovakia desperately needed radical social change. Peasants were hungry for land and workers were hungry for a life of economic and social dignity. The new land reform law and numerous other social laws offered a promising prospect for impressive improvement to both groups and, indeed, much was achieved. The Slovaks, however, were in equally desperate need of political awareness and education—qualities that cannot be acquired overnight. The ideas of a liberalism that would bring personal freedom, the concepts of socialism that heralded social equity were carried into a country submerged in a deep cultural sleep. To the ignorant, new ideas are objects of vast suspicion. In Slovakia, there was a second level of distrust, namely that the program of progress was voiced mainly by Slovak Protestants, nurtured in the intellectual climate of Prague, and their ideas sounded alien and disquieting to the ears of conservative Catholics. Their leader was Andrej Hlinka—the ardent nationalist rebel, romanticized by his brave stand before the war; or the priest of the picturesque town at the foot of the Tatra Mountains, Ružomberok, who commanded and received the submission of his flock; or, in city and village, the ever-present politician, dressed in a black cassock and with a halo of flowing white hair, who identified with the simplicity of the Slovak soul, but who also used that image of friend and father to defend conservative, parochial ends.

The conflict between conservatism and progressivism, endemic in the Slovak mind and aggravated by misunderstanding and circumstance, was personified in Hlinka and Šrobár. In political terms, the clash between them stemmed from Šrobár's centralist Czechoslovakism and Hlinka's insistence on Slovak autonomy—which would provide a legal basis for his patriarchal image of Slovakia's national identity. But there was more to the conflict than divergent political goals.

In the process of building his ministry, Šrobár offered Hlinka a post in charge of Catholic affairs, but the offer was declined. Hlinka would not serve under a liberal superior, nor would his political instincts permit him to turn into a bureaucrat. According to some sources, his ambition was to become a bishop, the first of Slovak extraction, and he suspected Šrobár of blocking his elevation. He was wrong; the Vatican delayed recognition of the new Czechoslovak state, wishing to prolong the jurisdiction of the Hungarian bishops and the archbishop of Esztergom over the diocese of Slovakia, and Hlinka's appointment would have conflicted with that policy.

Hlinka's suspicion and bitterness in this personal matter grew into a political hostility that engulfed both Czechs and Slovaks. In the eyes of Hlinka's followers, Šrobár and the Czechs were the very incarnation of evil: atheists, socialists, liberals, and anticlericalists, who would bring untold misfortunes upon the country if Slovakia were not guaranteed an autonomy that assured the preservation of her own culture.

Further Troubling
of the Waters

In November 1918, Hlinka himself had said ". . . we welcome with pleasure among us every Czech who wants to help us." [4] Little did he realize the numbers he would be required to "welcome with pleasure." The Czechs were eager to help, to offer their skillful hands and trained minds. Šrobár opened the door wide, and the Czechs poured in, swamping Slovak towns and villages, bringing their own progressive thinking into the conservative environment. Starting from scratch in a country nearly devoid of executives, professionals, teachers, and others of the intelligentsia, they quickly assumed profitable positions in industry, transportation, the judiciary, local administration, and education. On one hand, Šrobár's policy sowed the seeds of a resentment that eventually produced much hostility, but on the other hand, the overall effects of the Czech immigration were remarkably worthwhile, particularly in education.

Before the war, the educational situation in Slovakia was

4. Ibid., p. 18.

deplorable: there were 276 schools for 30,000 children, with Slovak as the language of instruction; there were no secondary schools at all; and illiteracy in the country was at 34.9 percent. By 1930 (and none of the achievements of the postwar years could have been approached without Czech assistance), Slovakia had over 3,000 elementary schools, serving some 43,000 children, and 48 secondary schools with 15,000 students. In June 1919, a university was established by law in Bratislava; by 1930 it was attended by 2,000 students. By the same year, illiteracy was reduced to 8.16 percent and, in another ten years, to 5.4 percent. Of necessity, most of the teachers were Czechs, but many of them learned Slovak and helped to educate a new generation of Slovak intellectuals. By 1937, there were 8,726 Slovak teachers, as opposed to 2,202 Czech teachers. In the period between 1919 and 1937, 867 new school buildings were erected and 771 were reconstructed. In 1918, there were only 2 Slovaks qualified to teach at the secondary school level; by 1937, secondary school positions were held by 493 Slovaks and 479 Czechs. Thirty Slovak professors taught at Comenius University, though the majority of the faculty was still Czech.

During the same period, there was a Slovak cultural awakening. The fine and performing arts, scholarship, literature, and poetry blossomed. Their representatives developed intimate contacts with Czech colleagues, and professional visits, concerts, exhibitions, and theatrical performances were exchanged. A publishing house in Prague specialized in bringing Slovak literature—almost unknown in prewar times—to Czech readers. Many prominent Czech scholars and intellectuals were critical of their government's centralist policy and supported the Slovak point of view.

The system of justice, with only one Slovak judge from the prewar period, had 227 Slovak judges by 1937, with 81 more awaiting permanent appointment, and 211 Czech judges. In local administration, 2,975 Slovaks were employed (not including 900 community clerks, or notaries); there were 1,133 Slovaks in the rural police forces, and 5,626 in the postal service. By 1937, the railroads employed 14,562 Slovaks, and over 400 kilometers of new railroads and 1,200 kilometers of new highways had been constructed. Industrialization and electrification, in spite of serious setbacks, had changed the economic structure of the country by the end of the interwar period.

Though they occupied key positions in all fields, the actual number of Czechs in Slovakia was relatively small; in 1921, 2.4 percent and in 1930 (the last pre-World War II census), 3.7 percent of the population of Slovakia was Czech, but they served as a visible target for the attacks of Slovak autonomists. By the more conservative, they were perceived as carriers of a dubious, perhaps dangerous, "progress," but there were other, more serious objections to their presence. They represented Prague centralism, and they persevered in holding preferential positions after the Slovak intelligentsia was qualified and ready to replace them. Samo Fal'tan, a Communist scholar, published some revealing figures on the subject (unfortunately, without a reference to the year): out of 417 employees in the Ministry of Education in Prague, only 4 were Slovak, and in its branch in Bratislava, there were 94 Czechs and 68 Slovaks; in the Ministry of National Defense, only 66 of 1,300 employees were Slovak; in the armed forces, of 139 generals, 1 was Slovak; there were no Slovaks among 436 colonels; and out of a total of 20,800 other officers and noncommissioned officers, only 830, or 3.9 percent, were Slovak.[5] While it makes a great difference whether this situation prevailed in 1920 or in 1937, it is clear that the Slovaks would have resented it, even in the earlier years.

Economic development was another aggravating factor in the relations between the two nations. Slovakia was predominantly agrarian; the Czech lands were highly industrialized. Forty percent of the Czech population worked in industry and some 30 percent in agriculture; in Slovakia, only 17 percent were employed in the industrial sphere, while 61 percent were in the agricultural sector. Theoretically, the two economies should have complemented each other, but the heritage of the past and subsequent economic turmoil distorted a promising prospect.

In prewar times, Slovak industry had been controlled by

5. Ibid., p. 88.

Hungarians, and its products found a natural market in Hungary. The north-south flow of rivers and construction of railroads gave a rational basis to this orientation. After the war, most of the Hungarian capital was bought off by Czech banks, since Slovakia had few resources of its own. This was sound financial policy, but it opened the door to the penetration of Slovakia by Czech capital. The years 1924–29 witnessed marked economic growth, but the preceding years had been punctuated by intermittent crises, and the subsequent period, until 1935, was plagued by the worldwide depression. The whole country suffered from these economic slumps, but the burden was particularly heavy in underdeveloped Slovakia. During the first period after the war, Slovakia lost the Hungarian markets, and the Czech lands were not yet able to replace them. Many factories and mines were closed. During the second period, additional enterprises were shut down, and Slovak industry worked at 20 percent of capacity. In 1930, Slovak industry contributed only 8 percent of the overall state industrial production, though Slovaks represented 23 percent of the population. Accusations of discrimination against Slovaks were rampant, but the blunt reality was that a system of free enterprise was at work, oblivious to political and social consequences.

Land reform brought Slovakia enormous relief from the prewar conditions of impoverishment and indignity. Close to 700,000 hectares of land were distributed among 200,000 families, but the average acreage of arable land was still below subsistence level, and when the economic crisis struck, the peasants' usual salvation of finding employment in industry was cut off. In the years between 1922–30, 170,000 Slovaks emigrated to the United States. By 1935, the economic situation had improved, and Slovakia's condition improved rapidly also, partly in response to the general recovery and partly because of the newly flourishing armaments industry in the eastern part of the country. Nevertheless, politics were by now radicalized, and both the mistakes of the past and the inevitable consequences of economic development continued to affect adversely the relations between the two nations.

Many personal, political, and economic factors accentuated

the stresses between Czechs and Slovaks. Some were the products of poor policy, others of uncontrollable circumstances, and still others of emotional tensions. The positive values of political, economic, social and educational progress in Slovakia, to which the Czechs undoubtedly contributed the lion's share, were overshadowed by temporary problems and immediate desires. For all the collective good will, some "ugly" Czechs in Slovakia besmirched the good name of the whole nation. It was a situation not unlike the relationship between developed and undeveloped nations, for the nationals of an industrial society are not immune to a condescending attitude toward those of a backward country, nor is the other side inclined to respond with unalloyed gratitude for the benefits it receives. On the contrary, resentment simmers and inevitably boils over.

It would be wrong to deduce that this resentment and wrangling, fierce as it was, seriously jeopardized the actual solidity of the Czechoslovak state or even disrupted the enduring ties between the two peoples. An overwhelming majority stood firmly for the unity and integrity of the Czechoslovak Republic and shared in the general progress. The Constitution was approved in 1920 by all Slovak members of the National Assembly, though six representatives of Hlinka's Populist Party qualified their votes with statements reaffirming their demand for autonomy. On many occasions Hlinka himself declared his loyalty to the Republic, even while insisting on autonomy for Slovakia. He pictured himself—and, to some extent, he was—a tribune of his people. To him and to the Populist Party, the Pittsburgh Agreement, which had promised the Slovaks their own administrative system, diet, and court, became a Magna Charta. Under the influence of two erudite Slovak renegades, Father František Jehlička and Professor Vojtěch Tuka (who were proven to be in the pay of Hungary), Hlinka became increasingly irresponsible and fanatic. He resented the position taken by the centralists, both Czech and Slovak, who maintained that the Pittsburgh Agreement was not a legally binding document, merely a declaration of intent, and that, it did not represent the will of the nation as it was not signed by any elected representatives, but by members of Slovak organizations in the United States, most of whom were probably American citizens. Since all other Slovak representatives in the government were centralists, resolutely set against Slovak autonomy, the demand for autonomy became the exclusive and attractive domain of the Populist Party.

Despite the fact that the Slovak centralists commanded the votes of the nation, they could not keep vast numbers of Slovaks from the conviction that they were a distinct national entity. With no evidence of any interest in autonomy on the part of the centralists, the Populist Party fed on the resulting discontent. During the critical days after the Munich Pact, through machination and terror, it became and remained (so long as it spoke for Berlin as well) the sole spokesman of the Slovak nation.

Thus, did the political freedom, economic improvement, and social progress brought into Slovakia by the Czechs produce a political backlash, a conservatism that grew more and more radical. It reached its ironic culmination with a post-Munich autonomy in 1938.

When the Prague government was finally forced to grant this autonomy to Slovakia, the Populist Party found itself with a strange and unexpected bedfellow: the Communist Party of Czechoslovakia. Their individual motivations for autonomy were born out of mutually exclusive ideological considerations and goals. But it was at just that moment that the continuing gyrations of Communist policy put it on the side of Slovak autonomy.

The intriguing history of the CPC's relationship to the problem of Slovakia deserves special attention.

The CPC
in a Quandary

From the beginning, the Slovak question provided a delicate, complex problem for the CPC. Essentially, this problem was part of the Communists' continuing dilemma involving the reconciliation of Communist theory on revolution with the fact of nationalism, and the construction of a strategy that would accommodate both.

The CPC was initially in trouble on the issue of "one or two nations." When a group of Czechoslovak Communists met in Moscow in May 1918, their message to the "Czechoslovak Proletariat in the Homeland" spoke of the "working class of the Czechoslovak nation." This error—violating Lenin's position on self-determination by lumping Czechs and Slovaks into one nation—might be forgiven; after all, the well-meaning comrades had been carried away, not only by revolutionary enthusiasm, but also (alas) by nationalistic emotions. But it was surely unpardonable that the CPC should continue this heresy for another four years. At its meeting in May 1921, the CPC drafted a resolution that still spoke of the "inseparable Czechoslovak nation" and its own loyalty to that united Republic. In February 1923, the error persisted as the CPC's First Congress adopted a thesis on the "Czechoslovak nation" in which a program of Slovak autonomy was condemned as an effort "to separate the Slovak people from cultural association and national unification with the Czech people." This thesis evolved from the Party's primary concern, which was waging a class struggle in economically depressed Slovakia. But it ignored the national sentiments of the Slovaks themselves, and it created dissensions, particularly within the ranks of the Slovak Party, which were never removed, whatever position the Party managed to adopt on the Slovak question.

The theoretical heresy of the First Congress clearly had to be eradicated. In the summer of 1924, the Fifth Congress of the Third International in Moscow stated that "there was not one Czechoslovak nation," that autonomy was a bourgeois concept, and that the Party must adopt the path of "self-determination up to separation." The Party obliged and, the following November, rejected the First Congress's thesis as "opportunistic" and branded the concept of one Czechoslovak nation a "bourgeois fraud."

Dimitrii Z. Manuilski, representing the Third International, defended "the question of self-determination up to secession as a matter of principle." As a matter of practical policy, however, he also argued that the right to secede represented "the best guarantee and assumption for cooperation of several nationalities on a brotherly basis within a federal state framework," since they will not be interested in secession if they enjoy real equality.

There was good logic in Manuilski's reasoning, but the CPC did little to remedy the old suspicions. The Czech comrades could not ignore the national feelings of the working class in the Czech lands, and the Slovak comrades wished to avoid the impression that their policy on Slovakia in any way resembled that of the conservative Populist Party. The Comintern instruction did prompt a regional Slovak conference held in July 1926 to speak of an independent Slovakia which would join the USSR. However, this proposition went too far for that moment and, on subsequent occasions, the Party propounded the idea of a socialist federation of Czechoslovakia, initiated by the Fifth Congress of the Third International.

In 1929, another order from Moscow to "bolshevize" the Party put new life in the "right of secession" argument, but the economic crisis during the first half of the 1930s only intensified the social aspects of the Party's agitation, and the Slovak national question was again put aside. By this time, Slovakia was known as a Czech "colony" in Communist parlance, but again Moscow's instructions kept changing. The Seventh Congress of the Comintern, focusing on the Nazi dangers, prompted the Party to adopt the policy of "equality of the Czech and Slovak nations," without—to save face—giving up the "right of national self-determination." [6] Then, after Munich, the Party endorsed Slovakia's autonomy, and since that time, several variations of the Slovak theme have been played again and again, down, indeed, to this day.

6. Miloš Gosiorovský, "K niektorým otázkam vzťahu Čechov a Slovákov v politike Komunistickej strany Československa," *Historický časopis* 16, no. 3 (1968): 360–62, 366, 367.

Chapter Six

The German
Minority

Czechoslovakia was ethnically heterogenous. Besides the Czechs
and Slovaks, who comprised, according to the 1930 census, 66.91
percent of the population, there was a wide variety of minority
groups: 3.79 percent Ruthenians; 4.78 percent Magyars; a scatter-
ing of Poles and other nationalities; and Germans, with over 22
percent of the population. The Germans, politically, economically,
and internationally the most significant group, provided yet another testing ground for what many Czechoslovak interwar intellectuals and statesmen perceived as the true meaning of the
country's history.

One cannot speak of the origins of the German minority in
the Sudetenland in any sense that implies a policy of imperialism.
The boundaries between the neighboring German states and the
Czech kingdom did not change significantly since the time of Char-
lemagne. In the tenth century, the Germans began to move into
the Sudeten area, rich with minerals, and into towns, as miners, fi-

nanciers, and priests. They brought along their own language, culture, and national habits. During the Hussite wars, which were both religious and national in character, many Germans were compelled (for either or both reasons) to leave the country, but their descendants returned en masse after the Czechs' defeat at the Battle on the White Mountain. These Germans were different from their ancestors: aggressive, imbued with a sense of superiority and the spirit of a unique German "mission." They acquired large land estates, opened new industries, occupied leading positions in the Austrian bureaucracy, took an ever-increasing part in the political life of the Empire, and became, generally speaking, *Kulturträger,* with an unconcealed contempt for everything Czech. Characteristic of the mood and relationship between the two nationalities were signs, posted in German hotels and cafés, that said "Czechs, Jews, and dogs not allowed here." During the nineteenth century, as the Czechs reawakened and searched for their own national, political, and cultural expression, the antagonism grew more intense.

With the collapse of the Empire, the privileged position of the Germans crumbled. Overnight, the *Herrenvolk* turned into a despised minority. Rejecting the existence of a new Czechoslovakia, German representatives sought rescue in association with Austria, which herself had proclaimed unity with Germany. Though the peace treaties put an end to this nonsense, the Sudeten leaders, living in Vienna and Berlin, organized financial support for irredentist activities in the Sudentenland. Political parties emerged along traditional lines in the territory, but all of them, including the Social Democrats, had one thing in common: an implacable hostility toward the Czechoslovak state. Some right-wing politicians had established contacts with Adolph Hitler even before he was arrested in 1923, and they frequently visited the German legation in Prague and received money from Berlin. During the early 1920s, the Sudentenland suffered from economic depression; but there the depression was aggravated by the disproportionate concentration of industry in the area and by political agitation. The general populace was apathetic, however, and local disorders were quelled by the intervention of small, improvised units of the emerging

Czechoslovak army. After the first national elections in 1920, the agitation was transferred to the Parliament, where the Sudetens continued to denounce the Republic (in German, of course) and to vote against any bills the government introduced.

The CPC:
Another Quandary

As in the case of Slovakia, the Sudeten German question posed special problems for the CPC and, similarly, its position on issues changed, according to altering domestic and international circumstances. The problem first arose when the Socialist Council in Prague was preparing a general strike—two weeks before the proclamation of the Czechoslovak Republic. Concerned that a strike by Czech workers not be viewed by German workers as an act of "national chauvinism," Šmeral drafted an appeal to the "proletariat of German workers," which recognized their own "right to self-determination" and expressed the view that "the representatives of the Czech and German peoples are called upon in this historical moment to decide in a contractual way about the mutual relations of the two nations." [1]

The developments, however, precluded any opportunity for the Czech and Sudeten German radicals to sign such a contract. Even as Šmeral, anxious to avoid a conflict with the national feelings of his followers, was opposing the idea of a Party that would include the German (as well as the Hungarian) minority, Karl Kreibich, the leader of the German radicals, and with Moscow's support, attacked Šmeral accusing him of provincialism. On the question of the future of individual nations, Kreibich stated, "Which nations will disappear in this development, which language will maintain itself longest, is to me as a communist an absolutely insignificant question. I am not concerned whether this world will be German, Slav, or Romanic, whether it will be a Caucasian

---

1. *Založení komunistické strany Československa: Sborník dokumentů ke vzniku a založení KSČ, 1917–1924* (Prague: Státní nakl. polit. literatury, n.d.), p. 23.

or Mongolian world; my goal is that it be a communist world." [2] In October 1921, the Sudeten German Communist Party, which had been founded seven months before, merged with the Czech comrades to form the Communist Party of Czechoslovakia.

For a while, the German faction of the CPC followed the line of Czechoslovak state unity. Indeed, at the Fifth Congress of the Cominform, Kreibich admitted that "there was no irredentist movement" in the German minority area, and that "no one would understand it if we—as if falling from the moon—came up with the proposal to separate this area and join with Germany." [3] Shortly thereafter, however, as Moscow's position shifted, the policy of the CPC changed in favor of the right of the Sudetenland to secede. By the late 1930s, when the country (and the Soviet Union) began to be threatened by Nazi Germany, the CPC stepped into the first ranks of the defenders of state unity and territorial integrity, and in the days of Munich, its members, including the Sudeten German Communists (the latter with particular courage), opposed the policy of secession of the Sudetenland and its attachment to Germany. Their complete about-face was fully understandable. The CPC obviously preferred to exist in Czechoslovak freedom rather than be decimated in Nazi Germany.

During and after World War II, any internationalist posture of the CPC was buried under a thick layer of nationalism. Together with the democratic leaders, the Communist leaders in exile advocated a policy of transferring the Sudeten Germans to Germany, and Karl Kreibich (who, in the early 1920s, had not cared whether the world be "German, Slav, or Romanic") turned into a Czechoslovak patriot. After the war, Václav Nosek, the Communist minister of the interior, took the lead in expelling the Sudeten Germans. It was still another interpretation of the principle of self-determination.

Back in the 1920s, however the majority of the Sudeten

2. Ferdinand Peroutka, *Budování státu: Československá politika v letech popřevratových,* 4 vols. (Prague: Borový, 1934–36), 4: 2, 208–9.

3. P. Reimann, *Geschichte der Kommunistischen Partei der Tschechoslovakei* (Berlin: Hoym, 1929), p. 217.

Germans declined to follow the extreme paths of either the CPC or the right-wing parties, and gradually they developed a positive attitude toward Czechoslovakia as their own state.

From Democracy
to Nazism

For their part, the Czechs handled the explosive situation with considerable caution. Aware that such a large and economically significant minority could not be permitted to persist in its inflamatory activity, the government approached the problem with firm resolve, yet in a spirit of reconciliation. There were mistakes, and there were shortcomings. Czech nationalism, already spurred by the achievement of independence, was further prodded by German hostility, and the conservative parties agitated for its resolute control. Land reform provided the authorities with an opportunity to move Czech families into the German-speaking territories and to extend preferential treatment to Czech farmers applying for allocations of land. Czech bureaucrats found employment in the Sudentenland, whereas very few German civil servants were located in central offices. During the depression years in the 1930s, the Sudeten region suffered more severely than did the rest of the country, not only because of the predominantly industrial nature of its economy, but also because the policy of the central government—for political as well as economic reasons—was to assist Czech, rather than German, industry.

These shortcomings in the official policy toward the German minority should not distort the general picture. All the progressive political parties strove for a constructive policy and sought cooperation with the Sudeten Germans. They sincerely wished to win them over to loyalty to the Republic. Two days after the Declaration of Independence, a spokesman for the minority visited Prague and, posing as a representative of a separate Sudeten German political entity which considered itself part of the Austrian state, proposed to negotiate with the National Council as an organ of a "foreign" power. In contrast, the National Council offered the

German minority a seat in the government. One National Council member, A. Švehla, told the visitor, "The Czechoslovak nation has carried the revolution, and that is the end of that! We now invite your cooperation." [4] The German representative declined the invitation.

It was Masaryk who set the tone and formulated the basic concept of the official policy toward the German minority. On December 23, 1918, only two days after his return from abroad and in an atmosphere of national tensions, he made a statesmanlike gesture by attending a performance in the German theater in Prague. He saw in that occasion, he said, a "prologue" to "a great political drama that we and the Germans living in our country can and should enact." At the same time, he made it clear in his first official speech as president of the Republic that the territory inhabited by the Germans was Czechoslovak. "No one can reproach us," he said, "if we are cautious after so many bitter experiences, but I guarantee that minorities in our state will enjoy full national and civil rights and equality. The American republic went into a civil war rather than to permit the secession of its South. We will never permit the secession of our . . . North."

Having established the scope, but also the limits, of accommodating the radical demands of the Sudeten German leaders, Masaryk worked untiringly for mutual understanding. In August 1919, he granted amnesty to all persons who had organized resistance against the Czechoslovak state. In April 1921, he suggested to the German representatives that they enter the government, but his proposal was rejected. During the same year, he stated that reconciliation had truly become his life task.

The government and the Parliament followed Masaryk's lead. The Constitution guaranteed "protection of national, religious, and racial minorities," fulfilling an international obligation stipulated for the ten countries in the Minority Treaty. A Language Law gave minorities the right to use their native languages in contacts with authorities at any level if more than 20 percent of their nationals lived in a court district. Two sets of laws that changed the

4. Jaroslav César and Bohumil Černý, *Politika německých buržoazních stran v Československu v letech 1918–1938*, 2 vols. (Prague: Čs. akademie věd, 1962), p. 102.

economic and social structure of the whole country—the land reform laws and the social legislation—were also beneficial to German farmers and workers.

In the area of education, the German minority was assured of preserving and developing its national and cultural identity. Documentary evidence records that the number of German schools in relation to the population was proportionately high: in 1930, with 22.32 percent of the population, 27.29 percent of the kindergartens, 21.49 percent of the elementary schools, and 20.98 percent of the secondary schools in the country were German. The student-faculty ratio was more favorable in German than in Czech or Slovak schools. Of all the German children in elementary and secondary schools, 95 percent received instruction in German from German teachers. The Germans enjoyed their own state-supported universities and equivalent institutions of higher learning on a highly advantageous level—32.5 percent of all state institutions. No other country in Europe offered its minorities such educational opportunity as did Czechoslovakia. In related areas, the Germans owned many publishing houses, had their own theaters and cultural and sports associations, and published sixty-three daily newspapers (as compared to fifty-three Czech dailies).

The German minority enjoyed full political freedom. Proportional representation in the electoral system assured German political parties of entirely equitable election results. Although most parties gradually developed a constructive attitude toward the Czechoslovak state, the German National Party and the German National Socialist Workers Party did not. They continued to agitate against the very existence of the Republic and were in contact with Hitler's Nazi Party. In 1927, Josef Goebbels participated in a rally in a town on Czechoslovak soil. Early in 1932, one year before Hitler came into power, Nazi headquarters sent instructions to its branch in the Sudetenland to be ready for the Führer's order "to take up arms in the cause of unity" as the day was "not far distant."

In the first three national elections (1920, 1925, 1929), democratic German parties represented an overwhelming majority of the Sudetenland populace. They had, on the average, fifty-

three members in the Chamber of Deputies, while the Nazi affili-
ates had only sixteen. In 1926, a breakthrough in the political position of the democratic German parties was achieved; two of them,
the Christian Social Party and the Agrarians, joined the Cabinet;
later, in 1929, they were joined there by the Social Democrats. To
allow a national minority party to sit in the government and be
privy to its confidential deliberations, which often concerned matters of state security, was an unprecedented act. Czechoslovakia
appeared to be well on the way toward a lasting solution to the
problem of her German minority.

Certainly the country tried to live up to its overall democratic and progressive program in this most sensitive area of minorities. As in the case of relations between Slovaks and Czechs, as
indeed, in the case of an assured existence of the Republic, an enduring solution of the minority problem would have required another thirty years of peace in Europe, and Czechoslovakia was not
granted this period of grace. The position of the German minority
developed into a critical international problem.

After the Nazi victory in Germany, the two nationalist German parties in the Sudetenland adopted a violent stance, agitating
and acting against the fundamental precepts of law. They were dissolved in October 1933, but were soon replaced by another chau-
vinistic, right-wing movement, which subsequently grew into
Konrad Henlein's Sudeten German Party. Nazism quickly infected
the masses of the German minority. In April 1935, Masaryk, true
to his democratic beliefs, declined to support a proposal to dissolve
the Sudeten German Party, and thus in the last national elections
held in May, that party scored a decisive victory, receiving 63 percent of all German votes and sending forty-four representatives to
Parliament. The representation of the three democratic German
parties was thereby reduced to twenty-one deputies. They worked
valiantly in the Cabinet until March 1938, but by then the Nazi avalanche was unstoppable. In the last free local elections held in
May 1938, the democratic parties were swept away by the Sudeten German Party, which gained over 78 percent of all German
votes. It now intensified its claims, demanding a territorial autonomy that would have created a state within a state. Thus it fol-

lowed the orders that Hitler gave personally to Henlein on March 20, 1938, to "make demands on behalf of the Sudeten German Party which would be unacceptable to the Czechoslovak government." Though the government made one concession after another, the spokesmen of the Sudeten German Party invariably advanced new and intolerable demands, until it became obvious that its actions were orchestrated by Berlin in keeping with its resolve to attach the whole Sudetenland to the Reich.

The rest is known: the Allied betrayal, Munich, the cession of the Sudetenland to Germany.

So did this experiment in cooperation, betrayed and thwarted, come to a dismal end. Its failure, resulting from international, not domestic, causes, cannot detract from the values of democracy and humanism that Czechoslovakia attempted to practice. Yet, questions always remain. Should the government have resisted—despite the pressure of friends and allies, despite the threat of war and revolution—the cession of these ancient Czech lands? The alternatives were awesome: to capitulate before pressures and violence, or to defend, even against foreboding odds, the nation's sell-esteem, dignity, and freedom—those qualities, which embodied the very essence of Czechoslovakia's history.

Chapter Seven

Munich!

Munich was the final crushing blow. But it was also the moment of truth. The anguished days of watching, imploring, cajoling; the disbelief at the perfidy of friends and the betrayal of allies; the desperate hoping and then the loss of hope—all were finally over, and Czechoslovakia faced the enemy, alone. The nation's independence was in grave jeopardy; indeed, it was all but lost. At that moment, Czechoslovakia's ideals of humanity, authentic or illusory, were cruelly tested. Would it prove to be a nation of Hus's truth, Žižka's indomitability, Comenius's morality, Palacký's integrity, and Masaryk's spiritual purity? Or would it be a nation of former servants, whose short-lived freedom had failed to "deaustrianize" them and eliminate the centuries-old habit of "bending the spine"? No analyst can submit final answers to these questions; he cannot even be confident that the questions themselves are justified.

Munich has been called a tragedy, and it did have the structure of a Greek tragedy. But the heart-rending question is whether there was about that moment more than the form of tragedy? Where was the "noble hero?" And did the final agony occur as the inevitable end of man, who in his flawed humanity, cannot triumph against the gods? Or was it, rather, a dreary series of events in which ideals were flawed by an acceptable pragmatism?

That Munich was pitiable, there is no doubt. But tragic? It was, perhaps, more a maelstrom than a tragedy, in which men and ideas and values were whipped about by forces too shattering to control. Trapped in the dilemma of choice between two evils, passions were lashed into a frenzy, the fainthearted were broken, and sturdy spirits were thrown into near manic exaltation. Imponderable values were swept away by the winds of physical force, as were principles by opportunism, the meaning of the past by the grim reality of the present and the terror of the unknown future.

The vast, inhuman forces of that fearful moment overpowered all. There was no man, no humanity, equal to the task that the times required.

There is no need to recount the complex events that led to Munich, but some aspects of the crisis, recently revealed from the archives of President Beneš, the Ministry of Foreign Affairs, the Ministry of National Defense, and the History Institute of the Communist Party of Czechoslovakia, permit an evaluation of the response of Czechoslovakia to the Munich dictate.

Let it be said, with an emphasis that cannot be overstressed, that Great Britain and France bear the primary responsibility for the shame of Munich. Every respectable source confirms this verdict. Great Britain was the principal influence in the outcome of events and, though it had no legal commitment to Czechoslovakia, it was a responsible member of the international community and the League of Nations; yet Great Britain acted counter to the fundamental article of international law—nonintervention in internal affairs. France had a formal international duty, embodied in a treaty signed in 1924, to come to Czechoslovakia's assistance if that nation became a victim of unprovoked aggression from Germany. Czechoslovakia also had a pact of mutual assistance with the Soviet Union, signed in 1935, which made Soviet participation operative only if France also fulfilled her obligation. During the Munich crisis, the Soviet government repeatedly stated that it would stand by its word and in the absence of evidence to the contrary, it cannot be faulted for its position and policy. The commitments of Yugoslavia and Rumania, based on their membership in the Little Entente, were limited to acts of aggression against Czechoslovakia from Hungary, though their ideological affinity with fascist Italy and Nazi Germany was antithetical to the cause of democracy which Czechoslovakia represented. Poland, whose relations with Czechoslovakia had been strained for many years, was waiting behind the scenes, hoping to join Germany in a play for its neighbor's territory. Very soon, however, Germany was to seize Poland's territory! The League of Nations, in which Beneš had worked tirelessly, was near collapse as its principal justification for existence—the system of collective security—turned moribund. The United States was very far away.

As early as 1935, the knell began to toll for Czechoslovak democracy. Great Britain and France took the first steps toward appeasement. They repeatedly ignored Germany's aggressive acts—violations of international treaties, unilateral armament, occupation of the demilitarized zone of the Rhineland, and the annexation of Austria. Czechoslovakia became the next target. On March 30, 1938, two weeks after the occupation of Austria, Hitler wrote, "It is my irrevocable decision to destroy Czechoslovakia by military means in the near future." Then Berlin's propaganda campaign began. Sudeten German Nazis enlarged the range of their violent activities and augmented their demands, all coordinated with Berlin's timetable and subject to its instructions. Hitler ordered the army to be prepared to take the Sudeten German territory no later than October 1, 1938.

Instead of stating that it would stand behind its obligations, France followed the lead of Great Britain, whose participation in an armed conflict with Germany France considered indispensable to its own. Simultaneously, these two nations brought ever-increasing pressure to bear on Prague, which ceded one position after another to the Sudeten German negotiators in an attempt to demonstrate the futility of appeasing them and their Berlin master. Beneš even indicated to the French government his willingness to surrender a portion of the Sudeten territory to Germany in order to avoid war.

After Neville Chamberlain's meeting with Hitler at Berchtesgaden, however, the British and French governments made Berlin's demands for cession of the Czechoslovak territory their own and, after an initially unsuccessful attempt to make the government in Prague accept these demands, they presented Beneš with an ultimatum: accede to Hitler's demands, or Czechoslovakia, denied their assistance, would be held solely responsible for the outbreak of war. In a calculatedly brutal gesture—designed, no doubt, to dramatize the precariousness of the moment—the ultimatum was presented to Beneš at 2:30 A.M. "The French envoy, handing over his government's message, wept. . . . The British envoy . . . remained cold and looked persistently at the floor. . . ." the president observed.

On September 21, Beneš and his government accepted the terms of the dictate. On the next day, at Godesberg, a triumphant Chamberlain reported to Hitler the results of his "peace" efforts, but found him in an ungratefully belligerent mood. Hitler presented additional demands, making it known that the German military occupation of the Sudeten territory must take place no later than October 1. For the moment, Chamberlain could stomach no more, and both he and Édouard Daladier, though they passed on Germany's claim to the Czechoslovak government, stated that they could no longer "take the responsibility of advising Czechoslovakia not to mobilize." In fact, Czechoslovakia mobilized on September 23; France ordered a partial mobilization; and Great Britain called her reserves to colors. All signs pointed to war in defense of democracy.

The signs were misleading. Chamberlain could not reconcile himself to the thought of entering a war with Germany "because of a quarrel in a far-away country between people of which we know nothing," as he put it. Having resumed contacts with Hitler, he initiated the steps that led to the Munich Conference, in which Germany, France, Great Britain, and Italy participated. The Soviet Union, an ally of France and Czechoslovakia, was ignored, and an agreement was quickly reached—in the absence of Czechoslovakia. The verdict that gave full satisfaction to Hitler's Godesberg demands was simply read to Czechoslovakia's representative. On September 30, the Czechoslovak government, alone and abandoned, faced an awesome choice: to resist or to accept. It chose capitulation.

In the final analysis, the decision to capitulate was exclusively the responsibility of the Czechoslovak government. Taking into consideration all the aspects of such a decision, its immediate as well as its far-ranging consequences, the dilemma is fundamentally reduced to the question of political ethics. Does a nation have a moral obligation to defend its rightful position against violence, even in the most adverse circumstances? Or is it morally justified in attempting to assure its biological survival, to "live to fight another day," at the cost of even the temporary loss of its moral integrity and fundamental values? The question is particularly pressing when studying such events in the light of Czechoslovak history.

Czechoslovak historians have engaged in the Munich controversy ever since the signature of their government appeared on the Munich dictate. Those who try to justify the capitulation point to what the devastating consequences of resistance would have been; those who favor opposition to German aggression find support for their position in the subsequent demoralization of the nation. Communist scholars analyze the Munich disaster in the light of the class struggle and see the capitulation as a deliberate act of treason on the part of the domestic and international bourgeoisie. It is certain that the controversy will continue in the future, for Munich was a catastrophe for Czechoslovakia, which haunts the conscience of its people whenever the country faces similar critical decisions, as it has on two occasions since 1938.

It is most likely that with the passing of time, the voices of condemnation will increase. But even as they enjoy the advantage of detachment, so their understanding of the realities of those dreadful days grows more abstract. So it is, then, that though future historians will deal more perceptively with the ethical aspects of the capitulation than did the Munich contemporaries, they will earn thereby no claims to a "higher wisdom."

A number of interdependent problems must be considered to reach any fair conclusion about Czechoslovakia's responsibility for its own capitulation: the dramatic speed of developments; the position of the leaders, particularly President Beneš; the weight of various arguments; the role of leadership in a revolutionary situation; the legal and political commitments to democratic processes; the country's geographical position; the will of the people; the anticipated consequences of the decision; the concrete power of realities and the intangible power of ideals; and finally, the question of whether or not a more perceptive reading of the meaning of Czechoslovak history might not have served as useful signposts for the future.

National Will

For many years, the Czechoslovak people were led to believe that their country's national life was sheltered (under the admittedly tenuous circumstances prevailing in Europe) by an optimal system of security. They continued to support the League of Nations, even when the actions of many of its other members weakened its authority and effectiveness. They trusted, within limits, its method of collective security, and beyond that, put their faith in the Republic's alliance with France and the Soviet Union and in the Little Entente. They expected, should circumstances demand it, a demonstration of solidarity in defense of democracy from other Western nations. The question is where, in all of this search for security, the development of faith in themselves was; such faith would certainly be a factor of decisive significance in an hour of national trial.

When the system of alliances dissolved in the chemistry of events, what was left to the Czechoslovak people? During the critical months preceding Munich, their leaders had made only perfunctory remarks about national self-reliance and the country's military strength. No psychological preparation had been even explored should the eventuality of facing the enemy alone ever arise. Even in the last days, when it became clear that France was desperately determined to extricate herself from her treaty obligations, the government concealed the real situation from the people.

It is, therefore, the more remarkable that the national will manifested a resolution far beyond that of its leadership. Every account describes both the enthusiasm of young men who were called to the colors and the eagerness of citizens who were anxious to speed up the process of mobilization. Within twenty-four hours, 800,000 soldiers were at their places of assignment. Meetings were organized all over the country to demonstrate the determination of the people; resolutions and individual messages poured into the *Hrad,* the seat of the president of the Republic, giving encouragement and calling for firm resistance.

Admittedly, the enormous pressures of precipitous events prevented the use of democratic procedures. In normal conditions, the government and its parties would slowly have prepared public opinion for its position; the opposition would have used available media for making its voice heard; a referendum could have taken place. But the situation in September 1938 changed from hour to hour: the shock of the British and French ultimatum; the news of its acceptance, and then the reversal; the call for mobilization; and, finally, the Munich dictate. Enthusiasm and the determination were in fruitless conflict with utter depression and despair.

Inexplicably and inexcusably, Parliament was not called into session. Instead, government spokesmen reported developments to a hastily conceived Committee of Fifty, composed of the chairmen and some members of the political parties. However, no adequate publicity was given to the committee's transactions and, consequently, rumors spread like wildfire, fanning optimism one day, fostering frustration the next. In this situation, the common people could only look to their leader to dispel the clouds of confusion and to add personal charisma to their energy and dedication to a national cause. It was one of those moments when the pendulum of history may swing one way or the other, depending on the will of a nation's leaders. In Czechoslovakia in 1938, the pendulum swung to capitulation.

The Role of Leadership

Who were the Czechoslovak leaders when the fateful hour struck? They were members of a government that represented nearly all the national political parties, their chairmen, and some prominent, popular individuals. They were experienced politicians, but they had never before been confronted with the necessity of making momentous decisions in a revolutionary situation, when all the weight of one's will must be thrown on one side or the other of the scale of a nation's destiny. The scope of the Munich crisis, in which the niceties of politics had to give way to a head-on confrontation, was beyond their grasp.

Some of those leaders played politics behind the scenes. Various members of the Slovak Populist Party maintained contacts with representatives of Henlein's Sudeten German Party and even with Berlin. In the chaotic days preceding Munich, these men secretly advanced the adventurous idea of Slovakia joining Poland, if Czechoslovakia should disintegrate. Rudolf Beran, the chairman of the powerful Agrarian Party, who was always critical of Beneš's foreign policy, particularly the policy of alliance with the Soviet Union, sent out feelers to Berlin, suggesting an "understanding" behind the government's back. These circles spread the vicious slogan that it was better to be Nazi than Bolshevik.

These were lonely voices, however; they were not the real problem. It was the indecisiveness of the most devoted leaders, who changed positions from day to day. Only two parties consistently opposed capitulation—the National Democrats (National Unity Party) on the Right, and the Communist Party on the Left. The others wavered from submission to resistance and back to submission again. Unable to move with any united front, they turned to an authority beyond themselves: the president of the Republic, Edvard Beneš.

The Role of Beneš

Beneš did not hesitate to accept the final responsibility for his government's policy during the Munich crisis. He could have withdrawn behind the articles of the Constitution, which gave the president no right to negotiate with foreign powers or make ultimate decisions. He could have thrown the awesome problem into the lap of the government and its prime minister, Milan Hodža. But his personality defied such considerations. He had been his country's foreign minister for seventeen years and its president for three. He knew all the statesmen of Europe, in addition to countless journalists and scholars. Endowed with analytical skill, he had a logical mind that reached well-reasoned conclusions. He was a "Westerner" with profound faith in the values of humanism and Western culture, a democrat dedicated to an evolutionary progress of justice and liberty. A man of courage, with supreme confidence in his own judgment, he sidestepped no responsibility; on the contrary, he reached for it. He surrounded himself with dedicated associates, while keeping his political adversaries at arm's length, and he overpowered opposition with the force of his arguments. His rational intellectualism earned him the nation's respect, but not its love, and his unprepossessing appearance deprived him of physical charisma. Beneš was a mathematician of politics. His empirical processes of evaluation rejected the idea that the values of pain, desire, and hope are important factors in society's complex decision-making processes.

Philosophically, Beneš followed in the path of Masaryk, his teacher, and became learned in sociology, history, philosophy, and political science. A respect for democracy and humanism permeates his written works, and ethics were the foundation of life to him. Nevertheless, his books and speeches convey the impression that he "learned" these values without ever having lived them. When faced with the task of defending them, he chose means that were neither ethical nor humanistic, though he was convinced that they were democratic. Since emotion was foreign to his reasoning, he hardly considered the feelings of his people in their moment of supreme crisis; he believed he knew better than they what was in the national interest.

Before the Western powers administered the coup de grace to his country, Beneš had applied his diplomatic skills to the task of forcing them to recognize their international obligations; he had confronted his friends and allies with incontestable facts. He had also tried to isolate the problem of the Sudeten German Party from the international issues, by demonstrating that no concessions would satisfy this agent provocateur who acted strictly on behalf of Germany. In order to prove his good will and in a futile effort to gain the good will of Great Britain, he accepted the humiliating mediation of Lord Runciman. After the ultimatum, he proposed that the conflict be resolved by arbitration, as provided by a treaty signed in 1925. He reacted favorably to President Franklin Roosevelt's appeal for an international conference. In the few days between the Godesberg and Munich meetings, when Hitler's intransigence seemed to leave England and France no other alternative than war, he carefully avoided any provocation and made it clear that Czechoslovakia, though now fully mobilized, would not renege on the conditions that it had already accepted in the first ultimatum.

But there was no way out. Great Britain and France were determined to avoid a war at any price—at least at any price that must be paid by Czechoslovakia. The decision on the "next step" was Czechoslovakia's and Czechoslovakia's alone. History records that Czechoslovakia's decision was to capitulate, but the drama of the internal conflict between the forces of submission and resistance, as it emerges from original documents, deserves to be related.

The Horns
of the Dilemma

As the storm gathered, General Ludvík Krejčí, the chief of staff of the Czechoslovak army, sent a memorandum on September 9 to the Supreme State Defense Council, warning against any "move by leading statesmen which—rightly or wrongly—might convey even the semblance of weakness." He wrote:

Our army is disciplined and has a high standard of morale and equipment. It would, therefore, be dangerous to undermine this discipline and high standard by actions which would be construed as showing that the helm of state is not in firm hands. The army is under the impression that all the interminable negotiations and humiliations are the result of an over-estimation of the strength of our northern neighbor and an underestimation of our potential strength.

The memorandum pointed to well-equipped frontier fortifications
and sufficient modern arms to "contain any enemy forces for a
considerable time," and thus enable "our allies to take all measures they consider necessary in the interest of their own security."
As to the German army, General Krejčí stated:

> . . . it seems to be more powerful than it actually is. In reality, the Ger-
> man army has only what can be seen in recent maneuvers: one and a half
> million imperfectly trained reservists. . . . It is a fact that the morale of an
> army greatly contributes to its value. At present, it can be stated that the
> morale of the German soldier is being artificially whipped up by the cult
> of the "superman" and intoxicated by the bloodless victories during the
> occupation of the Rhineland and Austria. The first failure of this soldier,
> when he approaches our fortifications . . . will suffice to break the
> morale of the German soldier. . . . Therefore, it is essential to evaluate
> our actual force and the actual force of the possible enemy correctly and
> to reject calmly and decisively all acts of intimidation which might weaken
> us physically and morally. The aim of these attacks is to beat down the
> morale of all public office holders. . . . But these momentous times fac-
> ing our nation demand momentous decisions. Germany's aim is the
> Black Sea. No mercy will be shown to our nation. If we do not defend
> ourselves, we will be miserably exterminated in the most inhumane man-
> ner.

General Krejčí added, in handwriting, "If death, then an honorable death." [1] In the light of what happened, Krejčí's memorandum is a fascinating document.

   Later, a few days before the British-French diplomatic note
of September 19 reached Prague, a group of politicians and journalists established an informal, secret council to prepare a plan of
action. Some members of the group were in contact with army
headquarters, which, on its own initiative, had already undertaken
precautionary military measures. As the government prepared
an answer to the ultimatum, the council's spokesman, Hubert
Ripka, a prominent diplomatic correspondent for *Lidové noviny*

1. Jiří Doležal and Jan Křen, eds., *Czechoslovakia's Fight: Documents on the Resistance
Movement of the Czechoslovak People, 1938–1945* (Prague: Čs. akademie věd, 1964),
pp. 15–17.

and a close associate of Beneš, addressed a letter to the president in which he said:

It depends solely on you whether we shall capitulate or fight. I am aware of the risk of resistance: we may be defeated. However, a defeat would not destroy the nation's moral force . . . while capitulation means moral and political disintegration, now and for generations to come, from which we could not recover. . . . I implore you not to be influenced by the reluctance and cowardice of some of our politicians.

There are in every party, Ripka continued, those who will support the president to the bitter end:

Mr. President, do not hesitate to apply entirely extraordinary procedures and measures: you will see that an overwhelming majority of the nation will stand behind you. So far, people stand firm, but the nation's morale will not stand for long. Otherwise, disintegration will follow. I am telling you frankly, and such is the opinion of many of my friends: we prefer the most terrible risk of war to a humiliating capitulation that will destroy everything that is clean, strong, and decisive. It would be, indeed, the first time in our history that we capitulated without a fight. We cannot permit such a devastating shame.[2]

Ripka obviously wished to allay Beneš's concern about the pusillanimous attitude of some members of his government and the machinations of some leaders of the Agrarian Party and the Slovak Populist Party.

The next day, at 7:00 P.M., the government handed to the French and British envoys its answer to their demands. In polite, diplomatic terms, it rejected the request, pointing to the fact that "these proposals were drawn up without previous consultation with representatives of Czechoslovakia." The note ended with the warning that ". . . it is not only the fate of Czechoslovakia which is in the balance, but also that of other countries and, particularly, that of France."

London and Paris remained deaf to Prague's appeal and

2. Jan Křen, *Do emigrace: Západní zahraniční odboj 1938–1939* (Prague: Naše vojsko, 1967), pp. 55–56.

delivered to President Beneš an ultimatum to withdraw his government's reply. The British note included a veiled threat that, should Beneš refuse, the British government ". . . must, of course, be free to take any action . . . appropriate to meet the situation. . . ." The French note stated bluntly, "Should the Czechoslovak government be unable to accept immediately the Franco-British proposals and reject them, and should war result from the situation thus created, Czechoslovakia will be held responsible and France will not join in such a war."

The government met four hours later, at 6:00 A.M. Monsignor Jan Šrámek, representing the Catholic Party, stated that he could not give his consent to the cession of territory because, according to the Constitution, such a decision belonged only to Parliament. František Ježek endorsed this position on behalf of the National Democrats. Beneš, however, still had hopes for a change in the French government's attitude, since it became known that its foreign minister, Georges Bonnet, had intrigued behind its back and sent unauthorized messages to Prague. Beneš asked the British and French envoys to give him their nocturnal ultimatum in a formal document and, using this short breathing space, inquired of Moscow whether the Soviet Union, as a member of the League of Nations, would come to Czechoslovakia's aid, even before the League's Council could deliberate on German acts of aggression. He received an affirmative answer: the USSR would help if Czechoslovakia turned to Geneva the moment she was attacked and notified Moscow of the action. A statement of such an action was drafted by Beneš's government, but, inexplicably, it was never delivered!

As the clock ticked away the hours of tension, maneuvers, inquiries, and intrigues, the French and British added to their formal diplomatic notes, delivered early in the afternoon, another pressing warning that any further delay in answering the ultimatum might lead to an immediate German attack. At 5:00 P.M., the government accepted "the Franco-British proposals with feelings of grief."

At a late hour that same night, a group of resisters—among them members of the coalition government and the leaders of the

Communist Party—met to organize a campaign to compel the government to reverse its decision. Accordingly, the next morning, a group of politicians constituted a special ten-member Committee for the Defense of the Republic which, it is noteworthy to record, included a Slovak Agrarian deputy and a Slovak Social Democrat deputy. A general strike was organized for September 22. That same morning, members of the committee, joined by other deputies (including General Gajda), and in the presence of representatives of the army, addressed a mass meeting before the Parliament and, manifesting their unity and determination, called for the rejection of the ultimatum and the resignation of the government. A statement was read, sent by General Syrový, the inspector of the armed forces, and a delegation was dispatched to President Beneš. The meeting was attended by 250,000 people—one-fourth of the Prague populace. The speakers represented a wide spectrum of political associations, from the Right to the Left, but all were of one mind concerning resistance. Among them were Klement Gottwald, secretary-general of the Communist Party of Czechoslovakia, and Ladislav Rašín, chairman of the committee and leader of the conservative National Democrats, whose father had been assassinated by a Communist in 1923. Rašín reminded the crowd of the crime against his father, but told them that now, when the homeland was in mortal danger, all forces must stand against the aggressor in a united front. "I, Rašín, am telling you that there is no difference between me and the Communists at this moment when it comes to a question of defending the Republic," [3] he stated, and then he and Gottwald embraced.

No record exists to indicate whether or not this public outcry influenced Beneš in his decision, but he did dissolve Hodža's government and nominate a new one, headed by the popular General Syrový, who had commanded the Czechoslovak Legionaries in Siberia during World War I.

Though the new government did not withdraw its predecessor's acceptance of the ultimatum, it was nevertheless widely acclaimed by the public. It was important to gain at least a few

3. Miloš Hájek, *Od Mnichova k 15. březnu* (Prague: Státní nakl. politické literatury, 1959), p. 65.

days for the skillful management of the crisis, and a breathing spell was offered by the need to elaborate the details of the occupation of the Sudeten German area. In addition, it was known that Chamberlain was to report to Hitler on the result of the British and French intervention in Prague.

On September 22, President Beneš went before the microphone to explain the realities of the situation as he perceived them. Despite his devastating revelations, he tried to convey the impression of being in perfect control, stating that he had never in his life had a feeling of fear for the state, "nor do I have fear today." He then added a mysterious sentence, "I have a plan for any eventuality and nothing will take me by surprise." Beneš later explained that he intended to offer a boundary rectification to Poland in order to gain her benevolent neutrality, at least.

The situation suddenly appeared more promising. Hitler's excessive demands at Godesberg seemed to have frightened and alienated England and France, who refused to support them. War seemed the inevitable solution. When Beneš, on September 23, received a communication of the British and French position, ". . . . he stood for a moment motionless, looking intently at the report," wrote his personal secretary Prokop Drtina:

It was obvious that he was reading the few sentences written on the paper again and again, and that it contained something extraordinarily important. Then, he put the paper on the desk, and said, "Yes," and began to pace back and forth across the room. . . . I observed that he was excited as I had never seen him before. Then he said, "This means war! The Englishmen advise us to mobilize." [4]

Beneš immediately convened the Ministerial Council and other representatives of the political parties and asked them to approve a declaration of general mobilization. Their decision was unanimous. The mobilization order was broadcast that same night, at 10:30 P.M. The following day, Beneš sent a message to the chief embassies:

4. Mîla Lvová, *Mnichov a Edvard Beneš* (Prague: Svoboda, 1968), p. 93.

The act of mobilization goes perfectly; the people are absolutely firm; the government is in full command of the situation. There have been no disturbances so far; our Germans, so far, join [the army] quietly. . . . No thought is given to any new concessions—one and a half million soldiers would not tolerate it, nor understand. . . . At the moment, we leave all roads and possibilities open except one: further concessions. After the country has been mobilized, further concessions are impossible. The military situation is good. Since we expected an air raid as early as last night, we now discern some hesitation in Berlin. It is a proof of weakness. If the mobilization is not disrupted tomorrow or the day after, we could stand against eighty German divisions with forty divisions. After full mobilization is achieved, we can withstand any attack, and for a long time.[5]

The country was poised for action, calm and determined, in full preparedness for the expected bloody struggle. "This will be a terrible war," Beneš said:

At the end, everyone will be fighting the Germans, uniformed and civilian men and women. Even if the great allies march with us, it will be neither quick nor decisive at the beginning, and we cannot prevent a German invasion of the Republic. But we shall fight to the last breath and will persevere to the end, happen whatever may. I will stay . . . permanently with the army. . . . I will stay with those who will fight till the last moment and will fall with them.[6]

The days passed in the tense expectation that war might break out at any moment. On September 28, the members of the Committee for the Defense of the Republic visited Beneš, pressing him to withdraw the government's concession to the British-French ultimatum, not to waver under any circumstances, and to appoint a strong new government.

The forces of appeasement were also at work. Beneš's appeal to submit the conflict to President Roosevelt for arbitration, or to convene an international conference as Roosevelt had suggested, went unanswered. Chamberlain was busy, planning an international conference of a different type—the Munich Confer-

5. Ibid., pp. 100–101.

6. Ibid., p. 127; Edvard Beneš, *Mnichovské dny:Paměti* (Prague: Svoboda, 1968), p. 302.

ence. On September 29, Chamberlain and Daladier met Hitler and Mussolini, and on the next day, at 6:00 A.M., the Munich verdict was read to representatives of the Czechoslovak government. Chamberlain yawned. The counselor of the German legation in Prague called on the Czechoslovak foreign minister, Kamil Krofta, at 5:00 A.M. and handed him the text of the Munich decision, which was to be accepted no later than noon. When apprised of the situation, Beneš exclaimed, "This is the end! It is betrayal and it will avenge itself. It is incredible. They think they save themselves from war or revolution at our expense. They are wrong!" [7]

During the morning, as the government was in session, the group of resisters met and sent a message to President Beneš, warning:

The undersigned deputies bring to your attention that relinquishing territory without the consensus of the constitutional representatives, the National Assembly, is treason according to the law. We implore you in this last moment to prevent the catastrophe which will transform the nation and the army into a desperate but determined mob. The only way of salvation is to reject the Munich treachery and to ask for an international conference.

A similar message to General Syrový added, "The nation did not call up the army to have it capitulate." [8] That same morning, Gottwald also called at the president's chancellery, where he made an urgent appeal to reject Munich, to turn to the League of Nations, to all nations, and chiefly, to the people, and to nominate a government of national defense.

During these fateful morning hours, the thought of turning to the Soviet Union again crossed Beneš's tormented mind. At 9:30 A.M., he called the Soviet envoy, Sergei Alexandrovskii, and asked him urgently to inquire of Moscow what its position would be "if Czechoslovakia entered the war against Germany, [assuming] that she would have England and France against her. . . ." For unexplained reasons, Alexandrovskii did not advise Moscow of Beneš's inquiry until shortly before noon. Meanwhile, in a session of the

7. Beneš, *Mnichovské dny*, p. 176.   8. Ibid., p. 179.

Ministerial Council, Beneš explained his real position on the question of Soviet help. "In the case that only Russia came to our assistance, a war of all against Russia would ensue and England would go against us." [9] Later, in a letter from exile in London, he explained privately to Rašín that going to war with only Soviet help meant that "the West would have believed that we [were] an instrument of Bolshevization in Central Europe; Poland and Hungary would have considered Soviet assistance an attack against them; the West would have, at best, waited and would have washed its hands of a German-Soviet war." He wrote further (and this part of the letter was omitted from Beneš's published account, *Šest let exilu a druhé světové války*) that to fight along with Russia would have meant that Czechoslovakia would have had "to take responsibility for all consequences, possibly also for a Bolshevik revolution, etc., in the whole area of Central Europe against the West's resistance." [10]

Without waiting to receive an answer from Moscow, Beneš dispatched, through Alexandrovskii, another message, stating that he did not expect an answer to his morning inquiry since his government had already decided to accept the Munich dictate. It did so officially at 12:30 P.M., on September 30, 1938.

At 5:00 P.M., General Syrový went before the microphone to announce the nation's capitulation to its people. He said that sometimes it was more difficult to live than to die for one's country. Millions of people shared his view, unable yet to see that it would be even more difficult to vegetate in the ruins of a country that for years had believed in freedom and progress. As the general was speaking, an airplane took off from Prague for Berlin, bearing a delegation that was to participate (the word meant very little) in the international conference which directed the dismemberment of Czechoslovakia.

On October 1, 1938, the German army began occupying the country, and it was conquered without the firing of a single shot.

9. Ibid., p. 182.

10. František Lukeš, "Poznámky k čs.-sovětským stykům v září 1938," *Československý časopis historický* 16, no. 5 (1968): 714.

Death Throes

In a desperate situation, the forces of resistance attempted to make a last stand. Their spokesmen drafted an appeal, signed by Rašín and sent to Beneš and Syrový, asking the government to oppose the capitulation, even at this last moment. Three members of the government resigned, among them Petr Zenkl, who became an inmate of a German concentration camp for the duration of World War II and died in 1975 as an exile from communism in the United States.

While the Munich Conference was still in session, President Beneš received the prime minister, General Syrový, General Krejčí, and three commanders of the land regions. Beneš subsequently described the scene:

The representatives of the Czechoslovak army, standing in front of me . . . took the floor, one after another, moved and sometimes excited. They tried to prove, unanimously and in different forms, this: "Let the big powers decide and agree on anything . . . the army will not tolerate acceding now to their pressure. . . . We must go to war, whatever the consequences. If we do, the big Western powers will be compelled to follow. The nation is absolutely united; the army is firm and wants to march. . . ." It was a most moving conversation. I noticed tears in the eyes of some generals and listened to their words of warning, pleas and threats, and these were emphatic pleas and warnings. They impressed and shook me again. I began to hesitate. . . .

The president commended the generals for their patriotic position. As for him, he stated, he could not consider "only the sentiments of the nation and the army." He had to see the situation as a whole and weigh the consequences. The generals were wrong in their expectations concerning France and England. "It would be irresponsible on my part," he said, "to lead the nation to a slaughterhouse . . . in an isolated war." However, he continued, "A war—a big European war—will come and there will be great upheavals and revolutions. They do not want to fight along with us now . . . they will have to fight hard, and for us, when we are no longer able to fight. . . . The generals left, dissatisfied, bitter, and in a desperate mood." [11]

At 2:00 P.M., Beneš received eight deputies, representing all political parties except the Agrarians, the Small Businessmen, and the Slovak Populists. The deputies belonged to the resistance group, and among them were Rašín and Gottwald. According to the notes of Josef David, one of the participants, Beneš "entered the reception hall pale, his face drawn, and his red eyes revealing that he had not slept that night." [12] Jaroslav Stránský opened the discussion:

Excuse me, but we cannot believe that a state which has such a disciplined and self-sacrificing people, such a magnificent army, would voluntarily give up. We have fortifications and there is fear the soldiers will not obey orders to lay down their arms. We should defend ourselves. Perhaps it would not be in vain, and the rest of the world cannot look passively on.

As David recorded the meeting:

. . . one saw that Dr. Beneš was very distraught; he seemed nervous and rambling as he said, "History knows no analogy to treating an independent state and nation in this way. You do not know what I lived through in these last days. It cannot be described. We are abandoned and betrayed. They are cowards, and most despicable in that they told us to mobilize, that there will be a fight. . . . It was a difficult decision to accept the conditions and save the nation, or to go to war and be massacred.

Gottwald answered:

Mr. President, I do not agree with you. Barefoot Ethiopians, without arms, defended themselves, and we yield! Look at the Spanish people, how they defend themselves! We have a great army; the nation is united!

11. Beneš, Mnichovské dny, p. 341.

12. Václav Král, Politické strany a Mnichov: Dokumenty (Prague: Svobodné slovo, 1961), pp. 160–64.

The rest of the world could not leave us to fight alone. Even now, we should demonstrate our strength. It still is not too late. The Munich demands should not be tolerated.

"I do not believe France and England would help us," Dr. Beneš replied, "Even Herriot implored us to accept." David reminded him that ". . . the President Liberator taught [the nation] that death was better than slavery. People cannot understand why we give away part of our territory without fighting." Beneš answered, "We are alone and encircled on all sides. It would mean the death of the nation, and the nation must live!" Then, Monsignor Stašek challenged him, "What ideals will you now present to the nation?" Beneš evaded, referring to the eventual question of his abdication, and Rašín retorted that his resignation would not resolve the problem of the nation's lost honor:

Excuse me, Mr. President, but I do not agree with you. In this castle, Czech kings reigned in an independent state and frequently determined the history of Europe. No one in this castle ever retreated! We should have defended ourselves. We ourselves retreated. Future generations will condemn us that we gave away our lands without fighting. In what should the nation now see its strength? In what should it now believe, when we have taken away its army, which must now abandon its posts without a shot? We are only adding our own to the cowardice of our allies. It is true that others have betrayed us, but now we alone are betraying ourselves.

Beneš was silent for a while and then said, "This would mean, in my opinion, the extinction of the whole nation. We could not bear this on our conscience. . . . We never betrayed; we were betrayed. It was not Hitler who defeated us, but our friends. . . . They have for the moment avoided [war], but for how long?" Gottwald repeated his protest against this reasoning, "You cannot convince me. . . . We should have defended ourselves. Perhaps then they would have come to their senses and would have come to our assistance." But Beneš again expressed his distrust of France and England:

. . . because they are afraid of war, indeed, mainly are afraid of social revolution. . . . We face a debacle of Western democracy. Our soldiers have said we can defend ourselves four to six weeks. And then? . . . The future of the nation depends on a resurgence of democracy . . . and we must maintain its life at any price. This must be the faith for the future. In spite of everything I have lived through and am living through, I believe in the ideals of democracy and humanity. True, in many ways, I have been disappointed. I have been wrong. I have now come to realize that the big powers and great nations, even in the present times, do not consider small states and small nations. They treat them as they find it convenient at the moment. We must in the future maintain our own freedom and democracy, we must build our own territorial entity, our own national life. . . .

"If the nation will not defend itself, moral disintegration will ensue," Deputy Tykal replied. "The people will trust no one and nothing. Everything must be done to prevent it." Beneš answered, "I am aware that morale will decline, that there will be widespread mistrust, but even this crisis must be endured." According to another documentary source,[13] Beneš elaborated his position at some length:

Had we not accepted [Munich], we would have waged an honorable war, but we would have lost our independence. An enforced acceptance of this dictate for the moment means saving as much as possible, receiving the West's guarantees—they may not be entirely worthless. It is necessary to adjust ourselves to international developments, to prevent social upheavals at home which Germany would like to exploit for an invasion. It is a hard decision, to accept the conditions and save the country, or to go to war and be massacred. . . . We can retreat without losing honor and prestige, preserve the state, and hold, as it were, a mortgage against the Western states . . . waiting . . . for a future accounting. This will certainly come, for the big powers have not solved anything for themselves by sacrificing Czechoslovakia, and events will go on.

Monsignor Stašek, probably sensing the president's distress, then said:

13. Lukeš, "Poznámky," p. 723.

Mr. President, in this hour of the whole nation's pain we pledge to you our faithfulness. You are not responsible for this end. It was, perhaps, a mistake that you trusted too much. However, history will not condemn you. You should not resign. We stand behind you.

No one appears to have seconded this promise of allegiance.

After a short conversation about the legality of the negotiations, the audience was brought to an end. Silent, solemn, Beneš shook hands with the visitors. "At the door, we stopped and many of us, with tears in our eyes, looked at the hanging maps of the Czechoslovak Republic."

As the German army moved, step by step, into the individual zones of the Sudeten territory, and the Czechoslovak soldiers prepared to withdraw from the zone which included the fortifications, a last attempt was made to stop the avalanche. A group of generals, led by Krejčí, planned to take over the government and even arrest Beneš. Some civilian leaders supported this plan. On October 3, four generals saw Beneš and, threatening to depose him if he refused, demanded his abdication. Allegedly, Beneš rejected the request, saying that he did not officially take cognizance of it, for if he did, he would have to punish the generals in his capacity as supreme commander.[14] The generals left; the plan aborted. It was the last attempt to ward off the ultimate catastrophe.

Two days later, Beneš did abdicate—under pressure from Berlin. Word had come from the German government that the negotiations of the international commission in charge of the details of the occupation would proceed more smoothly and, perhaps, some concessions in favor of Czechoslovakia would be achieved, if Beneš resigned. In the end, of course, Germany scored new gains in her peaceful aggression, which went even beyond the stipulations of Munich.

---

14. Křen, Do emigrace, p. 80. Five years later, when meeting Czechoslovak Communist leaders, Beneš harshly condemned commanders of the Czechoslovak army saying that "by their abilities they were just corporals . . . uneducated, incapable, and immature for their responsible role." Cesta ke květnu, document 3, vol. I-1 (Prague: Čs. akademie věd, 1965), p. 48.

The long night of struggle was over. A much longer night of darkness and suffering was to follow.

Which Conclusion?

Such were the complexities of the struggle that led to capitulation. It is clear that the decision to capitulate was almost entirely Beneš's. That his appeasement had no effect on the eventual destruction of Czechoslovakia is not, in itself, enough to condemn him. Rather, one must examine the legitimacy of the arguments calling for resistance to determine if there were, indeed, any meaningful alternatives.

First, was the hope of eventually receiving assistance from France and England, if Czechoslovakia chose to resist, based on defensible grounds? It was known that at least three members of Daladier's cabinet—Paul Reynaud, Georges Mandel, and Auguste Champetier de Ribes—opposed the prime minister's and Bonnet's policy, and France was not known for the stability of its government. Moreover, demonstrations in favor of Czechoslovakia were organized in Paris. Individual members of the Chamber of Deputies and a few journalists spoke up, reminding France of her international obligations and of the true nature and scope of the European conflict. After Godesberg, Daladier himself had appeared resolved to face the consequences of resistance to Hitler's aggression. On the other hand, such influential leaders outside the government as Léon Blum and Édouard Herriot vacillated, inclining toward appeasement, and public support for Czechoslovakia was organized chiefly by the Communist Party of France. There is grave doubt as to whether these forces could have delivered any effective assistance.

Similar developments took place in England. Winston Churchill and Anthony Eden raised their voices in opposition to appeasement; the Liberal Party and part of the Labour Party were critical of Chamberlain's policy; in the government, Alfred Duff Cooper did not approve and, at moments, even Lord Halifax, the foreign secretary, had doubts. Churchill sent a message to Prague, encouraging resistance, convinced that sooner or later, France and Great Britain would join in the war. This must have seemed a doubtful prediction at the time, however, considering England's yearning for peace and her lack of military preparedness.

Many documents (but not all) have been published, and much has been written about the position of the Soviet government. Moscow seemed ready to meet its obligations and, beyond this there is evidence that it promised immediate, unilateral assistance had Prague turned to Geneva and asked for Soviet help. However, even Czechoslovak Communist scholars admit that there is no hard evidence to prove that the Soviet Union would, indeed, have turned such promises into action.[15]

If, then, there was some validity to the prospect that the major powers would eventually have been drawn into the war, the second key question is whether the Czechoslovak army was in a position to resist a German invasion long enough to stir public opinion in the West and thus force a change in the West's policy. The military view, discussed earlier, was that the army could contain the enemy for a considerable time. For a short time, even Beneš believed that the army could withstand any attack and "for a long time." The army was well equipped; the fortifications were modern; the morale was unmatched. The Czechoslovak armaments industry was among the best in the world.

Recent studies, however, support neither the optimistic estimates of the military, nor the desperate estimates put forth by others.[16] Recognizing that Czechoslovakia was militarily well prepared, for a small country, they nevertheless point to weaknesses in its antitank weaponry; to unfinished fortifications; to an inadequate air force, artillery, and communications systems; and, cri-

15. Lukeš, "Poznámky," pp. 706, 712, 713. Lukeš further wrote, "Documents that are known up to the present do not justify the conclusion that the USSR was prepared to help Czechoslovakia under any circumstances, without any condition. If such were the case, we expect from the Soviet historians and archivists that they will support it by Soviet documents and will not demonstrate it with Czechoslovak documents—which are incorrect," p. 720, n. 72.

16. For example, Milan Hauner, "Září 1938: kapitulovat či bojovat?" Svědectví 13, no. 49 (1975): 151–68.

tically, they point to the unfavorable strategic location of the country. Out of some 2,000 miles of boundary, only 120 miles (bordering Rumania) were secure before an attack. The borders with Germany (including annexed Austria) stretched nearly 1,000 miles, and the remaining borders separated the country from hostile Hungary and Poland. On the other hand, the advantage was clearly Czechoslovakia's in terms of ground troops. The German army could field only some forty-eight divisions of freshly trained troops, but without adequate reserves, against forty-two divisions of the Czechoslovak army entrenched in defensive positions—for a limited period of time, clearly enough. Further, though supported by a highly developed industry, the German army's strategic supplies were estimated to be good for only two months and its raw materials for only four months. To compensate for his army's deficiencies, Hitler's strategy evisioned a blitzkrieg lasting only three days, the basic component of which was a surprise attack. This factor was lost when Czechoslovakia was given the opportunity to mobilize without interference. Further, Hitler vacillated between two concepts of waging the blitzkrieg: whether to develop a pincer movement from Austria and from the North into Moravia, thus preventing the Czechoslovak army from withdrawing into Slovakia; or to hurl his troops against the fortifications in southern Bohemia in a frontal strike. Hitler's chief of staff, General Ludwig Beck, warned against the war, for which, he claimed, Germany was not prepared; Beck was convinced that the conflict would not be limited to Czechoslovakia. Hitler might well have listened to his warning; years later, at the Nuremberg trials, Marshal Wilhelm Keitel stated that Germany "had no forces to break through the Czechoslovak fortified zone and had no soldiers on the western boundaries." Indeed, as late as June 18, 1938, Hitler wrote, "I shall decide on an action only if I am absolutely convinced . . . that France will not interfere and that consequently Britain will likewise do nothing." Moreover, a group of German generals planned to assassinate Hitler had he started a war.

In 1939, Germany's invasion of Poland disclosed serious deficiencies in her military machine, and today, when all substantial information on political and military matters is available, the evidence seems preponderant that a war in 1938 would have been short and that Germany would have lost. However, a judgment made in 1938 had to emanate from the knowledge of the relative strength of both camps that was then available. Clearly, a final victorious outcome would have depended on the eventual (and speedy) intervention of one or more of the Allied powers, Russia, France, or England. That was the gamble. But with at least four to six weeks to work with, one is forced to conclude that a leader—a real leader—would have taken the risk, grave as it was. He would have perceived that the valor of Czechoslovakia could be a catalyst to unite the frightened and diffused elements of the West. But in her hour of supreme crisis, Czechoslovakia had as her president not a leader, but a negotiator.

The term negotiator is not entirely pejorative. No responsible analyst can ignore the weight of Beneš's arguments. Subsequent events confirmed much of his cold reasoning: the war broke out eleven months after Munich and under much less favorable circumstances for England and France than would have been the case in September 1938. Indeed, France capitulated as a direct result of Munich, and England was left to face the German onslaught alone for one long year. In August 1939, the Soviet Union gained almost two years of respite by signing a pact with Nazi Germany that was a direct consequence of the Western powers' diplomacy at Munich. Under the protection of Soviet bayonets, Central and Eastern Europe experienced the radical social change which, according to Beneš, had been the fear of France and England, the fear that motivated their Munich policy. On the other hand, it can be argued that had Czechoslovakia's opposition to Munich been successful by involving the West, these things need never have come to pass.

Within Czechoslovakia, another aspect of Beneš's view proved correct: the country was spared massive physical destruction and annihilation. It emerged from the war less physically damaged than such nations as Yugoslavia, Poland, or Russia. No small nation can afford to overlook such considerations. But what of the moral consequences of the capitulation? Did Beneš ever fully realize their enormity?

As one sifts out all the arguments either defending or criticizing the capitulation, one cannot but conclude that the valiant ethos of the nation demanded from its leaders the ethical, not the practicable position. The Munich dictate should have been rejected, no matter what the consequences.

The spectre of Munich haunted Beneš the rest of his life. On every occasion, in conversations, in public statements, and in his books, he vigorously defended his decision. Undoing Munich, he frequently stated, was "the last goal of my life." His bitterness, however, was reserved for England and France, not for his own decision. He stated in his memoirs, "Since September 1938, I have thought about it, waking and sleeping. I have lived with it and suffered." Only in his posthumously published last work did he give way to doubts: "Did I decide in that terrible crisis correctly? Will not the events that ensued condemn me? These questions returned regularly at every important event. . . ."

Beneš was obviously concerned about the moral consequences of Munich, but he persistently maintained that the dreadful calamity could be transformed into a wellspring of moral strength. In 1942, he wrote to a friend:

It is a great drama from which we will come out the stronger. Our nation will always be able to see in all our attitudes great moral strength for its future struggles. We were the only one of all nations who, in this terrible crisis, was not internationally disgraced, did not harm anyone, and did not create a catastrophe through our own mistakes.[17]

Again, one senses Beneš's struggle for self-justification. But Munich did not turn into a wellspring of moral inspiration. On the contrary, that tainted fountain has not yet been fully cleansed.

Before he was burned at the stake, Jan Hus appealed to his nation to "defend truth till death." Žižka's Hussite chorale thundered, "Do not fear the enemy; ignore their numbers!" Masaryk considered self-defense a moral and spiritual duty. On the other hand, the first Czech king, St. Wenceslaus, when facing the power-

17. Václav Král, "Historická literatura o Mnichovu 1938," *Československý časopis historický* 22, no. 1 (1974): 51.

ful army of the Saxon king, Henry the Fowler, descended from his horse and, allegedly hearing the voice of God, offered Henry tribute and peace in preference to a bloody battle. In post-Munich times, Wenceslaus became known as "the first Munich man." Another great name, Palacký, condemned violence, claiming that "nothing worthwhile can be accomplished by force." Havlíček, while acknowledging that "at times men died for the honor, for the welfare of the country," maintained that the nation, "for the very same reasons, must live and work."

Expressed in the name of the nation these conflicting values embody the essentials of Czech history: 300 years of Hussite and pre-Hussite activism and 300 years of subjection. At the time of Munich both voices spoke: the one, to defend Czechoslovakia's humanistic convictions by military means; the other, to preserve them by passive moral resistance. Of course, the dilemma was never that simple: there were too many unknowns. Beneš had grave doubts about the army's ability to offer meaningful resistance; he believed that resistance was suicidal, and he wanted the nation to live. His opponents saw in capitulation the preservation of the nation but without honor, without dignity, without ideals. What neither side fully realized was that in capitulation, the nation suffered both death and demoralization.

In 1918, Czechoslovakia gained independence without firing a shot; twenty years later, the nation lost it without firing a shot.

Chapter Eight

Years of Darkness, Years of Struggle 1938–1945

Prague could never have been more beautiful than during the September days when its security hung by so slender a thread. Baroque towers— themselves unreal and ethereal—floated peacefully against skies in which the bright blue of autumn made way for isolated drifting clouds. . . . Yet rarely, if ever, has the quaint garb of this old city seemed more museum-like, more detached from the realities of the moment, than it did during these strange days. The world had taken final farewell, it seemed, of nearly everything that these monuments represented. . . . And again, a remarkable little people, whose virtues and whose failings are alike the products of adversity, found themselves standing out in lonely bitterness against what they felt to be an unjust and unsympathetic Europe.[1]

George Kennan wrote these poignant lines in October 1938, a few days after he had reached Prague as a young diplomatic officer. It was the first of his many reports, extending over a period of two

1. George F. Kennan, *From Prague after Munich: Diplomatic Papers, 1938–1940* (Princeton, N.J.: Princeton University Press, 1968), pp. 3–4.

years, on developments in Czechoslovakia, and the lines are characteristic of both Kennan's insight and his literary skill. It would require extraordinary talent for a Czechoslovak native who witnessed these dark days, however, to depict the sadness of the nation. Suddenly, after a few short days, everything seemed lost: the ideals of humanity, the reality of independence, the foundations of security.

During those days, Karel Čapek wrote "A Prayer for Tonight." With its litany of endurances as the meaning of Czechoslovak history, it sounded like a voice from the grave:

O Lord, Creator of this beautiful land, thou seest our suffering and despair . . . to thee we need not recount our woes. But for ourselves alone, our mouths and hearts strive to formulate what we must never lose, and that is faith: Faith in ourselves and in our history; faith that in history we have never stood and will never stand for wrong. . . . Greater than power is truth, for truth endures. . . . In our fate, a universal drama is being enacted, which will be carried through with great and glorious effort . . . [as] every resort of brutal force is brief, compared to the lasting need of man for liberty, peace, and equality among peoples and nations. We must work tirelessly among ourselves; we must love our nation even more than we have in the past; we must have greater love for each other. We believe that in this, and chiefly in this, is our mission on earth: to make of ourselves a nation in every way capable of building a better future. . . . We need internal strength. . . . Never can a nation be called small whose faith is great enough to build a better future.[2]

Čapek's prayer did echo the history of Czech endurance over the centuries, but it could hardly heal the wounds of day-to-day existence in the prostrate nation. It did not take long for the Munich generation to realize the enormity of its losses—in human lives, in the quality of material existence, in political freedom, and, worst of all, in moral values.

The material losses alone were staggering. In the wake of the Munich dictate and its sequel, the Vienna Award of November 2, 1938 (which allocated parts of Slovakia and the Carpathian ter-

2. Karel Čapek, "A Prayer for Tonight," in Czechoslovakia, Twenty Years of Independence, ed. Robert J. Kerner (Berkeley: University of California Press, 1940), pp. 448–49.

ritory to Hungary), Czechoslovakia lost 29 percent of her territory and 34 percent of her population, of whom almost one-third were Czech, Slovak, or Ukrainian. Industrial losses (58 percent in mining, coking, and briquette works; 65.3 percent in the glass industry; 59.8 percent in textiles; and 53.5 percent in the paper industry) stripped her of a tolerable economic base. Six months later, more material injuries followed.

Still worse were the moral and spiritual consequences. Few, indeed, responded to Čapek's prayer. Rare are the men of such moral fiber that they can withstand an anguish of such intensity. If there is no enemy to attack, men turn upon their former friends in bitterness and fear. Opportunism, defeatism, corruption, and denunciations were commonplace. The fruits of the labor of twenty years were spoiled in a single day.

Scapegoats were sought out, and Beneš was the visible target. Some elements of the population demanded his trial before a special tribunal, conveniently forgetting that other political leaders shared his responsibility for the decisions that had led to disaster. Even Thomas Masaryk was denigrated. Pictures of Beneš and Masaryk, hanging for years in government offices and private dwellings, were removed. When all the Czechoslovak legations abroad were ordered to destroy their photographs, the embarrassed staff in London, where the first president's son, Jan, was minister, could not bring themselves to do it. In grief and bitter awareness of the irony of the situation, Jan Masaryk took down the pictures himself—an act that vividly dramatized the death of the free and spirited nation his father had personified.

Berlin immediately began issuing directives. It instructed the German minority—which remained inland in isolated enclaves even after the Munich mutilation of the state—to incite disorders and stage demonstrations; it demanded that Prague oust Jews from government positions and free the nation from the vestiges of "Benešism." In January 1939, Hitler warned Prague that it must withdraw from the League of Nations, reorient its foreign policy toward Berlin, promulgate anti-Jewish laws, and reduce its armed forces. The guarantees for the security of Czechoslovakia, promised by the four Munich powers, were first mentioned gingerly in their diplomatic exchanges and then conveniently forgotten. Interestingly enough, Beran, who had sought an accommodation with the Nazis before Munich, complained in a confidential conversation that ". . . cooperation with the Germans [was] impossible; they [were] ruffians." His political confrere, Jaroslav Preiss, director of the Živnostenská Bank, seconded his view:

The Nazis are crazy; they ruin the economy. Just as it was a mistake before that we did not want anything to do with Germany, it would be a mistake now if we did not want anything to do with England and France; in the next war, the West will defeat Germany.[3]

If the true nature of the Nazi regime had been recognized by this powerful circle of the Agrarian Party before Munich, Beneš's posture might have been different. But by 1939, it was all rhetoric.

Meanwhile, the political life of the nation needed a concrete structure. For over two months after Beneš's resignation, the country had no head of state. All political parties, with the exception of the Social Democrats and the Communists, were fused into the amorphous Party of National Unity. The Communist Party was dissolved, and the Social Democrats, joined by some National Socialists, became the National Labor Party. The trade unions, organized previously along party lines, amalgamated into one movement. Legislative work ground to a standstill, and some members of the National Assembly refused to participate in a sham performance of democratic processes. The Communists and some National Democrats courageously continued to denounce the Munich Pact. The government wanted to rule by decree, but Slovak opposition delayed the National Assembly action approving the Enabling Act. On November 30, 1938, after Prague met the Slovak demands, Emil Hácha, the aging and apolitical president of the Supreme Administrative Court, was elected president of the ailing Republic, and the Enabling Act was passed two weeks later. Syrový's government resigned, and Beran was appointed prime minister. A new governmental structure was thus created,

3. Jan Křen, *Do emigrace: Západní zahraniční odboj 1938–1939* (Prague: Naše vojsko, 1967), p. 153.

but it soon proved to be a mere facade. Unable to offer any leadership to the nation, too weak to withstand intensified German pressure, ignored by the West, and unsuccessful in curbing fascist agitation, the government became wholly impotent, incapable of warding off the worst, which was yet to come.

Slovakia did not escape the deluge; in fact, its ravages there were even more devastating. After agitating for years for autonomy, the Slovak Populist Party wasted no time in exploiting Munich to achieve its goal. Less than one week after Munich, it convened a conference which outlined the program for autonomy. All the Slovak political parties merged with the Populist Party—again with the exception of the Communist Party, which was dissolved. An autonomous government was established, which included a representative of the German minority, Franz Karmasin. In the central government in Prague, the virulent Slovak leader, Karol Sidor, became deputy prime minister. To eliminate any doubt about his own and his fascist cohorts' position, he stated proudly:

Even in Prague I wear the uniform of the Hlinka Guards [a radical militia of his party] for I want to look like an honest young Slovak and not like the local gentlemen who prefer formal dress and silk hats. . . . In matters of foreign policy, I want a policy of collaboration with all nations which oppose Judaism and Bolshevism. The former regime associated with Red Spain, atheist Soviet Russia, and Jewish Geneva. In the future, as a first priority, we ought to cultivate cordial relations with our neighbors.[4]

So the Slovaks did, but the relations turned out to be anything but cordial. Slovak autonomy exceeded by far the pre-Munich demands, and its loosened association with the Czech lands found expression in a change in the name of the country; it became hyphenated—Czecho-Slovakia.

Even more chaotic events overtook Subcarpathian Russia.

4. National Archives, Diplomatic Branch, Record Group 59, General Records of the Department of State, 860F .00/589, George Kennan's "Review of Czechoslovak International Developments since Munich," December 20, 1938, p. 12.

Primitive, exposed for years to feuding cultural entities, even less prepared for national responsibility than Slovakia, it, too, demanded and received autonomy.

At a time when unity of spirit and determination should have been the moving force of the day, the whole country was crumbling. There was no moral imperative to "stand firm." The divided Czecho-Slovakia was an easy prey to Germany's aggressive plans.

On December 20, 1938, Foreign Minister František Chvalkovský told George Kennan that he had "entire confidence in the future independence of the country" and that he had received assurances from Hitler in a personal interview that Germany had "no desire to incorporate Czechoslovakia into the Reich." [5] Neither of those two diplomats could have known that only three weeks after Munich, Hitler had issued an order to the German high command to be ready "to smash at any time the remainder of the Czech state, should it pursue an anti-German policy." Aware of the absurdity of such a qualification, Hitler sent agents to seek out Slovak radicals and make them declare Slovakia's independence by the middle of March. He also ordered his generals to be prepared for military action. As in the Munich crisis, Hitler meticulously adhered to his timetable. The Slovak leaders were ready to oblige him. Vojtěch Tuka, once condemned to prison for high treason but by then one of Slovakia's leading figures, visited Hitler on February 12, 1939 and declared, "I put the fate of my nation in your hands." Hermann Goering promised financial assistance to other Slovak leaders if they could help dismember Czechoslovakia. Ignorant of Berlin's incitement of Slovak separatist plans, the government in Prague moved the military into Slovakia and deposed the rebel government. It was a futile, desperate gesture. On March 13, Hitler invited the ousted Slovak prime minister, Jozef Tiso, to visit him and directed Tiso to proclaim an independent Slovak state, threatening an Hungarian invasion if he did not comply immediately. Tiso agreed. The next

5. Ibid., p. 17.

day, the Slovak Diet proclaimed, amid partly spontaneous and partly contrived enthusiasm, a new Slovak state. On the same day, the Hungarian army occupied Subcarpathian Russia.

Once the Slovak problem was "solved," the Czech lands had to be dealt with. Hácha journeyed to Berlin and, in the early hours of the morning of March 15, Hitler ordered him to sign a document placing the future of his country in Hitler's hands and announced that the occupation of the Czech lands by the German army would begin at 6:00 A.M. If Hácha refused, Prague would be bombed.

A desperately sick man who had to be given several injections to keep him conscious, Hácha finally signed the infamous paper. As the tortuous scene unfolded, the German army was already crossing the frontiers and, by 9:00 A.M., had reached Prague. The weather provided a fitting atmosphere for the occasion: the skies were dark and leaden, the temperature below zero, and a blizzard raged over the country. The people of Prague, their faces grim, their arms raised and threatening, watched the German soldiers shivering in the tank turrets and the open trucks that rumbled through the streets of the desolate city.

The next day, Hitler entered Prague in triumph, and from the Hrad, the ancient seat of the Czech kings and of two Czechoslovak presidents, proclaimed the establishment of the Protectorate of Bohemia and Moravia. The illusion of Czechoslovak independence was finally dispelled. The country had been dismembered into a puppet Republic of Slovakia and an occupied German territory. The people, though again humiliated, were this time clearly in no position to rebel and, with what was nearly a sigh of relief, settled into the grim and total reality of occupation. From now on, there would be no burden of moral choice. The ultimate meaning of Munich was at last completely clear.

The Occupation

The British and French governments, responsible as they were for Munich, now refused (an easy morality) to recognize the dismemberment of Czechoslovakia. With more right to do so, the Soviet government also protested the act. In Washington, Acting Secretary of State Sumner Wells issued an official statement condemning the occupation as an act of wanton lawlessness, "which has resulted in the temporary extinguishment of the liberties of a free and independent people with whom, from the day Czechoslovakia attained its independence, the people of the United States have maintained specially close and friendly relations." The statement was sent to the American legation in Prague with a strictly confidential addendum: "We hope that you may be able to make this available to the Czechoslovak press and that the latter may find a way to give it publicity." The American minister in Prague responded, "The entire press here is under strict German control, the Gestapo is everywhere, and it would be virtual suicide for anyone to publish the statement unless, indeed, it first appeared in the Berlin press." [6] The minister was correct. All mass media had become mere Czech language instruments of German propaganda. This situation, however, was only one aspect of the new reign of terror.

Step by step, every authentic expression of political and cultural will was extinguished. Universities, the National Opera, and theaters were closed; numerous organizations were dissolved; political parties were forbidden. Prominent democratic journalists, writers, teachers, and priests were herded into concentration camps. The property of Jews was confiscated, and their tortuous trek to the gas chambers begun; it ended only after 140,000 Czech and Slovak Jews had been exterminated. It cannot even be said that there was a saving grace in the fact that anti-Jewish laws were introduced by the Nazis and not by Hácha's government. The grim reality remains that in the Czech lands, in the former Republic of T. G. Masaryk who had fought anti-Semitism throughout his long life, the results were the same as all over Hitler's Europe.

Hitler had given vent to his hatred of the Czechs as early as 1932, when he told Hermann Rauschning that he would ". . .

6. National Archives, 860F .00/690A.

transfer the Czechs into Siberia or the area of Volhynia and . . . assign them to reservations in the new federated states. The Czechs must be removed from Central Europe. As long as they remain there, they will be the focus of Hussite-Bolshevik disruption." During World War II, Berlin prepared several plans for solving the Czech problem. First, the Nazis planned to exile the entire Czech population in the East. When they came to realize that they were in need of the Czech labor force, however, the Nazis concluded that one part of the Czech people would be transported to the East, another part would be germanized, and the rest would be exterminated. Studies were undertaken to determine (by the measurement of skulls) which Czechs were anthropologically "suitable" for the process of germanization. If President Beneš had been concerned about mass slaughter had the nation resisted at the time of Munich, an equally grisly fate awaited its people later. Only an Allied victory saved them from Hitler's "final solution."

Human losses and suffering were accompanied by material privation. Once destined for the defense of the country, military equipment was transferred to Germany: 1,213 airplanes; 2,253 pieces of light and heavy artillery; 501 antiaircraft guns and 1,966 antitank guns; 810 tanks; 603,000 rifles, 57,000 machine guns, 114,000 pistols; and over 1 billion rounds of ammunition for the infantry and over 3 million rounds for artillery. Indeed, Czechoslovak equipment exacted a heavy toll from the Allies who had, in effect, turned it over to Hitler at Munich.

Economic losses were enormous, running into billions of crowns. Big industrial concerns and banks were simply taken over and losses in movable property alone were between $.5 and $1 billion. Some $100 million were extracted annually in taxes. Various financial transactions milked the country of another several billion crowns. Hordes of Germans—in high positions, gestapo and SS men, and regular army troops—battened on the land and the people, flaunting their racial superiority over the Czechs.

There were periods of relative calm in the Protectorate, when the German masters needed to extract a maximum war effort from recalcitrant Czech laborers. They tried to bribe workers with extra food rations and allocations of cigarettes. The chief target of German persecution, however, was the unreconcilable intelligentsia. According to the Central Committee of the Union of Anti-Fascist Fighters, before the war ended, 360,000 Czechoslovak citizens had been held in concentration camps and prisons, and 235,000 had died there.

Under these circumstances, the government of President Hácha was no more than a front for German policy. It was composed of a few genuine quislings, but there were also patriots in it who pretended to cooperate with the enemy while maintaining dangerous contacts with underground leaders. Two of these, Ladislav Feierabend and Jaromír Nečas, later escaped and joined President Beneš in London; another, General Alois Eliáš, who had succeeded Beran as prime minister in April 1939, was arrested and, in June 1942, executed. While the government did attempt to rectify some injustices in matters of minor significance, the German rulers ruthlessly carried out all important policies. Most people understood the helpless situation of the government and pitied its humiliating position.

In an exhaustive report from Prague in October 1940, George Kennan masterfully depicted the atmosphere there:

The outward changes under the Protectorate are neither great nor important. Bohemia has retained its muddy villages, its geese, its beer, its earthy fertility. And the city of Prague, to which Italian and Austrian architects long ago gave a grace and harmony unrivalled in central and northern Europe, has not lost its charm. . . . Under the surface, on the other hand, the changes have been profound.

After detailing the economic losses, Kennan turned to values of more lasting significance:

Czech cultural life still struggles on. It will never be entirely eradicated, as long as any appreciable part of the nation remains. . . . But if German authority in a physical sense is unchallenged, morally it does not exist. Whatever power the Germans may have over the persons and property of the Czechs, they have little influence over their souls. . . . Actually, the Czech nation today lives without moral guidance from any quarter.[7]

7. Ibid., 860F .00/692; Kennan, "Review," pp. 2, 12, 13, 15.

The wartime developments in Slovakia were more complicated. Since they had "independence" and their own president,
government, and other appurtenances of power, the Slovaks took
some satisfaction in their state. In fact, there was nothing to be
proud of. The government and all of political life took on the
shape of its fascist model. Jews were persecuted, and neither the
occasional half-hearted interventions of the Vatican and the epis-
copate, nor the feeble efforts of the somewhat conservative ruling
group could save them from the brutal fury of the radicals. Czechs,
who had once helped to build the country, were now ostracized
and evicted. Nearly every act of this Catholic Republic contradicted the basic principles of Christianity and humanism. The fact
that the Germans were in control was hardly a sufficient excuse for
the nation's overt complicity in such degradation. In August 1944,
Slovakia's name was finally cleansed by a true national uprising.

Resistance

It has often been pointed out that resistance activities in the Czech
lands and in Slovakia lagged behind partisan action in such countries as Yugoslavia, Poland, Greece, and France. The criticism is
largely justified, but some thought must be given to the reasons for
this difference. In the first place, no other occupied country had
suffered the betrayal and trauma of Munich. The Czechoslovak
people had not been attacked and conquered; they had been sold,
traded away by friends and allies. They had no incentives to
engage in sacrificial and suicidal resistance during the period of the
"phony war." Nor was there cause for resistance later, when the
Soviet Union was on the defensive, and the military strategy of the
West was limited to air bombing. Moreover, Czechoslovakia had
been occupied by the Germans for a full six months before the
outbreak of the war, and all her armaments were confiscated. In
addition, the relatively sophisticated communications system in the
Czech lands facilitated tight German control over the activities of
individuals and groups, and the terrain of the country did not lend
itself to guerrilla warfare. Nevertheless, the resistance movement in

Czechoslovakia—the last country to be liberated—did indeed exist throughout the war, and it grew as the Allied armies approached victory.

From time to time British officials questioned Czechoslovak representatives about the limited scope of their nation's resistance, and Molotov inquired about it when Beneš visited Moscow in December 1943. On the other hand, London and Moscow both appreciated Czechoslovakia's special contribution to the Allied war effort: a most effective intelligence service. Three months before the event, for example, Czechoslovak intelligence knew about the German invasion of Poland; it knew three weeks in advance of the German attack in the West; and it passed on information almost daily on the German army (code name, Werther), air force (Olga), and navy (Anna). Indeed, it had a spy in the center of German intelligence itself—code name, A-54.[8]

Even before President Beneš left the country in October 1938, a few of his close associates had established a clandestine group to be ready for underground activities in the war they considered inevitable. Slowly, other groups came into existence, consisting of prominent members of the former officers' corps, youth groups, and other people from all segments of society. In 1940, these groups formed one central body, the Central Committee for Home Resistance (ÚVOD), to coordinate their activities. Through radio and other means, the Central Committee remained in contact with the government in exile in London, but many of its members were discovered by the Germans, arrested, and executed. Others, civilians and officers, found their way to London, escaping through Slovakia with the assistance of the Slovak underground.

During 1940 and 1941, some 20,000 messages were sent to London. Intelligence information was delivered to Moscow regularly, even when political relations were suspended during the period of the Russian-German cooperation. Indeed, the most important information that came from the underground, passed through the British to the Soviet government, concerned Hitler's

8. Frantisek Moravec, *Master of Spies: The Memoirs of General Frantisek Moravec* (New York: Doubleday, 1975), pp. 170, 172.

"Operation Barbarossa"—Germany's invasion of the Soviet Union. A-54 advised Czechoslovak intelligence of the plan nine months in advance; in March 1941, he supplied detailed plans; and three weeks before the invasion, he provided the exact date.[9]

Ideologically, ÚVOD represented a wide spectrum, from the democratic Right to the democratic Left, without reference, however, to political parties, which were outlawed. The only party that preserved its structure and function (underground, of course) was the Communist Party, and therein lay its strength and effectiveness. Soon after Munich, and following a carefully planned action, some members of the Executive Committee of the CPC found refuge in Moscow, while others fled to London or Paris, and still others were instructed to conduct the Party's affairs on the home front. One illegal Central Committee after another was arrested, but the Party as such always emerged intact. The Party sought cooperation with the democratic underground, but this was declined since the latter did not trust the Communist leadership. Both camps published illegal newspapers. The Communists distributed *Rudé Právo* and the democrats, *V boj,* which was designed by Vojtěch Preissig, an American of Czech origin. He was arrested in 1940 and died in the Dachau concentration camp in May 1944.

The spirit of resistance among larger cross sections of the people found convincing expression on many occasions. Though these expressions did not hasten the end of the war, they strengthened the Czech and weakened the German morale. As George Kennan reported, for example, bouquets of flowers constantly appeared on the tomb of the Unknown Soldier and at the statue of Jan Hus. When the Prague orchestra played Smetana's *Má vlast* (*My Country*), the ovation lasted for fifteen minutes and the conductor kissed the score. The anniversary of Munich, as well as Independence Day, was marked by demonstrations in Prague. On other occasions, carefully planned boycotts of streetcars, or the Czech press under German control were carried out.

Toward the end of May 1942, the *Reichsprotector,* Rein-

9. Ibid., pp. 189–193.

hard Heydrich, was assassinated by a group of Czechoslovak para-
chutists who had been sent from London. The most widely acclaimed and spectacular Czechoslovak act of resistance of the war,
it was not necessarily the most effective. It was executed against
the advice of the underground leaders, who were concerned about
German vengeance, and indeed, the consequences were no less
striking than the act: some 23,000 Czechs were executed in repri-
sal, among them many democratic and Communist underground
leaders.

The German war machine was more directly affected by
frequent acts of sabotage, by "slowdown" campaigns in industries,
and, in the last phase of the war, by accelerated partisan actions.
According to the Documentary Department of the Central Committee of the Union of Anti-Fascist Fighters, there were 126 partisan units operating in Czechoslovakia, with 23,553 members;
they derailed and demolished 443 locomotives and 3,883 railway
carriages, and destroyed 120 railroads and 180 highway bridges.
Most of these actions took place in Slovakia, where the moun-
tainous terrain facilitated guerrilla warfare and where Soviet par-
tisans were parachuted in advance of the Red Army.

In Slovakia, resistance was generally more widespread than
in the Czech lands. Special conditions (somewhat more relaxed
under an "independent" government) made possible a buildup of
political organizations. In the summer of 1943, strikes spread over
the country and at Christmas of that year, democratic and Communist leaders reached an agreement on intensifying the national
struggle and on a program for a future, reborn Czechoslovakia.
They created the Slovak National Council and, from that time,
plans were readied for a national uprising. A number of generals in
the Slovak army cooperated with the resistance leaders in an effort
to win the army over to the resistance. On August 30, 1944, the
Slovak National Council called upon the nation to rise against the
oppressor. Within a few days, most of Central Slovakia was under
its authority. After a number of ferocious battles spanning four
months, however, the German army crushed the national uprising.
The event cost over 13,000 lives; some 30,000 persons were
deported; and 60 communities were destroyed. But the stain of

collaboration with the Nazis had been removed. The gain to the human spirit in Slovakia was incalculable.

Tasks Abroad:
Rebuilding the State

Though the Western Allied powers refused to recognize the dismemberment of Czechoslovakia, neither did they in the first phase of the war discuss the question of reconstituting the Republic. Thus, the task of reconstructing the state and regaining international recognition fell to a group of political exiles in London, Paris, Washington, and Moscow. Most of its members were unknown to the outside world, and Edvard Beneš, whose name was familiar to every statesman—held in admiration by some and in detestation by others—became the group's natural leader. Facing intricate diplomatic obstacles, he and his associates had literally to start from scratch.

On the day Czechoslovakia was occupied, Beneš sent telegrams of protest to Roosevelt, Chamberlain, Daladier, Litvinov, and the League of Nations. He was received by Roosevelt on March 28, 1939, and in the summer of that year returned from the United States to London. Immediately after the outbreak of war, he and his associates asked the French and British governments to recognize a provisional Czechoslovak government in exile. But the British and French authorities, still in the grip of the Munich mentality, treated Beneš as a private person. A few days before the outbreak of hostilities, Lord Halifax had sent a letter to Beneš beginning, significantly, "My Dear Monsier Beneš." Daladier had refused even to receive him. The Soviet Union, then pursuing a policy of appeasing Germany, recognized the Slovak Republic. Toward the end of 1939, modest progress was achieved when the French and British governments recognized the Czechoslovak National Council, though not as a government.

With the capitulation of France in June 1940, Chamberlain's resignation, and Winston Churchill's ascendance as prime minister, the new political atmosphere in London gave Beneš his first real opportunity to advance Czechoslovakia's interests. In July 1940, the British government granted recognition to the government in exile, though only as a provisional government. The British also declined to accept Beneš's contention that Czechoslovakia had legal continuity and that her pre-Munich boundaries should be recognized. At this time, however, Lord Halifax's official communication addressed Beneš as "Your Excellency."

After the German invasion of the Soviet Union, the international position of Czechoslovakia changed immediately and drastically. On July 18, 1941, the Soviet and Czechoslovak governments signed an agreement concerning the exchange of ambassadors and mutual assistance in the war. A few hours earlier, the British government, anxious to outmaneuver the Soviets, had recognized the Beneš government as a de jure representative of Czechoslovakia. In August 1942, the British government withdrew its signature from the Munich agreement, and in the following month, General de Gaulle declared the Munich dictate invalid ab initio. The consequences of Munich, of course, could not be so blithely undone.

In Washington, Beneš's efforts encountered serious opposition among some State Department officials. The U.S. government, though not a participant in Munich and not recognizing the dismemberment of Czechoslovakia, had nevertheless accepted the diplomatic consequences of these two events. It maintained a consulate general in Prague, and George Kennan followed the developments from his outpost in Berlin, where he served as first secretary of the American embassy. He visited Czechoslovakia on several occasions and, in his reports, he expressed understanding for Hácha's government and criticized Beneš, scorning the "dream of dramatic liberation and revenge." He ended his report of October 1940, "The heroics of irredentism are very well from a distance." In a memorandum dated February 5, 1941, Kennan elaborated this view:

. . . the Czech Committee in London, headed by Dr. Beneš, is not viewed with much seriousness in the Protectorate of Bohemia and Moravia. The publicity given to Beneš and Jan Masaryk adversely affects the

Czech people and, moreover, Beneš has never recovered his popularity with his own people. The feeling is fairly prevalent in the Protectorate that Czechoslovakia as it formerly existed will never be reestablished and that in the event of an Allied victory some sort of federation of certain Danubian states may be the ultimate solution to the complicated post-war arrangement.

Someone in the Department of State added a comment to Kennan's memorandum:

Mr. Kennan believes that such a federation may embrace Austria, Hungary, Bohemia, Moravia, and Slovakia, with the establishment of a monarchy. This coincides with certain remarks made to me by the Archduke Otto last spring. . . . In the light of the foregoing, Mr. Kennan expressed the strong feeling that this government should not give any formal recognition to the Czech Committee in London, thus causing embarrassment to the Hácha government, and that we should manifest a certain understanding of the position of the Hácha government. After all, said Mr. Kennan, the rallying of the Czech people in any ultimate revolt against German domination will center around the Czech government in Prague, and not around any absentee committee.[10]

The memorandum was passed on to Sumner Welles with a note to the effect that Kennan's viewpoint coincided with that of the Division of European Affairs.

In fact, as many authentic reporters testify and as history proved, the Czechoslovak National Council, together with an Allied victory, was the single hope of the Czechoslovak people. As its impotence increased, the Hácha government was viewed with pity, and it could not have served as a rallying point for resistance or revolt. Beneš, who had been held in low esteem after Munich, regained his popularity after the occupation, as his predictions about the forthcoming war were proven right. Jan Masaryk (1886–1948), little known before the war, was well liked by the common people who listened to his regular broadcasts from London. The idea of introducing a monarchy in Central Europe was absurd.

10. National Archives, 860F .01/461½.

In spite of the antagonistic position taken by the Department of State, political events and developments in the war moved President Roosevelt closer to the Allied cause and a position sympathetic to Beneš. At the end of July 1941, Washington granted the Czechoslavak National Council recognition as a provisional government. Still, it was "provisional" only.

Jan Masaryk and President Roosevelt reached an understanding on the matter in a way that was characteristic of both men. As Masaryk related the story, on one of his frequent visits to the United States, he talked at length with Roosevelt about the war and world politics. Czechoslovakia was not mentioned. At the end of the audience, as Masaryk was about to leave, the President asked him, "Jan, is there anything I can do for you?" Masaryk answered, "Yes, Mr. President. We have in England about one thousand pilots. Many of them fly over Germany on bombing missions. Some of them never return. They are shot down by enemy fire and they are killed. They are dead—not provisionally dead." Roosevelt answered, "I understand, Jan." Within a few days the American embassy in London was advised that on October 28, 1942—Czechoslovakia's Independence Day—President Roosevelt would send a telegram of felicitation that would address Dr. Beneš as "President of the Republic of Czechoslovakia" and that the Department of State would henceforth not use the term provisional.[11]

Beneš's Herculean efforts were finally crowned with complete success. His government was recognized by all the Allied states, and Czechoslovakia achieved the rank of a full-fledged ally. Considering the odds he had to overcome, no one can deny Beneš's diplomatic skills in this instance.

**Foreign Policy:
A New Concept**

While laboring for international recognition of his government, President Beneš also worked diligently on problems concerning

11. Ibid., 860F .01/463A.

the future of postwar Czechoslovakia and on a new concept of foreign policy. The latter task was a laborious undertaking too, involving complex issues of wartime diplomacy, and of dissension among the major Allies and their conflicting positions toward minor Allies, particularly Poland. In his efforts, Beneš was ably assisted by Jan Masaryk, minister of foreign affairs, and his deputy, Hubert Ripka.

The Munich betrayal had left ineradicable scars on Beneš's political psyche. By conviction a democrat, by philosophical and cultural orientation a Westerner, his political confidence was shattered by the failure of his principles and his policy. Munich had ruined the Republic's interwar concept of security and necessitated an analysis of the causes of its failure and a consideration of alternative policies. Understandably, a personal rancor against France and Great Britain played no small role in Beneš's thinking. As he looked beyond developments on the battlefield, he perceived new social and political trends that would significantly affect postwar Europe. He hoped that the "Big Three" would cooperate in common efforts to maintain peace and expected them to remain united in preventing Germany from rising again as a power that could unleash war. He assumed that France and England would play an important role in European affairs, and while he welcomed that prospect, he never regained his confidence in them. On the contrary, he remained bitter and distrustful, expecting little from the source of all his former hope. Not infrequently, he expressed these feelings to his political associates and once cryptically remarked that in the future, Czechoslovakia ". . . must not rely too much on diplomacy. It is a most vulgar trade" [12]—a strange comment from a man who had ardently engaged in that "trade" all his life and who was not immune to its vices. But the remark exhibited both his distrust of political commitments in general and his resentment of England and France in particular.

The Soviet Union, however, enjoyed Beneš's highest esteem, for it had been ready to meet its commitment to Czechoslo-

12. Julius Firt, "Cestou k únoru: Počátky byly v Londýně," Svědectví 13, no. 46 (1973): 211.

vakia during the Munich crisis. Also, Beneš envisioned the Soviet Union emerging from the war as a world power that would exercise great influence on international politics. In addition, he foresaw political and social upheavals and a danger of the communization of Europe. These factors were, to him, only more compelling reasons for cooperation with Moscow. He reasoned that a positive attitude would discourage the Soviet Union from interfering in the internal affairs of his country.

With all these perceptions of the postwar period, Beneš established in his mind a concept that he hoped would give his country a proper and secure place in Europe. The essence of his vision, and the aim of his wartime diplomacy, was to balance the potential and actual conflicting interests of the East and West—both ideologically and in terms of power—on the controversial ground of Central Europe, where the two cultures met. Geographically and politically, Czechoslovakia was at the crossroads of these two civilizations. Beneš constructed a concept of this obvious fact based upon the advantages, not the precariousness, of Czechoslovakia's position. As he subsequently wrote in 1947, the question of Czechoslovakia's orientation—West or East—was "consciously and clearly resolved by the answer—West and East." The idea echoed thoughts extending back many decades. Once again, under new circumstances, Czechoslovakia was to serve as the link between East and West, a bridge connecting the two cultures and mediating their differences. It was an ambitious theory, but its subsequent failure was anticipated by Jan Masaryk, who had a talent for reducing complex concepts to simple dimensions. "I don't like this bridge idea," he once commented, "Cows like to stop on a bridge and shit on it."

While pursuing his own vision of the future, Beneš was loyal to his British and American allies and sensitive to their views of postwar Europe. He missed no opportunity to argue the necessity of their making clear their policy on the future of Central Europe and committing themselves to active participation in the resolution of its international problems. There was no need to persuade the Soviet Union to pursue an active role. As the relations between the Western Allies and the Soviet Union grew in complexity and mutual suspicion, Beneš found himself in an increasingly delicate and risky position.

Even before the war started, Beneš had foreseen that the Soviet Union would play an increasing role in European affairs, in spite of the isolation into which it had been forced by the Munich Pact. In January 1939, he confided to his political associate, Jaroslav Drábek, his belief that "Russia will have a voice in Central Europe." "We will definitely be Russia's neighbor," he said, adding that Hitler "will help us" in this respect. According to him, war was inevitable; Germany would win at first, but "at the end, Russia and the United States will decide" the fate of Central Europe.[13] Jaromír Smutný, the head of Beneš's chancellery, noted in his diary that Beneš was "morally repulsed" by the Soviet-German pact, but not surprised or disheartened. Indeed, on September 11, 1939, a few days after the invasion of Poland and the outbreak of hostilities, Jan Šverma, a member of the Czechoslovak Politburo, conveyed a Soviet message to Hubert Ripka stating that ". . . it would be the greatest mistake to think that the Soviet Union had gone back on its promise of assistance to the Czechoslovak nation." Šverma indicated he had reason to believe that the Soviet Union would, in time, stand up against Germany, "but it will not be soon." Another Soviet source indirectly told Ripka that "nothing has changed in the attitude of the Soviet Union toward the Czechoslovak question . . . the Soviet Union insists as it did before the German-Soviet pact on its program of liberation of [your] nation from Nazi domination." Another Soviet message meant directly for Beneš stated that "the Soviet Union insists on the program of restoration of Czechoslovakia . . . roughly within its historical boundaries"; and it added that Beneš "should not be misled by Comintern agitation."[14]

Through this period of tense relations between the Western powers and the Soviet Union (which lasted until June 1941, when Germany invaded Russia), Beneš maintained regular contacts

13. Jan Křen, V emigraci: Západní zahraniční odboj 1939–1940 (Prague: Naše vojsko, 1969), p. 501.

14. Ibid., pp. 487, 495.

with Ivan Maiski, the Soviet ambassador to Great Britain, and it appears that the Soviet diplomat was equally interested in cultivating friendly relations with him. On September 19, 1939, Maiski visited Beneš (who was still, officially, a private person) and assured him that "the Soviet Union [meant] to stay on the Slovak borders" and that the pact with Germany was "not the end of everything," for there would be further developments in the East. He did not want Beneš to see the pact as "an alliance or collaboration" with Germany. "We are entirely free," he said. "There is nothing in the pact . . . in regard to any obligation to Germany. You will see it later." [15] The Soviet consul in Prague, Mokhod, took considerable initiative in establishing a working relationship with the underground intelligence service and constantly assured his contacts that the Soviet Union would be at war with Germany soon.

Encouraged by these assurances and predictions, Beneš sent a message to Prague, formulating his policy toward the Soviet Union as one of "loyalty, mutual sympathy, and friendship," based on his expectation that the Soviet Union would do nothing to damage his policy. Moscow did damage it, however, when in December 1939 it recognized the Slovak Republic and closed the Czechoslovak legation. To compensate for this official stand, unofficial Soviet sources, mainly military, assured their Czechoslovak counterparts that the recognition of Slovakia was "not a hostile act against Czechoslovakia" and that "the Soviet government stood by its program of the renewal of Czechoslovakia." Beneš apparently trusted these explanations and was not deflected from the basic direction of his diplomacy. When some circles in London and Paris contemplated sending troops to Finland after the Soviet Union invaded that country, Beneš rejected the idea of commanding the small Czechoslovak army that was being readied in France to join the battle.

Convinced that the Soviet Union would be drawn into the war sooner or later, Beneš avoided any move that might affront Moscow. Moreover, equally convinced that Czechoslovakia's fu-

15. Ibid., pp. 487–88.

ture safety required a strong Russia that would play an influential role in Central Europe, he felt the need of a common Czechoslovak-Soviet boundary. One week before the outbreak of the war, he had told Maiski, "After this war, we must become the Soviet Union's direct and permanent neighbor. This, too, is one of Munich's lessons." With this concept in mind, he alluded to Subcarpathian Russia,[16] stating in his notes on the conversation, "Either we will have it or, in case—as our neighbor—they should ask for it, we would have no objections." [17] Such statements, premature at best, illuminated a general policy that was to prove the truth of Beneš's own definition of diplomacy as "the most vulgar trade."

Jan Masaryk, Beneš's foreign minister, probably was not informed of this offer. On July 18, 1941, at a ceremony in the Soviet embassy in London marking the resumption of diplomatic relations, I observed an interesting exchange: Masaryk turned to Maiski and announced in his brash, unconventional fashion, "I Karpatskaia Ukraina nasha! [And the Carpathian Ukraine is ours]." Maiski, with equal bonhomie, answered, "Da, Karpatskaia Ukraina vasha [Yes, the Carpathian Ukraine is yours]."

Whatever the assurances of others, however, Stalin remembered Beneš's "neighborliness." When the Red Army was in the process of liberating the Carpathian Ukraine, individual communities, under the guidance of Soviet political commissars and local Communist organizations, passed resolutions in favor of the territory's attachment to the Soviet Union. According to an agreement with Moscow, the Czechoslovak government's delegate, František Němec, was supposed to take over the administration of the liberated regions; he was never permitted to assume his function and, in fact, was given an ultimatum to leave the Carpathian Ukraine in three days.

Suddenly less neighborly, the Czechoslovak government was seriously concerned about these developments and particularly fearful that such engineered enthusiasm might presage a simi-

16. The official name of the region was Subcarpathian Russia, but during World War II, for a variety of cultural and political reasons, it came to be generally called the Carpathian Ukraine.

17. Ibid., p. 505.

lar revolutionary movement in Slovakia. Stalin, sensing tension, sent a letter to President Beneš on January 23, 1945, which stated that the Soviet government could not forbid the populace of the Carpathian Ukraine to express its national will. He then reminded Beneš of their conversation in Moscow in December 1943, in which Beneš had stated that the Czechoslovak government was "willing to hand over the Carpathian Ukraine to the Soviet Union." Stalin noted, "you will remember I did not then accept" the proposition, and he assured Beneš that the Soviet government had no intention of violating the treaty between the two countries, "to solve the question of the Carpathian Ukraine unilaterally. Such an assumption would be offensive to the Soviet government." However, he said, since the question was now raised by the populace itself, it would be necessary to resolve it by way of an agreement.

In his answer to Stalin's letter, Beneš continued to woo the Soviet Union. He assured Stalin "most emphatically" that neither he nor his government ever thought the Soviet Union intended to solve the question unilaterally or to violate the treaty. He knew the "principles of Soviet Union policy" and that such actions were "absolutely unthinkable." Beneš assumed that Stalin remembered well his discussion with Maiski almost six years before and assured him that he had not changed his position and would not ever in the future allow the question to become a matter of dispute.[18]

It is difficult to fathom Beneš's mind. There were other occurrences in Soviet-Czechoslovak relations that gave cause for concern, but Beneš's persistent strategy of wooing Stalin's favor minimized the significance of all of them. In the case of the Carpathian Ukraine, it was not so much a question of the area's future, since it did belong culturally to the Ukraine. Rather, it was a question of a diplomatic process that was reminiscent of Munich. In his wartime policy toward the West, Beneš struggled intensely to undo Munich, to restore to Czechoslovakia her original bounda-

18. *Československo-sovětské vztahy v době velké vlastenecké války 1941–1945: Dokumenty a materiály* (Prague: Státní nakl. polit. literatury, 1960), pp. 205–7.

ries. Yet, he initiated a secret deal with Stalin that disrupted the territorial integrity of his own country.

Meanwhile, in other areas of Czechoslovak-Soviet relations, wartime developments offered Beneš continuing encouragement to pursue his foreign policy. Two weeks after the German invasion of the Soviet Union, Maiski visited Beneš and officially conveyed to him the news that Soviet policy favored an independent Czechoslovakia, with a national government; there would be no interference in her internal affairs, and the Czechoslovak people alone would decide on the Republic's structure and regime. Maiski's statement must have been music to Beneš's ears. It strengthened one of the fundamental premises of his own policy—that Czechoslovakia would be a loyal friend and ally of the Soviet Union, which, in turn, would respect the free, democratic development of her national life.

In other ways, the government in exile attempted to broaden the base of the country's future security. Partly at the instigation of Anthony Eden and partly because of the devastating lessons of the past, Beneš tried to improve Czechoslovakia's relations with Poland. He wished to bury their long history of disagreements and to forget Poland's invasion of Tešín at the time of Munich. He found a friendly partner in the person of General Wladyslav Sikorski, the Polish prime minister. Both men were aware, as had been Thomas Masaryk and Paderewski nearly twenty-five years earlier, that each country's independence hinged largely on their close cooperation. As early as November 1940, the two governments issued a declaration that laid the foundations for the establishment of various committees charged with preparing concrete plans for a future confederation. Though the committees' work was marred by mutual suspicion, by the end of January 1942, the two governments had signed a statement giving their plans formal expression. News of this document exploded in Moscow like a bomb.

During the war, Soviet-Polish relations were always tense and sometimes hostile. While Beneš considered Polish-Czechoslovak cooperation a step toward improving Poland's relations with the Soviet Union, the Polish government apparently considered such cooperation a means of backing up its own hostile attitude toward Moscow. Though Maiski had originally raised no objections to the confederation plans, Soviet diplomats in London subsequently questioned, sharply and aggressively, the implications of the agreement. Beneš immediately cooled in his commitment to the idea of confederation. He had now the choice of cooperation with either Poland or the Soviet Union. He opted, understandably, for accord with Russia. However, he did not abandon the idea of trying to bring Poland into the picture of a future political constellation embracing Central and Eastern Europe.

In May 1942, Beneš raised the question of a visit to the Soviet Union with Moscow, and later inquired, on several occasions, whether the USSR would consider signing a treaty of alliance with Czechoslovakia, before the end of hostilities. He further suggested that Poland might join in such a pact. The Soviet government first reacted most cautiously and then with increasing interest, but it rejected outright the proposition that Poland participate. Anxious to avoid the isolation of Poland, the British government intervened, and Anthony Eden urged Beneš to postpone his trip to Moscow and to refrain from signing the treaty of alliance. Beneš vacillated, not wishing to compromise his own position in London or to complicate British-Soviet relations, and, at one time, he decided to postpone his plans. At the Moscow conference of the foreign ministers of the "Big Three," however, after a brief explanation by Molotov, Eden reversed his position and approved of the treaty.

The door was open for Beneš's trip. Before journeying to Moscow, however, he paid an official visit to Washington at the end of May 1943. He explained his policy toward the Soviet Union to President Roosevelt, who received it "with obvious satisfaction" and recognized that Beneš "proceeded . . . correctly." [19]

The visit to the Soviet Union did appear to be a triumph for Beneš's policy. On December 12, 1943, the Soviet Union and Czechoslovakia signed the Treaty of Friendship, Mutual Aid, and

19. Ibid., p. 60.

Postwar Cooperation, to which was attached, at Beneš's request, a protocol that made provision for Poland to join the alliance. The document contained all the clauses common to international treaties of that kind, including mutual respect for state sovereignty, territorial integrity, and noninterference in the internal affairs of the signatories. On the face of it, it was a good treaty, and in the light of Beneš's vision of postwar Europe, entirely justified. From the military point of view, Czechoslovakia was being liberated by the Red Army. The U.S. army was poised to liberate the Czechoslovak western lands, but General Eisenhower declined the opportunity. From the political point of view, Great Britain and the United States had no concrete plans for the future of Central Europe beyond such general statements as the Declaration on Liberated Europe and, in any case, political developments were realistically related to the advance of the Allied armies, including, of course, the Red Army. Beneš was well aware of all these factors and sought in the complex situation an outcome of optimal benefit to his country. Anxious to keep the international position of Czechoslovakia in balance, he would have liked to sign a similar treaty with England, but its government was unresponsive to his diplomacy. It did not want to be committed in time of war to an obligation related to postwar developments and problems which, in its opinion, ought to be considered at a peace conference. Britain ignored the fact that, historically, wartime decisions, both military and political, have affected postwar settlements.

The American government took an analagous position. While no records have been found to indicate that the Czechoslovak government approached Washington about a treaty, it suffices to note that the United States declined treaties of alliance with both Great Britain and the Soviet Union. However, Jan Masaryk once related that, in the course of an audience, President Roosevelt had asked him, "Jan, why did you sign a treaty with the Soviet Union?" Masaryk answered the question in his typical way. Taking a blank sheet of White House letterhead from the president's desk, he signed it at the bottom and remarked, "Here is my signature, Mr. President. I am willing to sign anything you are willing to sign with me."

It must be admitted that Beneš had reason to believe that in order to restore democracy in Czechoslovakia, he needed Soviet cooperation and good will. Had he insisted on pursuing the plan of confederation with Poland, had he not gained Soviet understanding, had he declined to sign the treaty after negotiations reached the final stage, it is by no means unlikely that Moscow would have created a Communist-led Czechoslovak government on Russian soil, as it did in the case of Poland. In such a situation, Beneš could not have returned to a free Czechoslovakia, but would have had to watch the communization of his country from abroad. His return was essential to ensure the nation's democracy, and his passage home was open only through Moscow.

Thus, it is not Beneš's concept that should be criticized here, but rather his actions and his style: his offer of the Carpathian Ukraine to Maiski; his quick abandonment of a Polish-Czechoslovak confederation at the first sign of Soviet displeasure; his unwillingness (because he was afraid of Soviet displeasure) to withdraw Zdeněk Fierlinger, his ambassador to Moscow, knowing as he did that Fierlinger served Soviet, not Czechoslovak interests. In short, in all his relations with the Soviets, he lacked the dignity required of a statesman representing a sovereign, independent country.

In Moscow in December 1943, Beneš was eager to assure Soviet statesmen of his loyalty. According to the notes taken by Jaromír Smutný, he inquired on several occasions about the Soviet position on Germany, Poland, Hungary, Austria, and France, always stressing his desire to proceed in complete accord with Soviet policies. He spoke with Soviet statesmen at some length about future economic policies for Czechoslovakia, such as the confiscation of enemy property, land reform, and the nationalization of key industries, always implying that his country would pursue a program of economic socialization which would be pleasing to Moscow. To give the point special emphasis, he said that Czechoslovakia could not cooperate with Poland if that country did not change its economic and social structure. Envisioning renewed conflicts between Czechs and Slovaks, he invited Molotov to request the Czechoslovak government to punish members of the Slovak puppet government, so that their condemnation would not appear to be an anti-Slovak move perpetrated by Czechs. This, of course, was a direct enticement to the Soviet government to intervene in Czechoslovak internal affairs. Even Molotov was startled and remarked that "it would hardly be understandable" if the Soviet government appeared to "put the Slovaks on the same level as the Germans and Hungarians."

This kind of diplomacy, unbecoming to the head of an independent country, can once again be explained by Beneš's obsession with assuring an ever-suspicious Soviet government of his absolute sincerity, in the hope that Moscow would, in turn, give him a free hand in the postwar reconstruction of Czechoslovakia, including the handling of the Communist Party and its revolutionary designs.

There is great pathos and tragic truth in the words Beneš wrote a few days before his death to his former secretary, Edward Táborský, "My greatest mistake was that I refused to believe to the very last that even Stalin lied to me cynically . . . and that his assurances to me . . . were an intentional deceit." [20]

Home Politics Abroad

It must not be forgotten, however, that personal freedom and social justice were the philosophical concepts that drove Edvard Beneš from the outset of his political life. In this, he followed the path of his illustrious predecessors. He took that path again during World War II, because he realized that the mortal struggle between Nazism and democracy would bring to the surface new political and social forces, demanding material social change. He welcomed these prospects, as he saw in them progress toward the ideals of humanity. As in the area of foreign policy, however, his methods tainted his philosophy and goals.

The Munich experience did not weaken Beneš's faith in

20. Edward Táborský, "Beneš and Stalin—Moscow 1943 and 1945," *Journal of Central European Affairs* 13 (1953–54): 162, n. 29.

the value of democracy. When lecturing at the University of Chicago early in 1939, he constantly expressed his conviction that the
democratic ideal would in the end emerge victorious, for it was
"the expression of a genuine human morality and of modern civilization, and is alone worthy of twentieth century humanity. It will
be victorious because it is also the law of social evolution and of
the philosophy of history." Condemning both fascism and communism, he saw that if democracy were to survive, then, while political freedom must be maintained, society's manifold problems
must be resolved. He pleaded for an extension of the principle of
liberty, equality, and fraternity to the social and economic sectors
of life. To the Communists, he said:

I was always in favor of social justice, but it ought to be realized by evolutionary methods and not by violent and bloody social revolution or the
dictatorship of the proletariat. . . . My conclusion is that it is the essence
of human nature on the one side and of human society on the other that
man must struggle constantly for this reasonable and well-balanced relation between collectivity and individual freedom, and that he can fight
through to this balanced relation only in a political democracy.[21]

In practical politics, too, Beneš took steps to avert the dangers to
his democratic concepts in general and his country in particular
that stemmed from Communist revolutionary activities and agitation. He was certain that Nazism would be defeated, but he feared
that democracy would be in jeopardy from the radical Left.

On the day that hostilities broke out in 1939, Beneš sent a
message to his associates in Prague. After analyzing the international situation, he pointed to the Soviet expectation of a "social
upheaval in the spirit of their ideology." Therefore, he warned,
"we . . . must be on guard . . . ready for all possibilities, upheavals, attempts at social revolution in Central Europe. . . ."
Two months later, he revealed to a Czech émigré in London his
fear that it was "quite possible that the whole of Europe will pass
through a period of Bolshevik government before it returns to de-

21. Edvard Beneš, *Democracy Today and Tomorrow* (New York: The Macmillan Co.,
1939), p. 141.

mocracy." He brooded over the danger of Germany succumbing to communism first, leaving Central Europe exposed to intolerable Communist pressure from two sides. He assured his Western listeners that "should there be, after the war, a social revolution in Central Europe, under the protection of Communist Russia . . . we, the Czechoslovaks, will recover fastest . . . and will begin to build anew a democratic republic, a republic in the spirit of Masaryk." In another message, he pointed to the necessity of making decisions with a clear goal in mind, "to construct after the defeat of Nazism, by a swift fait accompli, as quickly as possible, a firm regime . . . and to see to it that, domestically, we do everything not to fall into a Bolshevik chaos." [22] As early as October 1939, he anticipated the Soviet Union's participation in the war and its subsequent efforts to foment revolution in Germany and Central Europe. He returned to this theme frequently, exposing at times a conviction, at other times a hope, and always a concern, that his country, politically mature and socially progressive, would escape the plight of communization.

In view of this danger, his messages to Prague constantly propounded the necessity of a constructive program of social and economic democracy. However, Beneš's vision of a future democratic Czechoslovakia was distorted by his personality. He had supreme confidence in his own judgments, believing too much in his ability to manipulate political forces and channel developments according to his views. Therefore, he seriously underestimated the profound impact of powerful societal forces upon national affairs. He did not take into account the fact that history is made by the encounter of ideas and the interplay of leadership and mass desires. His democratic ethics and daily political practice were ever at war. Reminiscing about his contacts with Beneš, Ambassador Maiski commented:

When I met him, he was a split person, with his soul there, with his mind elsewhere. He understood that the future of Czechoslovakia could be assured only in close cooperation with the Soviet Union. That was his mind

22. Křen, V emigraci, pp. 506, 512.

. . . but Beneš was not enchanted with an Eastern orientation. His soul had grown entwined with the West.[23]

As the Communist scholar Jan Křen observed in an article, Beneš went "with revolution against revolution"; he was a radical "with conservative ammunition." Though in favor of reform, he was basically nonrevolutionary, though not, Křen summed up, a counterrevolutionary, either.

This characterization of Beneš's passion for social justice— his revolutionary inner openness to change—is not inaccurate. Beneš's broadcasts to the nation stressed the need for a program of social and economic democracy. He promised to overcome past weaknesses, to eliminate social tensions, and to move along the path of political freedom and social justice in all areas of national life. A new sense of the meaning of Czechoslovak history burned brightly in his view of the future.

Beneš was not alone in these programmatic exhortations. Despite differing political beliefs, the members of the government in exile shared his views. Three men, Jan Masaryk, Jaroslav Stránský, and Prokop Drtina, appeared before the microphones regularly throughout the war. Masaryk's speeches expressed a tender love for his country; Stránský's dominating themes were spiritual and moral values and Thomas Masaryk's stern moralistic convictions; and Drtina's words emphasized Beneš's libertarian concepts. But all three spoke of freedom and justice.

More importantly, the democratic voices emanating from within occupied Czechoslovakia expressed the same political and social convictions. Collections of documents concerning the ideological program of the resistance movement clearly reveal this. The introduction to one of these documents states that the authors of the ideological program, fully aware of the far-reaching consequences of the war, wished to link "our Masarykian, West-European tradition with a modern understanding of socialist society," foreseeing many essential reforms, but always maintaining the spirit of democracy and democratic socialism.

23. Ibid., pp. 502–3.

The first underground group to formulate a program for the future consisted of left-wing intellectuals who had been closely involved with the working class, since they had been in charge of the Worker's Academy, a prewar educational institution. They called themselves the Petition Committee: "We Shall Remain Faithful (*Věrni zůstaneme*)." By May 1938, they had collected 1 million signatures in their effort to resist Nazism and avoid what was to become the Munich capitulation. After the outbreak of war, the group sent messages to Beneš, predicting a development toward the Left. They stressed that the country could not return to the pre-war situation, as there would be political, social, and economic progress toward real democracy and socialism. "The workers want a real democracy, in the political as well as in the economic and social sense," one message read. Though its ranks were decimated by periodic arrests by the Germans, the Petition Committee, created several subcommittees that prepared proposals for a new constitution, a new economic order, financial reform, a new agricultural policy, reorganization of the army, and educational programs. All such programs were framed within the principles of a socialist democracy, but their democratic political character prevented the Communist leaders from endorsing them. After several redraftings, they were published in the clandestine press and in a brochure in the spring of 1941.

Another elaborate program was called "For Freedom (*Za svobodu*)." Its introductory section recognized that World War I resulted in political, but not social and economic liberation. It recalled T. G. Masaryk's writings and convictions, and advanced propositions for provisional arrangements to be implemented immediately after World War II. It then spoke of the need for reforms of the constitution and parliamentary practices, and it discussed a revival of the defunct League of Nations and plans for international cooperation. In addition, it advocated the nationalization of some industries and the principle of the right to work. All this was to be accomplished within the context of complete political freedom.

Similar programs were advanced by an illegal newspaper, *Český kurýr,* published by a group of members of the Evangelical

Church of Czech Brethren. In one of its issues in September 1940, the newspaper stated that, ". . . . from all that has happened, it is obvious that we are moving toward the Left. . . . The ideal of mere political democracy will not be enough. A future democracy will be possible only if a populist democracy encompasses as well the economic and social fields." Such ideological pronouncements found their way to the ÚVOD, which adopted them and passed them on to Beneš's government in London. The pronouncements were accompanied by statements by individual leaders, some of them smuggled out of German prisons.

One such statement deserves special mention. It was written by Antonín Pešl, a former prominent journalist who, during the first phase of the war, was a courageous liaison between underground fighter groups, and who finally became a "guest" in the death cells of the gestapo. "I am far away from daily work, compelled to think and 'preach,' " he wrote with a touch of humor some eighteen months before his execution, in a letter addressed to the ÚVOD and smuggled out of the prison at Gollnov on the Baltic Sea. The letter expresses Pešl's view of the future:

At the end, everything will be resolved on a grand scale—the main thing will be not to miss the bus, not to pass it by. Value the free life—a poor one is better than the best jail. . . . Spiritual and moral power will finally decide—that is the compass that guides us. . . . We are moving irresistibly toward a planned socialist order . . . the quicker and the better we think it through, prepare for and then realize it, the less there will be of misery and terror. Our nation is directed in an extraordinary way by categorical moral and rational imperatives. . . . The task will be to swiftly put prostrated and desperate small nations back on their feet. . . . In this respect, we have always marched in the front rank. . . . It will be necessary to employ all possibilities of word and deed to strengthen integrity, honesty, solidarity. . . . A stony path leads through the valley to the peak—in the midst of the greatest revolution of mankind.[24]

The government in exile was greatly encouraged by these messages from the home front which pointed unmistakably toward

24. Jaroslav Vozka, *Hrdinové domácího odboje* (Prague: Práce, 1946), pp. 75–76.

the convergence of modern needs and timeless humanitarian ideals. The government itself drafted laws and statements that were intended to serve as the basis for the future social order: guarantees of personal freedom, a multiparty parliamentary system and a decentralized administration; land reform; and the nationalization of key industries. On the surface—and in contrast to the plans of other exiled governments—all measures appeared to ensure a peaceful, constructive transition from six years of enemy occupation to an independent, progressive national future. However, all these plans were threatened by the politics, jealousies, opportunism, and in the final analysis, conflicting ideological goals which beset the government in exile itself.

Political émigrés are strange people. Uprooted from their national environment and deprived of a political base, they struggle among themselves for power. Often they cover their personal ambitions with high-sounding patriotic pronouncements; they dream and scheme, enter into constantly shifting coalitions and, in search of security, frequently find themselves with very strange bedfellows indeed. They must do all this not only without embarrassing the host country in its domestic or foreign affairs, but also without ever losing sight of their ultimate goal of returning home and resuming positions of leadership. Émigrés' motives are more patriotic than not, but their methods are inevitably tainted by their frustrated condition. An apt term had been coined for this condition in reference to the Russian émigrés after the October Revolution: *emigranshchina* ("émigré sickness"). Many of the Czechoslovak political émigrés were not immune to the disease.

In London, President Beneš had to deal with a host of people touched by or in advanced stages of *emigranshchina*. The cases of Štefan Osuský and Milan Hodža were particularly difficult. Both were Slovaks, the former the Czechoslovak minister to Paris for twenty years and the latter a prominent statesman and prime minister before Munich. They considered themselves authentic spokesmen for the Slovak nation and declined to accept Beneš as the leader of the liberation struggle. The Slovak question, which was the Achilles' heel of Beneš's policy, served as an instrument to further their claims for national and international recognition. They found considerable support among Slovak Americans, and the U.S. Department of State had voluminous files of letters, proclamations, petitions, and warnings from them and from separatists. The separatists, however, received no support from Osuský or Hodža. They both believed firmly in a united Czechoslovakia. Neither man could be reconciled by governmental appointments. Osuský stopped attending Cabinet meetings, and Hodža would not participate in the sessions of the State Council—a quasi-representative body which served in London as a substitute for the National Assembly. Though Osuský was supported by the French government and Hodža by some British government circles, both men ended up in political isolation.

Another serious problem was Rudolf Bechyně. A talented politician and a leader of the Social Democratic Party, he had been a member of several Cabinets and a determined fighter for democracy and against communism. In London, he aspired to speak on behalf of his party and claimed a decisive position in Beneš's government. The president, however, conducted political affairs on the premise that party politics must be excluded from the critical struggle. He felt this was not only his personal opinion, but also the clear mandate of the numerous messages from Czechoslovakia. Bechyně violently disagreed and, in anger and bitterness, went so far as to support a postwar attachment of Czechoslovakia to the Soviet Union. The idea led to his political demise. Beneš rejected him, and the Czechoslovak Communists rejected him as well.

Despite these difficulties, Beneš's national and international stature increased as time passed. He could point with pride to the international recognition of his government, to the "undoing" of Munich, to the prestige garnered abroad and the popularity restored at home, and to the consolidation, to a remarkable degree, of the democratic forces in the émigré colony. In addition, a small Czechoslovak army, organized in the East and West, contributed significantly to Beneš's struggle for the liberation of his country.

After the demoralizing military debacle in France, Czechoslovak units were organized in England and grew into an armored brigade of over 5,600 men. Czechoslovak air units distinguished themselves in the Battle of Britain and in bombing missions over Germany. According to official statistics, they flew over 27,000 flight hours and downed 319 German planes. In the East, units in the Soviet Union, established in 1942, grew to 20,000 men and participated in a number of battles. The crossing of Dukla Pass into Czechoslovakia was, perhaps, the most famous of these battles and also the most costly. Total casualties among the Czechoslovak units in the Soviet Union amounted to 80 percent of the total force: 3,000 killed, 11,000 wounded, and 2,800 men missing in action.

Policy on Major
Domestic Problems

The government in exile faced three major problems of national policy: the future of the Sudeten Germans; the structure and status of Slovakia; and the relationship of the various democratic forces to the Communist Party of Czechoslovakia. The first two questions were resolved; the third, in spite of an apparent accord, proved to be insoluble.

From the outset of their exile, and particularly after the outbreak of the war, Czechoslovak democratic circles were aware of the necesssity of seeking a solution to the problem of the Sudeten German minority. Its Nazified political party had been one of the forces that led to Munich; during the occupation of Czechoslovakia, its leaders were the most cruel oppressors of the people and were, in turn, cordially hated. On the other hand, a tiny German Social Democratic Party remained loyal to the Czechoslovak state and valiantly faced the terrorist onslaughts of Henlein's Sudeten German Party in the tense pre-Munich days. The leader of the German Social Democrats, Wenzel Jaksch, found refuge in London and, after the war began, Beneš invited him to participate in Czechoslovak political activities there. Jaksch, however, demanded too heavy a price for his cooperation: a formal guarantee that the Sudeten Germans would be granted autonomy in postwar Czechoslovakia.

The two men parted, and the idea ripened in Beneš's mind

that the troublesome problem of the Sudeten German minority could be solved, once and for all, by transferring the German population to Germany. This major move could only be achieved with the consent of all the Allied powers, and Beneš set to work patiently and systematically to gain this sanction. By the summer of 1942, the British government had approved of the idea in principle, and during the following summer, the American and Soviet governments also acceded. At the Potsdam Conference in August 1945, the "Big Three" laid down a general plan for the transfer.

The mass deportation of the German minority has been severely criticized as being cruel and undemocratic. The charges are justified as far as the execution of the transfer is concerned. It was a disorderly operation, accompanied by ugly acts of vengeance. These cannot be excused, committed as they were by a country that thought of itself as devoted to the ideals of humanity. Nevertheless, the fact of such acts can be understood. For nearly 1,000 years, the relationship between the Czechs and the Sudeten Germans had been more painful than peaceful. Then came the Nazification of the Sudeten Germans and their brutal persecution of the Czechs. Small wonder that the inevitable outbreak of hatred and revenge after the war was impossible to control.

The movements of the Sudeten Germans to Germany did enable Czechoslovakia to emerge as an ethnically homogeneous country and, most importantly, it put relations with Germany on a new, solid basis, free from the burden of the unpredictable political behavior of this minority with its historically divided allegiance. These two factors were—and are—of such far-reaching significance for European peace as to justify the transfer of the Sudeten German minority.

The second critical problem was the old question of the position of Slovakia in a future, free Czechoslovakia. Dissatisfied with their interwar experience, the Slovaks during the war had acquired a certain pride in the illusion of managing their own house, and six years of nominal independence only intensified their ardent nationalism. There was no doubt in the minds of most responsible Czech and Slovak politicians that the relation between the two nations must be built on a new foundation. The Slovak

Populist Party, which was responsible for the proclamation of the Slovak Republic in March 1939 and for the adoption of Nazi principles and methods during the war, was utterly compromised, and all took it for granted that it would fall into oblivion with the defeat of Nazism. The serious and urgent questions concerned what political forces would fill the vacuum and what would be the place and program for Slovakia in the reunited state.

Prominent democrats in Slovakia developed regular contacts with the government in exile. Fraudulent as it was, Slovakia's status of independence facilitated transmission of messages via Rome, Geneva, and Istanbul. One document, dated February 10, 1943, glorified the old Republic and called it an "example of social justice and national and religious tolerance." Such messages were received in London with joy. They appeared to confirm Beneš's past position on Slovakia and encouraged his sense of the inevitability of its place in a future Czechoslovakia. On the other hand, Beneš often criticized Slovakia's betrayal and condemned the Slovaks as a people who must not be "pampered" as they had been before the war.

Such Slovak messages to London were misleading. They emanated from honest but isolated individuals, most of them Protestants, who continued to cherish a romantic post-World War I illusion of Czechoslovakism. The president, sincerely sharing and publicly expressing this same view, headed inevitably for a conflict with the real mood of Slovakia.

Until the end of 1943, there was no organized democratic opposition to the Nazi-like government in Slovakia. As in the Czech lands, the only well organized group was the Communist Party of Slovakia, and its position on the country's future changed several times.

Yet Another
CPC Quandary

The Party found itself in the whirlwind of conflicting interests between the Czech and Slovak factions, and it was further disrupted by special Soviet considerations. It wavered from one position to another, always claiming to follow Lenin's theory of self-determination.

In June 1939, the Party Secretariat, temporarily in Paris, issued a secret directive for work abroad, advocating "full reestablishment of Czechoslovak independence" and further exhorted its followers to "excel in devotion" to that cause. In the fall, the underground Central Committee of the Party in Prague issued the watchword, "For a Free Slovakia in a Free Czechoslovakia," and the Slovak faction, which was now constituted as the separate Communist Party of Slovakia, altered it slightly—but not for long—to "A Free Slovakia in a Liberated Czechoslovakia and a New Europe." Soon thereafter, the concept of a reestablished Czechoslovakia was condemned—but, once again, not for long.

By the end of 1939, illegal Slovak publications had begun to coin such slogans as "Independent Slovakia" and "An Independent Soviet Slovakia." Then, in August 1940, the incorporation of the Baltic states into the Soviet Union provided an attractive example for the Slovak Communists. On May 1, 1941, the Party's programmatic proclamation spoke of national liberation for Slovakia along the path that "led to the final national and social liberation of the Baltic states, Bessarabia, Moldavia, Bukovina, Western Ukraine and Bielorussia. . . . Their path is an example also for us." [25]

This sudden shift presented serious problems to the CPC leadership in Moscow. Stalin had signed a pact with Hitler in August 1939 and subsequently established diplomatic relations with the "independent" fascist Slovakia. The Moscow group could hardly "excel in devotion to the cause of Czechoslovak independence" under those circumstances and Gottwald, accordingly, associated himself with his Slovak partners, deciding, in March 1940,

25. Za svobodu českého a slovenského národa: Sborník dokumentů k dějinám KSČ v 1938–1945 (Prague: Státní nakl. polit. literatury, 1956), pp. 85, 154, 198; V. Plevza et al., eds., Prehlad dejin KSČ na Slovensku (Bratislava: Pravda, 1971), pp. 244–46, 267; Ferdinand Beer et al., Dejinná križovatka: Slovenské národné povstanie—predpoklady a výsledky (Bratislava: n.p., 1964), pp. 75–76; Miloš Gosiorovský, "K niektorým otázkam vzťahu Čechov a Slovákov v politice Komunistickej strany Československa," Historický časopis 16, no. 3 (1968): 369–70.

that the calls for the "reestablishment of Czechoslovakia" were "imperialistic and anti-Soviet." His directive emphasized that "the policy of the complete right to self-determination for Czechs and Slovaks" was valid for the Party, and explained, "The right of self-determination means the right to an independent state existence" and "fighting for the complete sovereignty of the present Slovak State. . . . The future relationship between the Czech and Slovak nations is a question of self-determination of both nations and depends on military developments." The message was approved by Georgi Dimitrov, the secretary-general of the Comintern, who added two significant words—"and results." Under the compelling circumstances then prevailing in Moscow, the Party leadership shelved the program of reconstituting Czechoslovakia, though, for the same compelling reasons, it did not openly approve the Slovak comrades' goal of a future Soviet Slovakia. Nevertheless, as late as April 1941—two months before the German invasion of the Soviet Union—Karol Bacílek brought a message from Moscow to the Slovak leadership at home in which Gottwald still clung to his "imperialistic" characterization of the war, stating that it could "be brought to an end only by a united struggle of the proletariat under the leadership of the Communist Party . . . by a proletarian revolution . . . for a Soviet Slovakia." In May, he issued another directive which was only slightly adjusted to the new, developing situation. With Dimitrov's approval, he considered it "*now* incorrect to use slogans on Czech or Slovak Soviet Republics," but neither was "the time ripe to speak about a Czechoslovakia [italics added]." In fact, in a conversation with another Slovak Communist leader, V. Široký, Dimitrov expressed "serious doubts that there will be again a Czechoslovakia," since the establishment of an independent Slovakia "left insurmountable scars." [26] (This was at exactly the same time, it should be remembered, that Soviet officials were assuring Beneš that their program was to restore an independent and united Czechoslovak Republic.)

On June 22, 1941, everything changed again overnight: the

---

26. Samo Falťan, *Slovenská otázka v Československu* (Bratislava: Vydav. politickej literatúry, 1968), pp. 116, 117, 145, 149; Křen, *V emigraci*, p. 566, n. 100.

"imperialist war" became a patriotic war; the Czechoslovak government and the Soviet government became allies and, one month later, signed an agreement renewing diplomatic relations and reaffirming Czechoslovakia as a sovereign state with recognized pre-Munich boundaries. The Party leadership in Slovakia was left with only a shattered dream of a Soviet Slovakia. It recognized the Soviet-Czechoslovak agreement, not as an act of two states, but as an "allied and military pact of the Slovak and Czech nations with the USSR," a pact that was not concerned with "future government, future state structure, and future boundaries," which were matters to be decided by "the liberated nations."

The sudden switch presented no problem to Gottwald. While he had never before mentioned Czechoslovakia in articles or broadcasts, addressing himself strictly to Czech audiences, he immediately assumed the role of a Czechoslovak leader and, to alleviate the fears of his Slovak followers, advocated a policy of complete equality for Czechs and Slovaks in the restored Czechoslovakia. His closest associate, Václav Kopecký, found a way out of the dilemma by sending a message to Bratislava which asked Slovak comrades to pursue their demands for Slovak freedom, thereby "not harming anything, neither from the Slovak nor the Czechoslovak point of view."

Then, the Presidium of the Executive Committee of the Third International decided to cut through the Gordian knot of conflicting attitudes. In a carefully worded (and deliberately vague) resolution, passed in January 1943, it stated that "the common struggle of the nations of Czechoslovakia against Hitlerism *today* will facilitate and accelerate the *future* solution of the national question on the basis of equality [italics added]." [27] Armed with this authoritative statement, Karol Šmidke, a Slovak Communist, reached Slovakia in early 1943 and persuaded the leadership there to adopt a new policy, to broaden its militant base and seek cooperation with democratic elements. The 1943 directive eventually led to the "Christmas Agreement" between the Communists and democrats; the agreement subscribed to the policy of Slovak

27. Ibid., pp. 137, 139, 149–50.

autonomy within a united Czechoslovakia, but stipulated that there must be full legislative and executive powers for Slovak organs.

Still, the problem of Slovakia's fundamental orientation lingered on. During the days of the Slovak uprising in August 1944, in the midst of general enthusiasm for a united Czechoslovakia, Gustáv Husák, a member of the Slovak Politburo, raised at a Party meeting the question of declaring Slovakia one of the Soviet Republics. In October, he publicly acknowledged in an article in *Nové slovo* that "the working people in recent years were politically and nationally oriented toward the USSR and called frequently for including Slovakia in the Soviet Union." In London, his position was seconded by another leader, Laco Novomeský, who "did not conceal his doubt as to whether it was wise for Slovakia to remain within a small Czechoslovakia when it could join the great Soviet Union."

The Slovak Communist Party, always suspicious of Beneš's concept of Czechoslovakia and of the attitude of its Czech comrades, wanted to let it be known that Slovakia enjoyed the freedom to choose between rejoining Czechoslovakia or becoming part of the Soviet Union. On September 17, 1944, it passed a resolution approving a "new Czecho-Slovakia" (significantly hyphenated), but warning everyone against claiming any "prejudicial rights which would compel our nation to seek alignment with other brotherly nations."

These Slovak voices conflicted with the interests of the Soviet Union, which had signed a treaty of alliance with the Czechoslovak government in exile in December 1943; in that treaty, the USSR unequivocally recognized the unity and territorial integrity of Czechoslovakia. Once again, Georgi Dimitrov (though the Third International had presumably been dissolved in May 1943) extended his assistance. Toward the end of December 1944, he met with Gottwald and Novomeský and told them, "A separation of Slovaks from Czechs is not *now* in the interest [of the Soviet Union] and it would be harmful for the Slovaks themselves [italics added]." Stating that he favored a federation, he added, "Dr. Beneš will be president of the Czechoslovak Republic, if for no other reason than for the sake of continuity, and who will be president later—that will be solved later." Dimitrov's position was in line with Stalin's remark to Beneš (back in December 1943) that it would be "necessary to keep the Slovaks firmly in hand." [28] Encouraged by such an incontestable authority, President Beneš tried, indeed, to be firm.

Beneš and the Slovak Question

The first occasion for confrontation arose in December 1943 when President Beneš met with the Czechoslovak Communists in Moscow. Even as the Christmas Agreement was being drafted on the soil of Slovakia, he was vigorously opposing the Slovak claim for recognition as a distinct nation. According to notes taken by the Communist participants in the discussions, Beneš rejected the autonomist position utterly, saying, "You will never compel me to recognize the Slovak nation. That is a conviction based on science and therefore I shall not change it. . . . I resolutely take the view that Slovaks are Czechs and the Slovak language is one of the dialects of the Czech language. I do not object if someone says he is a Slovak, but I will not permit the statement that there is any such thing as a Slovak nation." [29]

It is hard to believe that Beneš used such strong words; such was not his style. Nevertheless, the substance of the Communist account is undoubtedly correct. Beneš's position characterized the chasm separating him not only from the Communists, but also from the general feeling in Slovakia. Eight months later, the Slovak national uprising forced the issue. Representing the Communist Party and the newly formed Democratic Party, the Slovak National Council issued statements on behalf of the Slovak nation, which, while firmly supporting Czechoslovak unity and recognizing the

28. Ibid., pp. 168, 177–78, 179; Gosiorovský, "K niektorým otázkam," pp. 376, 377.

29. Cesta ke květnu, document 3, vol. I–1 (Prague: Čs. akademie věd, 1965), pp. 53–54.

government in exile as the supreme state authority, also named the National Council as the sole executive power of an autonomous Slovakia.

Beneš had no choice but to retreat from his evidently obsolete position. When a delegation of the Slovak National Council visited in London in November 1944 and presented its program to him, he recognized that it made no sense to dispute about the terminology of a Slovak or Czechoslovak nation if the majority of the population considered itself exclusively Slovak. "I simply respect facts," he said, "and request complete tolerance in these matters in the [renewed] Republic. I maintain this tolerance unconditionally and will respect it also in the future." [30]

The constitutional question of Slovakia's position in Czechoslovakia was still far from solved. In March 1945, President Beneš and a group of other émigré politicians, representing all Czechoslovak political parties, reached Moscow; in negotiations with the Communist representatives and a delegation of the Slovak National Council, they were to prepare, among other things, a new program for Slovakia. The groups were deliberating in the shadow of the Soviet government, whose army was advancing victoriously into Slovakia, and it soon became obvious that decisive power lay in the hands of the Communists and the Slovak National Council. The latter, considering itself the exclusive executive and legislative organ for Slovakia, not only succeeded in eliminating two other Slovak representatives who had journeyed to Moscow, but also insisted that a forthcoming governmental declaration include the promise of a constitutional guarantee of Slovakia's autonomous rights. Without denying the Slovak right to autonomy, the Czech democrats wished to assume only a provisional obligation in the matter and, in an entirely democratic manner, leave the final decision to the people. There were moments when the conflict over Slovakia's future seemed to endanger any positive outcome of the negotiations. On several occasions, Gottwald threatened that those not wishing to build the country on new

30. Jaroslav Opat, O novou demokracii, 1945–1948 (Prague: Čs. akademie věd, 1966), p. 37.

foundations would be excluded from participating in the task of reconstruction.

It is difficult to conjecture about what the outcome would have been had the Czech democratic representatives acted more resolutely than they eventually did. On one hand, Gottwald's threat was well-taken, since the negotiations took place in Moscow, where all power, including that which would allow the government in exile to return to Czechoslovakia, resided. On the other hand, Gustáv Husák stated later that even before the negotiations began, Stalin had advised Gottwald to "work with Beneš, reach an agreement with him, accept him as president." After the troubles of the Polish question, Husák said, Stalin "wanted to avoid similar problems and complications with Beneš." [31]

It was not a matter of denying the Slovaks their rightful place; indeed, the plan presented by the Slovak National Council and the Communists was a good solution. Rather, it was a question of respecting the inalienable right of the Czechoslovak people not to be presented with a fait accompli. Put on the defensive, the democratic representatives made concessions in matters of political ethics and fundamental principles of democratic procedure that augured ill for the renascent nation, for the confrontation over Slovakia foreshadowed a conflict of much greater seriousness with more far-reaching consequences—the question of the balance of political forces in the future Czechoslovakia.

Beneš and the CPC

The third major problem concerned the role of the Communist Party of Czechoslovakia in a democratic government. Once again, Beneš found himself torn between principles and politics. And once again, he trusted his strategic skills, ethically questionable as they were, to achieve ends that would clearly justify the means. Short is the memory of man, and sure is the judgment of history.

As in other significant events in modern Czechoslovak his-

31. Ibid., p. 39.

tory, the attitude of the CPC toward wartime developments and President Beneš underwent a number of opportunistic changes, dictated by the political strategy of the moment. During the year between Munich and the outbreak of war, the Party rode the crest of the wave of patriotism and publicly recognized Beneš as an important factor in the struggle for liberation. But in a secret directive of June 1939, the Party, while acknowledging the need to cooperate with Beneš, assigned the role of real leader to Klement Gottwald. After the war broke out, the Party openly and systematically attacked Beneš. In London, its pamphlets compared him to Hitler and accused him of being a stooge of imperialist capitalism. The Party's own program was ambiguous, as it could not entirely ignore the fact that Czechoslovakia was occupied by Germany, but at the same time, it wished to follow the directives of the Comintern. Therefore, the Party was vague about the future of Czechoslovakia and advocated a policy of cooperation with the nonexistent Communist parties of Germany and Austria and with the working classes of these countries.

Along these lines, Gottwald sent a message home, saying, "Beneš' action abroad is in the service of imperialists and enemies of the Soviet Union. It will not be the imperialists, Chamberlain and Daladier . . . who will free us from foreign domination, but the Czech nation itself in alliance with the German and Austrian working class. . . ." [32] Under a complete delusion about the prospects for revolution in Germany and Austria, the Communist parties of Czechoslovakia, Germany and Austria, in November 1939, issued a common proclamation—under Comintern aegis, of course. The proclamation spoke about self-determination for Czechs and Slovaks (as well as for Austrians and Poles), but said nothing about Czechoslovakia.

With the German invasion of the Soviet Union, the Communist characterization of the war changed overnight from an imperialist to a patriotic conflict, and the attitude of the Party toward the Czechoslovak liberation movement and President Beneš changed with equal velocity. The Party issued appeals for partisan

32. Křen, V emigraci, p. 554, n. 74.

activity and sabotage; it enthusiastically supported a Czechoslovak army abroad (which it had denigrated in the past) and professed loyalty to Beneš and his leadership role.

Beneš quickly seized this opportunity, which appeared to fit his grand design. He reasoned that Communists would be an important political force in postwar Czechoslovakia, and that if he succeeded in blunting their penchant for violence and bringing them, with the blessing of the Soviet Union, into the stream of democratic politics, he could maintain a firm democratic framework for a program of radical social change. Thus, he brought Communist representatives into the State Council, appointed a few Party members to government posts, and established contacts with the Party leadership in Moscow. In the light of subsequent developments, it is easy to censure his actions. However, just as Churchill and Roosevelt cooperated with Stalin, so Beneš wished to proceed with the Czechoslovak Communists, hoping to spare his country the ravages of possible violence, including civil war. No other exiled government tried such an experiment, but the governments of Poland and Yugoslavia never returned to their native lands. Beneš's government did. As in his policy of cultivating the good will of the Soviet Union, so in his effort for cooperation with the Czechoslovak Communists, the fault was not in the principle— there was no alternative—but in the method. Once again, he neglected to defend the principles of freedom, courage, and integrity. In his eagerness to win new friends, he shut his eyes to the methods of the Communists, to their cynical disregard for democratic processes in an open society.

Once the door to cooperation was ajar—and the Communists were eager to push it wide open—Beneš presented his plan for postwar Czechoslovakia. He expected a future political stratification to emanate from the unity of the working class, and he also expected the Communists to participate in the national reconstruction and in the government (a sort of *front populaire*); though the prime minister would be from the Left, the government would enact a program of radical social and economic reform with the participation of the progressive bourgeoisie. In return, the CPC would work loyally with the president. It was a bold proposition and, theoretically, entirely in harmony with the traditional concept of combining personal and political freedom with a program of social progress.

However, sincere Communist-democratic cooperation was a lost cause from the outset. Conflicting views escalated into open clashes, and these accumulated and grew in intensity, encompassing almost every area of political life. For example, during the first phase of the war, Beneš maintained secret contact with the collaborationist government in Prague. Hácha kept the government in exile informed about the situation in the Protectorate, and Beneš, in turn, advised him on how to react to various German measures. Beneš's goal was always the same: not to waste the lives of his countrymen in an uneven and premature struggle. In the same spirit, he refused to appeal to his people to organize partisan units in the occupied country and rise in revolt against the enemy.[33] This was the first issue over which Beneš and the Communists quarreled. The dispute, increasingly bitter, was evident in the contrast in tone and substance of the radio broadcasts that originated in London and in Moscow. While Beneš and his spokesmen were cautious, the Moscow broadcasts rang with rousing appeals for a national uprising and guerrilla warfare.

Their appeals met little response at first, but when the Red Army was approaching the borders of Czechoslovakia, the Communists stood ready to organize and lead partisan activities. Though decimated, the Party's ranks had maintained a tight organizational cohesiveness and, accustomed as they were to obey instructions, they engaged in effective but sacrificial acts of sabotage. Since their leaders in Moscow and Czechoslovakia spoke about a struggle for democracy and freedom—not communism—the Communist units were joined by courageous democrats. In the battle

---

33. It was only toward the end of the war, when victory was in sight, that Beneš consented to step up calls for an active fight, assuming (as he did toward the end of World War I) that patriotic, revolutionary action and spirit could really be timed and made to order from abroad. Colonel František Moravec, chief of the Czechoslovak Intelligence Service in London, explained that Beneš refused to call for active resistance because he and his associates were doing "the revolution according to science." It should be recognized, however, that because of indiscriminate German oppression, an early appeal for partisan struggle would probably have fallen on deaf ears.

between Beneš and the Communists about the nature of the struggle, Beneš's policy of caution was defeated by an ideology backed by organization and action.

Another problem plagued the relationship between the London and Moscow political forces. This concerned the preparation for the eventual administrative and political takeover in Czechoslovakia on the local level. Local organization was to be entrusted to National Committees, and Communist leaders persistently appealed to their radio listeners to create these committees. During the war, they were to organize resistance activities in factories, in the communications and transportation systems, and in city blocks and villages. After the liberation, as the Germans withdrew, they were to take over and administer their respective areas. It was a most resourceful plan, designed to penetrate the centers of local political power under the cloak of nationalism, since the very name—National Committee—had had an attractive ring from the time of World War I.

Beneš was most reluctant to accept the idea. First, his attitude was guided by the same consideration that affected his policy on partisan warfare—concern about German reprisals and unjustified sacrifice. Second, he saw in the Communist concept of National Committees a subterfuge to secure power by way of "street democracy"—managed, demagogic, and using force or the threat of force. Toward the end of the war, in an attempt to minimize the differences between their views, he spoke in favor of National Committees, but his guarded, halfhearted attitude was more than evident in his broadcasts.

Other matters also created dissension. Communists in Moscow and their comrades in London criticized Beneš's government for harboring reactionaries and for tardiness in preparing legislation for the confiscation of enemy and collaborators' property and for the punishment of war criminals and traitors. This situation was aggravated by a serious conflict among the Czechoslovak spokesmen in Moscow. Themselves united, the Communists received support on the issues at stake from the commander of the Czechoslovak army in the Soviet Union, General Ludvík Svoboda, and from the Czechoslovak ambassador, Zdeněk Fierlinger, both of whom undermined the authority of the government in London and weakened its position vis-à-vis the Communist group. Against this integrated and well-orchestrated coalition, General Heliodor Píka, chief of the military mission in Moscow, stood alone. His secret messages informed Beneš of the Communist-oriented politicization of the Czechoslovak unit and of the political dangers that were rapidly mounting. In one of his telegrams, dated December 17, 1942, Píka advised London that, in a conversation with him, the leaders of the CPC had strongly attacked the government, alleging that before the war, the majority had been opposed to socialist reforms and now, in time of war, protected Hácha. One Czechoslovak representative (and Píka's message does not make clear whether he meant a Communist or, perhaps, Fierlinger) told him, "If the President will not support the program of the Czechoslovak group in the USSR, he will not be president." [34]

It is unlikely that Beneš underestimated the significance of that message. But he had his own plans for postwar political life in Czechoslovakia, and skirmishes over wartime questions did not cause him to swerve from his predetermined path. As always, he was entirely confident of the correctness of his progressive, democratic goals, of the power of his arguments, and above all, of the success of his shrewd political craftsmanship. His rationalist mind told him that a policy that was to him fair, reasonable, and logical would inevitably lead to the desired results.

As a starting point for postwar planning, Beneš envisioned a new structure of political parties. First of all he wanted a reduction in their number, as the proliferation of parties before the war had weakened political democracy. His simplified concept pictured a conservative party, drawing support from right-wing elements; a center party, for mediation and balance; and a united socialist party, encompassing the whole spectrum of the Left and serving as

---

34. *Československo-sovětské vztahy*, p. 52. Beneš was fully aware of Fierlinger's disloyalty and Svoboda's subservience to the Communists and the Soviet army commanders, but he did not dare remove them for fear of affronting Stalin and roiling the smooth surface waters of his relations with the Soviet Union. Fierlinger and Svoboda were rewarded for their fellow-traveler services after 1948 with membership in the Politburo; Píka, for his services to Beneš, was sent to the gallows.

the backbone of a government that would carry out far-reaching social and economic reforms while adhering to a democratic, pluralistic system. This new socialist party would consist of the National Socialist Party, the Social Democratic Party, and the Communist Party of Czechoslovakia. Beneš's plan was ingenious; it meant to assure peaceful democratic and socialist development, taming the Communist Party by legitimatizing its share in public responsibility.

There was just one flaw: the plan was devoid of any realistic assessment of fundamental Communist goals and strategy. It ignored the original objective of the Third International, which stipulated that every party must maintain its exclusive Communist identity and its separation from all other political parties. This principle was strictly observed at all times, as far back as the 1920s when the Communist Party of China entered the ranks of the Kuomintang or as recently as the 1930s when Moscow initiated the Popular Front policy and adhered to it throughout the war. Even before the outbreak of war, the Communist Party of Czechoslovakia had issued a statement approved by the Comintern in June 1939, pointing to the necessity of taking part in resistance activities abroad, without, however, "giving up its independent position, without renouncing its own, independent tasks"—a declaration completely in accord with Lenin's dictum of maintaining "class separation of the proletariat which may tomorrow find itself in armed conflict against its allies of today." It is incomprehensible that Beneš, a learned man, could have so naively cherished the idea that the Communist Party of Czechoslovakia would tamely accept a program that called for the submersion of its identity within a broad, democratic socialist movement. What actually happened, was that in all the countries of East Europe, including Czechoslovakia, the Communist Party devoured all social democratic parties.

When Beneš arrived in Moscow in December 1943, he invited the Communists to join the government before the end of the war and sounded them out on the question of participating in a united socialist party. The Communists declined the first offer, arguing that while they supported the government in general, they did not wish to share in the responsibility for its policy, which they had severely criticized. The second idea, they simply ignored.

Beneš held six meetings with Gottwald and his associates, which altogether lasted seventeen hours. Apparently no stenographic record was kept, but the Communist participants subsequently compiled detailed notes and sent an exhaustive summary to their comrades in London. These documents were published in Prague in 1965.[35] Beneš's own impressions of the meetings were documented in his brief telegram to London from Moscow, in public statements made after his return to London, and in a message to the resistance leaders in Czechoslovakia. In addition, an unpublished memorandum by Beneš was found in London in the 1950s, and Julius Firt, a former member of the State Council, summarized in an article a memorandum concerning one part of the meetings that had been written by a Czechoslovak diplomat, Jaroslav Kraus.[36]

If the notes prepared by the Communists are accurate, they present a vivid picture of the disparate and unequal forces engaged in the discussion: a head of state who approached his Communist countrymen in the spirit of a friendly exchange of views; and the countrymen who forced him to yield to their demands on all major points. Beneš's sense of isolation in the overpowering atmosphere of Stalin's Moscow cannot be ignored. Nor can his role as president of the Republic, a respected leader, recognized both abroad and at home by democratic politicians who loyally supported him throughout the war, be excluded from consideration. But the fact remains that the Moscow documents provide a dismal picture of a man who sacrificed his dignity and his principles in order to gain the confidence of the opposite side, acting, as usual, in the belief that his diplomatic finesse would ultimately lead to his goal—freedom and progress for his country.

The consequences of the Moscow meetings were not immediately apparent, as the Communist group also spoke of democracy, but in the light of present knowledge of what later transpired, the origin of the communization of Czechoslovakia in

35. *Cesta ke květnu,* pp. 40–68.   36. Firt, "Cestou k únoru," p. 246.

February 1948 can be identified in that fateful occasion. Given the international situation and the disequilibrium between democratic and Communist forces throughout Europe, it may well be that the final denouement would have been no different had Beneš himself acted differently. However, in his negotiations in Moscow, Beneš lost sight of the point of his strategy of gaining Stalin's trust, which was principally to enable him to deal firmly with the Czechoslovak Communists. He overlooked the fact that the Communists, at least temporarily, needed his cooperation in both domestic and international affairs (as Stalin, indeed, had advised them). He gave away this strength out of fear that too much opposition to Communist aggressiveness might prevent his own return to Czechoslovakia. This was his principal concern, since he believed that the mature, sober Czechoslovak people, given his leadership and Stalin's benevolent neutrality, would reestablish democracy and cope successfully with any Communist design to seize power.

According to Firt's article, Václav Kopecký, a member of the Politburo and a participant in the meetings, engaged in a brutal attack on Beneš's policy of capitulation at Munich, his ambiguous attitude toward Hácha, and a number of other issues dividing the London government and the Communists. The documents published in Prague do not refer to Kopecký's attack, but they do give the impression that President Beneš, who held the floor almost exclusively during the first four lengthy sessions, was on the defensive from the outset. He explained his contacts with Hácha and vigorously defended his Munich policy. Outlining his postwar plans, he told the Communists that at the end of the war, the government in exile would resign as soon as it had moved to Czechoslovakia. The new government of the Left would represent the Communist, Social Democrat, and National Socialist parties, which could act independently, as a bloc, or as one party. Then, speaking to the CPC, he volunteered the comment, "You will be the strongest of the labor parties. You will also be the strongest in the leftist bloc. If you know how to go about it, you will inevitably win."

In discussing the situation among the émigrés in London,

Beneš had nothing but praise for the Communists, who "are the most constructive group, have a firm line, and enjoy the greatest influence in the State Council today." He may have been speaking out of frustration with some other groups and individuals who, hungry for ministerial positions, were continually fighting each other and intriguing against him. He called the London émigré group "a horrible society." Beneš's characterization of the Communist group was entirely justified, but his summary condemnation of others, while not without provocation, was not the best statesmanship. Beneš had special praise for his Moscow ambassador, Zdeněk Fierlinger, for whom he had "a warm feeling, as for all people who sincerely assisted him." Fierlinger was, he said, "a man of character. He does not belong in the category of careerists . . ." and added that there existed between them, "the best relationship." [37]

From the Communist notes on the Moscow meetings, it is apparent that Gottwald did not present the position of the Party until the fifth session. He then asked that Beneš's government change its vacillating attitude toward partisan warfare and its lukewarm position on National Committees, and he stressed that the Slovak question must be resolved. Speaking of Beneš's concept of the transition to a new government, Gottwald said he considered it "impossible that the present London government return home and govern there—not even for one day," though some of its members might be carried over to the provisional government. The socialist bloc would be its pith, he continued, but it would not pursue an exclusive policy of the Left; rather, it would be a "real representative" of the whole nation. As Beneš himself had recognized, the Communists would be the strongest party and, according to constitutional tradition, the prime minister should come from its ranks. The Communists did not wish to claim this right in the first provisional government, however, since "the circumstances will be extraordinary. We do not want to cause you difficulties and we think that your man should be prime minister." However, it

37. Less than five years later, during the critical period preceding the Communist takeover, the "man of character" betrayed Beneš, who then, finally seeing the light, warned Firt, "Remember, Fierlinger is a swine," ibid., p. 240.

was self-evident that the Communists must receive significant posts in the new government, such as the Ministries of Interior and National Defense.

Gottwald's proposal concerning the prime minister was ingenious, even if transparent in motive. He knew that Beneš considered Fierlinger "his man," but Gottwald was sure, in fact, that Fierlinger was "Gottwald's man." Further, he knew that to control the two ministries he mentioned meant to hold the real centers of power.

Beneš accepted Gottwald's plan only with some reservations. Indeed, on some points, he even offered additional encouragement. He acknowledged that Gottwald's proposal about the prime minister was a "more suitable formula, and internationally more appropriate," and further advised, "Insist, however, as Communists that you want to uphold the tradition" of the strongest party nominating the prime minister. "It will be important for the future, after the elections, when the people will probably confirm you as the leading party. All other parties are in crisis. You Communists are in the strongest position." Elaborating on his theme, Beneš admonished, "The proximity of the Soviet Union will play a great role in the growth of your influence. You must be cautious, however, and not push too fast, so that no one can say that everything is being 'bolshevized' at one stroke."

When the question of Beneš's future role came up for discussion, Gottwald confirmed that Beneš would hold the presidency in the transitional period, but added significantly that the Communists would "determine their ultimate position in the future regular elections of the president according to their experience during the transitional period." The Communist account renders an exchange that ensued:

Beneš. You will be the strongest element in the new regime and I will always support that element. I want the situation in the Republic to be more solid. I will need a government that will know its obligations, so that I can be just a president [unquestionably alluding to his past experience when he made personally the decisions on most serious questions].

Gottwald. If our agreement is frank and honest, the Communists and Beneš will together represent a force that no one can overcome.

Beneš. I will always act openly. You will always know what my opinion is. I would hope that you, too, as the leading party, hold freedom as the primary tenet of your position. It is possible that our views will be different, but we will together keep and follow the basic line.

Gottwald. Mutual respect and understanding in our relations is necessary. We are Communists and will remain Communists. We have not only principles and views of our own, but have also our own Communist moral code, and this, as you know, is not one of the worst.[38]

It was a fascinating but, in a way, pathetic conversation: a Stalinist and a democrat reaching a consensus based on mutual trust! One wonders what was really in their minds as they uttered those banalities. Gottwald could not have forgotten Lenin's statement that "Communist morality is the morality which serves the [Communist] struggle . . . and 'moral' is only that which facilitates the destruction of the old world." As for Beneš, since he was not a fool, one can only believe that he was once again engaged in the "vulgar trade."

The conversation continued. Beneš had some apprehensions on the question of the role of the National Committees and, in particular, on the way they would be elected. Worried about Communist-managed mob action, he stressed the need to safeguard democratic principles. "We will not permit any tricks," he said. "All parties must have the same chance." As to the distribution of ministerial portfolios, the president was reluctant to make any promises, since this was a matter for negotiation with other parties. He had no objections, however, to reserving the Ministries of Interior and Defense for the Communists, and commented, "There could be an ideal cooperation between me, as the supreme commander of the army, and a Communist, as Minister of National Defense."

With these thoughts and many others on his mind, President Beneš returned to London, carrying with him a detailed summary of the meetings that Gottwald had sent in an open envelope to his comrades in the British capital. In London, Beneš painted his negotiations in Moscow in rosy colors. He sent reassur-

38. *Cesta ke květnu,* pp. 55–56.

ing messages to the democratic leaders of the resistance movement at home and spoke in the same optimistic manner to his political associates in London. No available document reveals any doubts in his mind—except one. In the 1950s, a note was unearthed in London that reveals his real impressions. It reads:

(1) The Communist Party will also stay after the war (lack of agreement about one unified party). (2) National Committees, in the communist understanding, are in fact soviets. (3) The totalitarian tendencies of the communists remain; under the guise of the National Front; in fact, one party only should govern. (4) The participation of the communists in the government has one aim: to get hold of positions and have the decisive influence in preparation for seizing all power in the state.[39]

Obviously, Beneš saw through the Communist game. Why, then, did he concede every critical point to the Communist antagonist and why, especially, did he proceed in a manner that could only encourage the Communists eventually to push him to the wall? There is no satisfactory answer.

A Communist source offers its own interpretation of the Moscow negotiations:

Dr. Beneš' positive attitude toward the majority of the CPC proposals, some of his progressive views about the development of our national and democratic revolution, and some of his indisputably surprising evaluations of the policy of the Czechoslovak bourgeoisie, had a series of reasons. Dr. Beneš acted again, in these negotiations, as an experienced politician of the Czechoslovak bourgeoisie who always did serve his class faithfully, but, in contrast to other bourgeois politicians at home and in the emigration, he was capable of a realistic evaluation of the political situation. Dr. Beneš was an extraordinarily able political opportunist, who never openly opposed a revolutionary development, but nevertheless, he always tried, through the most varied tactical maneuvers, to defend the class that he represented. Thus, his position at the Moscow negotiations in December 1943 testified that he understood it would not be possible, at least temporarily, to govern in the liberated Republic without the Com-

39. Josef Korbel, *The Communist Subversion of Czechoslovakia, 1938–1948: The Failure of Coexistence* (Princeton, N.J.: Princeton University Press, 1963), p. 91.

munists. . . . But it must be duly appreciated that his attitude, both at the time of signing the Czechoslovak-Soviet treaty and of the negotiations with the Moscow leadership of the CPC, and in contrast to other representatives of the bourgeois government in the emigration, played, objectively, a positive role.[40]

No wonder, as another source revealed, the Moscow Communists "agreed that the conferences had taken a satisfactory course and that results had been reached which they themselves had not expected."

The Communist analysis makes a great deal of sense. Beneš was, indeed, a democrat who could never accept political coercion or the Communist ideology. But, while he sincerely believed in and worked for democratic socialism and wished to represent all strata (and here the Communists misjudged him) in a truly national program, he also was influenced by the compelling pragmatic aspects of the situation. Still, the whole question of Beneš's position and behavior in Moscow remains baffling. Lacking his own authentic explanation, one can only speculate.[41] As his personal note about the Moscow experience indicates, he did not trust the Communists, but he knew that he could not rebuild the national life without them. Perhaps, he naively hoped that they would mend their ways, once they faced the rooted democratic traditions of the Czechoslovak people; or perhaps, he thought that their participation in the government would teach them a sense of responsibility toward the people and restrain their uninhibited agitation, once economic socialism had brought them closer to the Marxist goal. Though it did fail, this concept was not as fatal as were Beneš's quick concessions to such crucial demands as Communist control of the Ministries of Interior (the police) and National Defense. If Beneš did not fully trust the Communists, he must have realized that this act alone could destroy Czechoslovakia's democracy. Also, his failure to insist on an orderly process of elect-

40. *Cesta ke květnu,* p. 58, n. 6.

41. An authoritative study of Beneš's political and personal life is badly needed. I understand that Professor Edward Taborsky, Beneš's personal secretary during the war, is working on his biography.

ing National Committees severed the only healthy roots of democratic procedures. At some point, surely, he could have stood firm, could have tested, at least, the possibility and the dimensions of a conflict. Perhaps, just perhaps, Stalin and Gottwald felt they needed Beneš. There was some meaning in the statement that emanated from the Communists' own evaluation of the Moscow negotiations—"results had been reached which they themselves had not expected."

After the Moscow conference, developments moved irrevocably toward the final denouement. The democratic groups in London organized into formal political parties in order to enable them to negotiate with the Communist Party on a nominally equal level. In March 1944, the three left-wing parties—Communist, Social Democrat, and National Socialist—established a "national block of the working people of towns and countryside." This clumsy name was intended to appeal to all strata of the population and to provide, at the same time, the rationale for a Communist-led coalition. Influenced by increasing Communist pressure, the government prepared a number of decrees concerning postwar political, economic, and social programs for the country.

The Slovak national uprising in August 1944 completely altered the situation in Slovakia and assured the Slovak National Council of the position of exclusive representative of Slovak national rights. The Soviet Union was most reluctant to aid the uprising, not knowing whether its leadership was in proper, that is Communist, hands. When, in the fall, the USSR finally did send limited assistance, it was too late to sustain the Slovak action. The Soviet government took a similar position on the Warsaw uprising that occurred at about the same time and on Marshal Tito's home-grown Yugoslav partisan struggle. Stalin obviously preferred to liberate Central Europe and the Balkan areas with the bayonets of the Red Army, owing nothing to the contribution of local patriots, even if led by Communists.

Events now gained momentum. By the beginning of January 1945, the Red Army was liberating eastern Slovakia, and the Soviet government suggested that the Czechoslovak government transfer its seat to Moscow. Beneš welcomed the invitation, commenting that he had "waited for the proposition," though after the experience with the Carpathian Ukraine, he must have waited with some misgivings.

In the last week of March 1945, Beneš and a delegation from London, composed of representatives of all political parties, arrived in Moscow to negotiate with the Communists and representatives of the Slovak National Council. The atmosphere was tense. President Beneš, this time accompanied by his foreign minister, Jan Masaryk, withdrew from the meetings, claiming that according to the Constitution he must stand aloof, above the political parties. His stance was indeed strange, for during the Munich crisis, when he could and should have acted according to the Constitution, he had taken it upon himself to make decisions that were clearly unconstitutional; in 1945, in a revolutionary situation, without an elected government and parliament, he took refuge in the technicalities of a suspended constitution. By this time, his prestige had reached a peak: he had signed a pact with the Soviet government, legally guaranteeing nonintervention in Czechoslovak domestic affairs; and he had constructed his whole strategy on the assumptions that he enjoyed Stalin's trust and that the democratic forces had the ability to defuse a Communist revolutionary explosion. But in this most critical moment, he chose not to use these precious advantages and, once again, failed to seize the chance to stand firmly for Czechoslovakia's democratic principles.

A detailed program, prepared by the Moscow Communists, was accepted as the basis for negotiations among the political parties. The discussions were at times fierce, as two members of the Czechoslovak National Socialist Party, Jaroslav Stránský and Prokop Drtina, objected to the Communist plans concerning the Slovak question and the functions of the National Committees. After considerable wrangling, a general agreement was reached, with minor concessions on both sides.

The negotiations climaxed with a discussion of the crucial question: the composition of the new government. First, the principle that each party would have three representatives in the government was accepted. However, since the Communist Party insisted that its Slovak branch was an independent party, it slipped six representatives into the government. In addition, with Fierlinger ("Beneš's man") as prime minister and General Svoboda (technically an expert but in fact a tested fellow-traveler) as minister of defense, the Communists acquired two key allies in the Cabinet. Professor Zdeněk Nejedlý—an avowed Communist who had spent the war years in Russia where he was delicately coached as a replacement for Beneš, should the latter not "behave"—entered the government as an expert on education. Thus, without any test of their popularity at the polls, the Communists, secured seven positions in the twenty-five-member government (besides the premiership and the Ministry of Defense), including the all-important Ministries of Interior, Information, and Agriculture. Gottwald became one of five deputy prime ministers. Jan Masaryk, who entered the government as an expert with no party affiliation, was to be watched by the highly knowledgeable and intelligent Slovak Communist, Vlado Clementis, who was state under secretary in the Ministry of Foreign Affairs, thus increasing the direct Communist representation in the Cabinet to eight positions.

Visiting Moscow for the first time, Masaryk was given particular attention by Gottwald. Masaryk dictated a memorandum (which has not been published and is in my possession) about his two-and-a-half-hour conversation with the Communist leader. Reading the document, one gets the impression that Gottwald subjected Masaryk to a vigorous third degree.

Jan Masaryk was known throughout the free world as a kind and jovial man, delightfully unconventional in the expression of his views. If politics is a combination of science and art, he was abundantly endowed with the latter quality. The son of a Czech scholar, who had been particularly impressed with Anglo-Saxon literature and philosophy and American democracy, and an American mother—an erudite, artistic, and highly sensitive woman—Jan Masaryk led a life that exemplified the finest qualities of Western culture.

Fundamentally conservative, he nevertheless possessed a refined social conscience and was profoundly concerned about social problems and the people's poverty. His weekly wartime broadcasts from London and the United States were filled with warm concern for his people and dedication to his country, wholly humane in content and original in expression. He had no ghostwriter for these broadcasts, as no one was able to approach his inimitable style. These qualities made Masaryk one of the most popular spokesmen for Czechoslovakia during and after the war.

Masaryk's wit concealed other qualities. Behind the facade of gaiety and improvised perception was hidden an acute sense of scepticism, with an inclination toward melancholy and loneliness, and a sensibility that was easily hurt by unkindness. It was both a gift and a burden to him to be the son of one of the greatest men of his epoch in Europe and in Czechoslovak history.

Masaryk confronted his antithesis in Gottwald: a leading representative of the international Communist movement; a trained Marxist and Stalinist, with firm class convictions and goals. Devoid of sentiment, Gottwald was a superb tactician and a ruthless fighter. In every respect, the two men stood at opposite poles, and their conversation in Moscow reflects this difference.

Gottwald's opening sentence zeroed in on Masaryk's future. "We Communists," he said, "are interested in individuals only to the extent that they execute this or that function; we are concerned with programs, not with persons." He first criticized Masaryk, as minister of foreign affairs, for not accompanying Beneš on his earlier trip to Moscow, noting that the Czechoslovak comrades, and the Russians as well, saw this as an anti-Soviet gesture. Masaryk retorted that he had offered to accompany the president, but that Beneš and the government in London had decided that he should attend a UNRRA conference instead. When Gottwald alleged that Masaryk had, on other occasions, expressed contempt for Moscow, Masaryk flatly denied the allegation.

Gottwald then attacked the London government in general, and Masaryk in particular, for not pursuing a foreign policy of unalloyed friendship with the Soviets, either before or after signing the Treaty of Alliance, and for compromising the alliance by having too much regard for the Western democracies. Masaryk reacted to this attack in some detail, explaining the delicate position of the government in exile and recognizing, in the last part of the conversation, that the closest foreign policy cooperation with the Soviet Union "must become an unquestionable and unchangeable cornerstone of Czechoslovakia's future." When Gottwald objected to the "London witch hunt" against Fierlinger, Masaryk's response was rather lukewarm, but he added that his only criticism of the ambassador was that, "from the day when he became the envoy of the London government in Moscow, none of his reports contained a single word even mildly critical of the Soviets," which gave the impression that Fierlinger "was more papal than the Pope." Gottwald significantly concluded this part of the discussion with the reminder that Fierlinger was the Party's candidate for chairman of the Ministerial Council.

Going on to the developments in the Carpathian Ukraine, Gottwald recommended that an agreement with Stalin and Molotov be reached now, in Moscow. Masaryk referred to the frequent public statements in which he had stated that he did not recognize boundaries of Czechoslovakia other than those which had existed before Munich and pointedly commented that the Allies would interpret such a step in a light unfavorable to the Soviet Union. Gottwald reminded him aptly of Beneš's conversation with Stalin in December 1943.

Masaryk resolutely protested Gottwald's assertion that he was a "quasi-representative of one class" and possibly harbored "some reactionary inclinations." He retorted that such allegations, if made publicly, would compel him to defend himself, "whatever the consequences." This personal attack was followed by "a little lecture about Communist philosophy, Communist practice, historic materialism that is as solid as a rock, a profound, correct political doctrine—the only one that in the future can assure freedom and prosperity to mankind." American and English journalism, Gottwald went on, was a farce, while Soviet journalism was a serious and truthful occupation, giving the nation facts, not titillating sensation. Gottwald also asserted that parliamentary democracy, with periodic formal elections, was a sham—a position Masaryk refuted.

At the end of the conversation, Masaryk engagingly expressed his wry understanding that a man ". . . doubly burdened as he was . . . bearing the mark of both his father's old world humanism and his mother's American nationality, must sometime expect such a sudden foray out of the dark." Masaryk's memorandum ends, "In conclusion, only one sentence. In the first Republic, when the political parties did not dare to attack the president [T. G. Masaryk], they attacked the foreign minister [Edvard Beneš]. Today, the president is Dr. Beneš and the foreign minister is Jan Masaryk. That is all." It is most unlikely that when he read this memorandum President Beneš failed to grasp the import of its concluding sentence, nor was he unaware of its truth. By March 1945, however, it was too late to change the onrushing course of events which Beneš himself had helped to channel.

All agreements sealed, President Beneš and the politicians bade farewell to their hosts in Moscow on March 31; their special train, moving across the Ukraine, reached the liberated town of Košice in eastern Slovakia at 6:00 P.M. on April 3. The future sovereignty of Czechoslovakia and the independence of her government was symbolically revealed on this journey, for Valerian Zorin, the Soviet ambassador to Czechoslovakia, was the only diplomat attached to the company. In spite of their insistence, all other Allied diplomats accredited to the government were denied the opportunity to accompany Beneš on the first return to his native soil. The wartime drama of the Czechoslovak anabasis was approaching an end; the peacetime drama was about to begin.

Even in the last few weeks of the war, military developments could have considerably affected the political outcome. As the Red Army approached the Czech lands with heavy and heroic fighting, the American forces were advancing rapidly in pursuit of disintegrating German troops. On April 18, without any previous planning, the Third Army under General George Patton crossed the Czechoslovak western frontier. Poor Beneš, guarded by the Soviet ambassador and the Red Army, had never before been seen so caught up in emotion. "Thank God, thank God," he murmured in a quivering voice, according to the account of his personal secretary, Edward Taborsky. Beneš immediately dispatched a telegram of congratulations and welcome to Patton. The roads

further east were open; Prague, the ancient capital of the kingdom
of Bohemia and of the democratic Republic of Czechoslovakia, expected to be liberated momentarily by the American army; the
whole of Bohemia and parts of Moravia could have been liberated
by the Americans. Their Third Army was 60 miles from Prague;
the Red Army was 120 miles from the capital. On April 22,
Anthony Eden told Ambassador John G. Winant that "it would
be most desirable politically for Prague to be liberated by the
United States Army." [42] But it was not to be. Once again, a small
nation was to be the pawn of the big powers in the game of international politics.

On May 5, the day of a national revolt in Prague, the Soviet high command asked General Eisenhower not to cross the
previously agreed-upon line. A group of American tanks, unauthorized, advanced to within ten miles of Prague, but were ordered
to withdraw. On May 9, twenty-four hours after the armistice had
been signed, at about 4:00 A.M., the Soviet tanks of General Ry-
balka reached the outskirts of the city. Prague, and most of
Czechoslovakia, had been liberated by the Red Army alone. No
politically mature citizen could misunderstand the implication of
the military strategy of those last days. The West was not interested in Czechoslovak democracy; its fate was left to the Communist and Soviet forces. This realization had a shattering effect on
the morale and psychology of the Czechoslovak people: after six
years of agony, as in a kind of nightmare, they watched something
like Munich happening once again.

This history of those years of "darkness and struggle"
(drawing on new documents published mostly in Prague) depicts
the aftermath of Munich, the disintegration of the state, the German invasion and occupation, dismemberment, and then the long
and tortuous road back (aided at long last—as Beneš had predicted—by the might of Allied arms) to the restoration of the
Czechoslovak Republic.

Despite the arduous and frustrating diplomatic tasks that
Beneš faced in reviving the Republic, he nevertheless kept his eye

42. National Archives, 860F .01/4-2245.

firmly on the goals of Czechoslovak tradition, freedom and social justice. In substance, his accomplishments in the establishment of such goals were not too different from what Masaryk's might have been, given the years of added experience and progress in social thought. It must also be noted that Beneš operated in an atmosphere far more charged with peril than did Masaryk. The latter became president of the new Republic on the crest of the Allied triumph in World War I, and his goals and ideals were oriented toward and supported by the West.

Beneš, on the other hand, was once again (as he had been at the time of Munich) largely neglected by his Western friends and under the menacing shadow of a potentially fearsome enemy—the Soviet Union. Indeed, the last episode of this story of the road back to full nationhood ended with the rumble of liberating Soviet tanks in Czechoslovak streets, not only by reason of force of arms or the accidents of war, but also by an "understanding" among Beneš's allies, reached without consultation with the Czechoslovak government in exile. Once again, Beneš (unlike Masaryk) was to confront superior forces from outside the borders of his country, forces intent on shaping lives of the people of his nation to their will.

But whatever variations there may have been in the pressures Masaryk and Beneš faced or in the atmospheres of political tension in which they worked, one absolutely critical difference emerges: Beneš placed his reliance on his allies and on his skill at diplomacy; Masaryk placed his on what he regarded as historic Czechoslovak moral principles. To Beneš, the risks inherent in a confrontation with the Soviet Union were realities that must be dealt with; to Masaryk there could be no realities save those moral values for the preservation of which risks must be taken. Thus it was that during the war years, Beneš saw and dealt with the Soviet Union not as one of the inescapable influences of Europe with which Czechoslovakia would necessarily have to reckon, but as an influence so compelling to the physical reemergence and preservation of Czechoslovakia as to justify the bargaining away of his country's central values. It was a compromise of principle for practicality that was to cost him and his country dearly.

During the first few months of peace, the coalition government (as it had been agreed upon in Moscow) not only was established, but also—as long as the Soviet Union thought it to be in its best interests to engage in rapprochment with Czechoslovakia— seemed to work. On the surface, there was hope. But the dragon's teeth had been sown, and still another inevitable confrontation awaited Beneš and his unhappy country.

Chapter Nine

Years of Hope, Years of Fears 1945-1948

Evaluating the events in Czechoslovakia during the spring of 1945, in the light of her history, the scholar Albert Pražák saw a logical link between the revolutions of 1918 and 1945. To Pražák, the first was essentially a national liberation, with a strong tendency toward social change; the second was an attempt toward both national and full social liberation. In terms of concept, Pražák was right; in terms of implementation, brutal realities outweighed the ideals.

The Košice Program

On April 4, 1945, the day he reached Košice, President Beneš appointed a provisional government, the political composition of which reflected the terms of the Moscow agreement, and its program was made public on the following day. In its broad outlines, the government program represented new concepts of political and social equality. It assured the people of constitutional liberties, particularly "freedom of the individual, of assembly, association, expression of opinion by speech, press, and pen; the privacy of home and mail, and freedom of learning and conscience and religion." In addition, it offered a "Magna Charta" to the Slovak nation, guaranteeing its national individuality and autonomy. In rather cautious terms, it stipulated the limited nationalization of key industries, the credit and banking systems, the insurance business, and mines, while extending support to private enterprise and initiative. It also promised new land reforms. Further, the provisional government, consisting of all political parties, was to be responsible to a provisional National Assembly, which would be replaced by a Constitutional Assembly chosen in free elections taking place "in the shortest possible time." National Committees were to assume political and administrative responsibilities on the local level.

Generally acceptable to all strata of society, the program also embodied some measures that gave cause for concern. Though correct in outlawing fascist organizations and in committing the government to the punishment of collaborators and traitors, it carried a sweeping collective guilt clause forbidding a "renewal, in any form, of the political parties which transgressed so gravely against the interests of the nation and the Republic. . . ." This prohibition extended not only to the small, conservative National Democratic, Small Business, and Fascist parties, and to the irreparably compromised Slovak Populist Party, but also to the large Agrarian Party, whose varied constituents could not conceivably be held responsible for the political machinations of some of its leaders at the time of the Munich crisis and during the war. The democratic members of the government shortsightedly agreed with this Communist-inspired policy in the expectation that farmers, conservative as they were, would now give their votes to the democratic parties. Their self-serving calculations misfired on the day of the elections.

Moreover, the program carried disturbing stipulations concerning the armed forces; they were to be commanded by "officers of sincerely democratic and truly antifascist convictions" and were to be given "political education" by select "educational officers." Such phrases were ominous, inviting abuses and special interpretations.

In spite of such foreboding elements, the Košice Program, as it was called, provided the foundation for a peaceful transition from the experience of enemy occupation to that of reconstruction and progressive social change. The government soon realized the enormity of its task, however, as the dynamics of the forces confronting each other behind a facade of national unity became apparent in growing political conflicts. Again, the ideal and again, the failure. What had promised to be the first invigorating experiment in the socialization of a democracy in an industrial society became, after three hard and bitter years, a Communist dictatorship. Again, one must probe for the reasons.

It was not that the material damage caused by six years of occupation and war could not have been remedied by diligent work and planning. Though the index of industrial production in 1945 fell thirty-two points below the 1913 level, though the railway system was disrupted, and though the patterns of foreign trade were shattered, the country still had suffered less physical damage than had some other Allied and enemy countries. Rather, it would seem that ethics and ideals had been the principal victims of the war years.

Official professions of national unity to the contrary, the Czechoslovak national will had been fragmented on several levels. German and Hungarian minorities had been deprived of citizenship and their property confiscated if they were unable to prove their political reliability—and very few of them could. Vast areas of the Sudeten lands were depopulated by the expulsion of the Sudeten Germans—a development that impelled a mass migration of Czech peasants into those territories. The Ministries of Agriculture and Interior, both controlled by the Communists, were in charge of the resettlement of the Sudeten lands, and they set one stratum of the population against another by extending privileges to those land-hungry farmers who were willing to support the Party. Industrial workers, too, were wooed toward active participation in nationalized enterprises by promises of advantage over other groups.

The war years had also wrought strange psychological changes in the workers. In those days, to "go slow" was a patriotic deed. But after the war, when the country depended on the workers to put an extraordinary effort into the task of rebuilding the economy, it seemed that no one dared to call upon their patriotic spirit. Traitors and collaborators were punished and isolated from the rest of the nation, but various retributive decrees were also exploited by the Ministry of the Interior to dispossess propertied individuals, to encourage vengeful denunciations, and to spread a psychosis of fear. On several occasions, the American ambassador in Prague, Laurence A. Steinhardt, referred in his dispatches to a "fear complex" that hampered the solidification of political liberties. A fragmentation time bomb was ticking in the edifice of "national unity."

The problems in Czechoslovakia were by no means limited to the two incompatible ideologies of democracy and communism and their irreconcilable strategies, though those divisive factors were obviously vital to the ultimate success of a Communist coup. Nor did the difficulties just concern wrangling over the implementation of the Košice Program. A proliferation of other divisions surfaced, most of them stemming from the varied traumatic experiences of the war. Most of the politicians who had escaped the concentration camps by retreating into obscurity, and who were subsequently beset by guilt, lost any leading role in the reconstruction. The few who survived the Nazi prisons justifiably aspired to key positions in all sectors of life in the new nation, but their ambitions were frequently thwarted by appointments that had been made at the Moscow conference in March 1945. In addition, the concentration camps had particularly decimated the non-Communist elite, and the health and will to engage in democratic struggle of those who returned was undermined. Equally important, a mutual estrangement grew between the former inmates of concentration camps and the returned émigrés, since the latter could hardly understand the psychology of those who had undergone torture and witnessed terror and death in the camps. A similar thorny hedge grew between those who fought for the liberation of the country in the resistance movement at home and those who worked for the same goal in exile. There were divisions, too, among the émigrés themselves, such as the easily understandable one between the so-called "Londoners" and "Muscovites." The hostility even permeated the military ranks, dividing officers and men who fought on the eastern or western fronts.

Looming behind all these conflicts was the psychologically oppressive presence of the Red Army, during the first six months after the liberation, and, at the roots of it all, an inescapable dichotomy between the desire for a sincere friendship with the Soviet Union and the spiritual essence of a traditional Western orientation. Thus, every pressure toward disorientation and disillusion existed, and in this mood, the people turned away from any patriotic support of the new government and moved toward personal advancement in mass organizations and political parties, in professional groups, and in antifascist or resistance associations, youth movements, and trade or farmers' unions. Social consciousness dissolved under selfish personal and class pressure.

It is no small wonder, then, that the three-year experiment in democratic socialism recorded some remarkable achievements. The benefits, like the dangers, arose from a combination of factors. The Czechoslovak people did feel some sense of common purpose: they wished to live in freedom and at the same time, construct a socialist economy. For a time, there was hope. The democratic forces were growing, and their leaders demonstrated increasing courage when facing Communist pressures. Most important, the Communist Party refrained (on instructions from Stalin) from attempting to seize the government. As Gottwald frequently stated, the Party pursued a "specific Czechoslovak road to socialism."

Political Struggles

As mentioned earlier, the CPC was the only organization that entered the scene immediately after the liberation as a coherent political entity. In spite of severe Nazi persecution, it had preserved skeleton cadres throughout the war and, after each wave of arrests, succeeded in reconstructing its leadership. According to

Party sources, 28,485 members (out of a prewar membership of 70,000) remained in the Czech lands at the end of the war. After the liberation, acting against the Leninist principle of a small, strictly controlled party of dedicated revolutionaries, the CPC aspired to become a mass party. Anyone who wanted to join its ranks was welcome, and there were many who did. Many of the new members were opportunists who sought material favors from the Party, whose exponents occupied influential positions in all sectors and were able to offer patronage to eager newcomers. Two months after the liberation, CPC membership rose to 475,000 and in another two months, to 712,000; during the same period, its local and factory organizations grew from 3,460 to 10,934. By March 1946, the Party counted 1 million members and 14,700 organizations, and by January 1948, it had 1.3 million members— more than all other political parties together.

Though the democratic parties had to start from scratch, their followers responded well to the newly established leadership's efforts in organization. By the end of 1945, the Catholic Party had some 350,000 members and almost 7,000 local organizations. The National Socialists numbered some 450,000, with around 7,000 organizations, and grew to 562,000 members by the end of 1947. At that time, the Social Democrats had 363,000 members. Though the Communist Party in Slovakia grew from 23,615 members to 120,000 members between April and the summer of 1945 (of whom only 12,000 were prewar Communists), they remained far behind their Czech comrades proportionately, as well as behind the Slovak Democratic Party which recorded 240,000 members. All in all, the mass influx to membership in all parties resulted in an unhealthy politicization of every aspect of national life. Before the three-year period of political freedom was over, one out of every 2.5 citizens, eighteen years of age or older, belonged to a political party. Such politicization inevitably gave the Communist Party, with its tight organization, firm discipline, and carefully structured plans for the infiltration of all segments of life, an enormous advantage.

The press enjoyed considerable freedom (though only political and professional organizations were permitted by law to publish newspapers or periodicals), but editors exercised cautious (though voluntary) restraint in reporting about the Soviet Union and in commenting on Soviet-oriented foreign policy. In addition, since newsprint was a scarce commodity and its distribution was in the hands of the Communist-controlled Ministry of Information, Communist publications received preferential treatment. For instance, in 1946, five Communist-controlled dailies in Prague printed 1,030,000 copies, while all four democratic parties together published no more than 743,000 copies. The same "technical" limitations were imposed on the publication of books; non-Communist authors and publishers suffered—not from ideological censorship, it was insisted, just from a lack of paper.

For a time, there was an impressive cultural renaissance. After six years of closed institutions of higher learning in the Czech lands, of closed libraries, of books and archives transferred to Germany, of theaters showing imported Nazi films, and after the fascistization of schools in Slovakia, the Czechoslovak people had a burning desire to satisfy their cultural and educational thirst. Universities were reopened and new educational institutions founded; the theater and arts flourished; concerts proliferated; new periodicals were published, and books were written and read throughout the country.

In the midst of political battles about freedom, the socialization of the economy, and the place of the nation in the increasingly intense Cold War, intellectuals raised their voices about some fundamental problems. Confronted with the heavy artillery of Marxist propaganda and swamped with translations of Lenin and Stalin, they evoked the ideals of humanity and searched once again for answers to the troubling question of the meaning of Czechoslovak history. There was general agreement that its contemporary meaning required a reinterpretation encompassing a new social and economic environment and the prevailing cultural trends in Europe, where Western values confronted Soviet-interpreted Marxist ideology. In the course of the great debate about a philosophical orientation for the country, many non-Communist writers envisioned a synthesis of individualism and collectivism, a harmonious amalgamation of the worthy qualities of the Western and Eastern systems. They were the forerunners of the Western scholars who, years later, presented the theory of convergence.

Ferdinand Peroutka, the renowned publicist of the interwar years who had miraculously survived the concentration camps even though he refused to put his pen to Nazi use, remarked that "the great weakness of socialism was that it was the Communists who tried to bring it about."

Václav Černý, a leading philosopher, plunged into the polemic concerning a Western or Eastern orientation of the Czechoslovak culture with the theme that "the essence of Czechoslovak culture" was Western and must remain so in the future, "as it was in the best periods of our history . . . truly humane." The meaning of the theme was familiar to students of history, but in the context of the battle raging on the political scene, it pointed far beyond the world of culture to a total way of life. The depth and breadth of these exchanges evoked all of the excitement of the interwar controversies. Ideas flourished, and greater growth seemed inevitable.

It was not to be. The relentless struggle for political power inexorably politicized even the nation's cultural life. The Ministry of Information exercised control over the state-owned radio network, theaters, and over film production. It signed a contract with the Soviet government film agency, guaranteeing that 60 percent of all foreign motion pictures in 1946 would be Soviet imports, 70 percent in 1947, and 80 percent in 1948 and thereafter. Soviet literature and drama, often mediocre, was presented in great quantities, promoted by the state-subsidized League of Czechoslovak-Soviet Friendship. No formal act forbade the resumption of close contacts with the Western cultural world, but in a financially exhausted country, no individual initiative could compensate for the official cultural policy, and attempts to establish a balance were often thwarted by the lack of foreign currency.

The process of systematic penetration of key government positions by the Communist Party was apparent on all levels, local and national, as well as in the bureaucracy, the officer corps, and the economy. By 1947, Party members held 57 percent of the chairmanships of community National Committees, with 80 percent at the district level, and 100 percent in the Provincial National Committees. These committees, which had not been elected by a democratic process, soon became a primary instrument of the Communist Party in the Czech lands.

In the upper echelons of the bureaucracy, Communist ministers pursued a policy of communization in the Ministries of Interior, Information, Agriculture, and Social Welfare, and for shorter periods, in the Ministries of Education, Internal Commerce, and Finance. The Party fared less well in the ministries whose heads were members of the democratic parties. An analogous situation, determined by party affiliation, existed in the administrative offices in Slovakia, except that there the ratio was reversed, due to the strength of the Democratic Party over the Communist Party.

The policy of nationalizing industry occasioned a similar development in industrial administration. Of eleven central industrial offices, Party members controlled the two most powerful industries sectors, employing 322,000 persons out of 598,000 employees in all nationalized enterprises. In seven additional central offices, the deputy directors were members of the Party. As to individual enterprises, in heavy industry, 35 percent of the managers and 33 percent of the deputy managers were Party members; in light industry, the percentages were 34.4 and 49.6 respectively; and in the food industry, 34.4 percent of the managers and 35.2 percent of the deputies were Communists. More often than not, key positions in industry were awarded on the basis of Party allegiance, and not for expertise or other qualifications. This distribution of political spoils, intolerable in any enterprise dedicated to productivity, wreaked havoc on the country's economy. The workers, who took an active part in planning and supervising production, were controlled by the powerful unified trade unions, which were, in turn, controlled by the Party. Immediately after the war, individual enterprises organized cadres of factory guards whose original purpose was to protect nationalized property against possible sabotage by the remnants of enemy forces; these later became Communist-dominated workers militia.

The police force, controlled by the Ministry of the Interior, was slowly communized, and the State Security Guard (SNB)—

the secret police—was thoroughly infiltrated. In the armed forces, under the command of the minister of national defense, General Svoboda, "compromised" generals were removed; these were mostly people of merit who were in London during the war and had opposed Svoboda's subservience to Moscow. According to two Communist scholars, the National Socialist Party and the Slovak Democratic Party had a plan to establish their own control over the army, but if such a plan ever existed, it was illusory. It was further alleged that President Beneš had intervened to remove Communists from leading positions and opposed the concept of building a true "people's army." Nevertheless, effective work by the CPC frustrated the designs of the "reactionaries" and, by the second half of 1947, the army was reported consolidated as an instrument of the "people's democracy," though still not imbued with sufficient revolutionary spirit.

Of sixty-eight key positions in the army, almost one-third were held by Communist generals. In the Ministry of National Defense and in the chief of staff command, twelve of thirty-five men were Communists, as were two of four regional commanders, three of ten army corps commanders, and four of nineteen divisional commanders. Only five positions in all (7.3 percent) were held by members of other political parties, while the rest (61.8 percent) of the examined positions were nonaffiliated. The Communists claimed that an overwhelming majority of noncommissioned officers were "on the side of the revolution" and that only some 10 percent of all officers belonged to the "reaction." The educational officers were almost exclusively Communist, and it was due to their efforts that up to 70 percent of some garrisons voted for the CPC in the 1946 elections. Nevertheless, though the armed forces were highly infiltrated with Communist Party members, the die was by no means cast.[1]

In November 1947, in Belgrade, I had an interesting conversation with General Koča Popović, then chief of staff of the

1. The data on Communist positions in industry and the armed forces are based on Miloš Klimeš and Marcel Zachoval, "Příspěvek k problematice únorových událostí v Československu v únoru 1948," Československý časopis historický 6, no. 2 (1958): 195–97, and on Milan Špičák and Ján Lipták, "Únor 1948 a československé ozbrojené síly," Československý časopis historický 21, no. 3 (1973): 309–34.

Yugoslav army, who had recently returned from a visit to Czechoslovakia. He found the morale of the army there very low and was
concerned about its effect on the nation in a moment of crisis. Analyzing the international situation, he expressed the conviction that
war between the East and West was inevitable (with Yugoslavia at
that time firmly in the Soviet bloc) and that Czechoslovakia was
apparently undecided as to which side she would support. He continued:

I sense that your political situation is unsettled. Too many parties are taking part in political life. In foreign policy, you have not decided whether
you will go with the West or with us, and there is no campaign of hatred
against western imperialism in your press, which should be systematically
educating the nation on the inevitability of war. You will understand that
all this must deeply concern me as chief of staff of an Allied army.

Communist scholars also acknowledge that the situation in the
armed forces was complex and delicate. Unlike the secret police,
the army could not be fully trusted to play a decisive role in a
Communist takeover.

Slovakia Again

The political and cultural developments, both positive and negative, in the Czech lands were echoed in Slovakia, though the character of the struggle for freedom and social progress there had a
specifically Slovak flavor. Developments were further complicated
by steadfast efforts to implement, in the name of national identity,
the right to autonomy enunciated in a general way in the Košice
Program. The proclamation of the principle and its realization,
however, were two different things, and Slovakia's autonomy
created strange problems.

       The body of Slovak commissioners and the Slovak Na-
tional Council (established during the Slovak uprising) continued.
Matters of common interest, such as foreign policy, national defense, and finances, remained the domain of the central govern-

ment and the National Assembly in Prague; other concerns, such as transportation and social welfare, came under the combined authority of both the Slovak National Council and the National Assembly, while still others, such as education, were entirely in the hands of the Slovak authorities in Bratislava. The Czech lands had no comparable executive and law-making institutions—an arrangement that led to an anomalous situation, called assymetrical by Czechoslovak scholars, in which the central government in Prague passed decisions, some of which extended to the whole country, while others were limited to the Czech lands. As might be expected, confusion and clashes over the delineation of authority between Prague and Bratislava abounded and even three separate formal agreements failed to resolve the newly resurgent problem of Czech-Slovak relations.

This time, the critical moving force behind the controversy was the struggle between Slovakia's two parties, the Slovak Democratic Party and the Communist Party of Slovakia, for Slovakia's ideological allegiance. The new situation was not analogous to the interwar developments, which had been characterized by conflicts between the forces of progress and conservatism. After the war these ideological contrasts could not be clearly identified. Though the conservative forces of the prewar period had been compromised and corrupted by six years of fascism, the Slovak people, still predominantly peasants, remained basically conservative, pious, and Catholic. Nor was the Communist Party considered representative, in all respects, of the progressive elements within Slovakia.

The Democratic Party, therefore, after reaching an agreement with the Catholic church, quickly gained in popularity, and its program combined a devotion to personal freedom with a kind of Christian socialism. The nationalization of key industries was accepted by the Democratic Party, but it stressed the necessity of preserving human rights and private initiative in the process. In appealing to Slovak nationalism, the party wished to bridge the gap between the spirit of renewed allegiance to Czechoslovakia and the memories of the wartime Slovak Republic as an independent state. The Slovak Democratic Party's vigorous pursuit of Slovak autonomy was a policy which gave the party resounding victories in the elections. Thus, the old-time provincial outlook of the Slovak nation deepened, and the rifts grew wider, not only between Slovaks themselves, but also between Slovaks and Czechs. This divisive movement reached a crisis during the trial of Father Tiso, the former president of the Slovak Republic, when Archbishop Kmetko expressed the view that every Slovak would certainly prefer an independent state, but since that was impossible, Slovakia should support the Czechoslovak Republic. This grudging recognition of unity compelled Beneš to speak out strongly, saying the country "could not survive another crisis in Czech-Slovak relations" and adding that "Slovakia would never emerge from such a crisis as an independent state. It would most probably become part of Russia." [2] The last part of Beneš's admonishment had a cooling effect on Slovak politicians, as well as on the masses, but the cauldron of divisions and problems continued to simmer.

The Communist Party of Slovakia found itself in a perplexing predicament. Only the working class and some intellectuals had responded to its general program for democratic revolution and progressive socialization. Because the Party had little chance of broadening its base and increasing its popularity in a fair contest with the Democratic Party, it devised a typically acrobatic approach to the problem—a sudden volte-face in support of the central government in Prague. Here was something wondrous to behold: a party which had in the past agitated for Slovakia's autonomy—even to the point of proclaiming her right to secede—a party which had, during the first period of the war, agitated for a Soviet Slovakia and which by the end of the war had returned to the policy of autonomy, suddenly supporting the centralizing measures that emanated from Prague. The strategy stemmed from the hope that, since it was making little headway against the conservative forces in Slovakia, the Party might at least strengthen its position in the Czech lands, where people were also concerned about

2. National Archives, Diplomatic Branch, Record Group 59, Records of the Department of State, 860F .002/2147.

the extent of Slovak autonomy. Moreover, by advocating centralization, the Communists could gain power positions that were denied to them in open competition with the Democratic Party in
Slovakia. These machinations culminated in the months preceding
the Communist seizure of power, when the Communist Party accused the Democratic Party of harboring reactionaries and pro-
pagating a program of separatism. Needless to say, these developments opened the old wounds of mutual suspicion between the
Czechs and Slovaks, wounds which have not healed to this day.

Lenin Revised

It is a fascinating exercise to reread, with the perspective of thirty
years, the statements made by Czechoslovak Communists during
the years following the end of World War II. They contain the
sounds of humanism, and thus they were not unattractive to people that yearned for peaceful progress toward freedom and social
equity. They seemed to ignore Lenin's teaching about revolutionary violence, the dictatorship of the proletariat, and the necessity of smashing the existing society without regard for law or life.
The CPC did, indeed, become a member of the National Front,
and its representatives occupied important positions in the government. After years of experience in opposition politics—experience
that had created certain habits—the Party was to engage in constructive, responsible, nation-building politics, and these were to
be conducted along the lines of a "democratic, not socialist, revolution."

   At a meeting of Party functionaries in Košice, when the
war was still in progress, Gottwald defended his policy of joining
the government and replied to some Party members, who were
unwilling to revise Lenin's theory on revolution, by saying that "no
other tactic is possible *today*" [italics added]. That did not mean,
however, that "the class struggle has stopped; it continues in different forms and these are advantageous to us." These words
sound strangely contemporary, though they were spoken ten years
before Nikita Khrushchev made similar statements which ushered

in an era of peaceful coexistence, subsequently extended to an era of détente.

In the same vein, Gottwald further stressed that the Party's *"immediate* goal" was not a "Soviet Republic, a socialist state," as it would be a "great strategic mistake if the Party had such *immediate* perspectives [italics added]." (The words were probably uttered gently, with the transient thought that in this time of exhilaration and euphoria, on the eve of final victory over Nazism, only a few would notice the time qualifiers.) Still facing some discontent within the Party, Gottwald found shelter in Stalin's protection and in September 1946, secretly informed the Central Committee that on his last visit to Moscow Stalin had told him that "as experience has shown and as classics of Marxism-Leninism teach, not just one way exists, leading to the dictatorship of the proletariat. Rather, in a certain arrangement of circumstances, there can be a different way." Stalin pointed to an increase of self-esteem among broad national masses and stated, "In such historical occasions, there are many possibilities and paths for a socialist movement." He expressly mentioned Czechoslovakia as a country with "a possible special road to socialism." [3] Gottwald's statement was not published then, nor was it included in his collected works. During the period of Stalinism in the 1950s, the Party kept it secret, for it would have contradicted Gottwald's subsequent dictate, in January 1953, that there existed "only one road, the Soviet road, toward socialism in Czechoslovakia."

Meanwhile, the Party was marching along the "pathway of national and democratic revolution," claiming to be "the sole heirs of all the finest and best in the national tradition from the Czech kings in the Middle Ages to the distinguished life of Masaryk." To Gottwald, cooperation with the democratic parties was not "opportunistic, temporary," but an act of national unity. Even such sensitive matters as religion were tolerated in the Party's "immediate goal." For the moment, religion was not even the "opium of mankind." Antonín Zápotocký, an old-guard Communist from the days of World War I, a member of the Politburo and later presi-

3. Jaroslav Opat, *O novou demokracii, 1945–1948* (Prague: Čs. akademie věd, 1966), pp. 51, 218, 226–27.

dent of the Republic, spoke on Christmas Eve, 1945, of the "beautiful, unforgettable, and mystical poetry of Christmas," of the "midnight Mass in the church, from which resounds the rejoicing carol, proclaiming the birth of the new man—the Savior," of the value of religious education, and of the "mystical magic, the secrets and miracles, ennobling the whole Christian mind." [4]

In matters of foreign policy, the Party spokesmen, while emphasizing close ties with the Soviet Union, did not neglect the West and, at first, gave full support to negotiations with France concerning a treaty of alliance. In June 1945, the American chargé d'affaires in Prague, A. N. Klieforth, reported to the Department of State on a conversation with Gottwald, who "appeared anxious . . . to establish friendly relations with the West and with the East," and who said further that "the alliance with Russia was principally a military alliance . . . and not intended to prevent Czechoslovakia from re-establishing its former relations with the friendly Western powers." In a conversation with Klieforth, Zdeněk Nejedlý, the Communist minister of education, acknowledged that a great deal of Russian history and language would be introduced in the schools, but stated that English and American schools would be reopened and English taught in all schools as a secondary language. Nejedlý recognized that the "American education system was more suited to Czechoslovakia than Russian or European ones." Klieforth also reported that General Svoboda spoke to him about the excesses of the Red Army, but had called the situation "a blessing in disguise in that they will cure the Czechs of radicalism." [5]

Klieforth's dispatch does not indicate whether or not he was impressed by the friendly remarks of the Communist ministers, but it was a generally accepted view that diplomats in Prague were received warmly by Communists in government posts. As late as May 1947, President Beneš said to Sir Robert Bruce Lockhart, who was for years intimately acquainted with Czechoslovak politics, that "Gottwald was a reasonable man who believed in parlia-

4. Josef Korbel, The Communist Subversion of Czechoslovakia, 1938–1948: The Failure of Coexistence (Princeton, N.J.: Princeton University Press, 1959), pp. 139–40.

5. National Archives, 860F .002.

mentary democracy." The aphorism, "Communists are first Czechs and then Communists," acquired popular currency. The Communist strategy of cooperating with the democratic parties and professing faith in democracy and fidelity to a parliamentary path to socialism, used in conjunction with a pragmatic use of power, paid off handsomely. Success came to the Communists in the 1946 elections for the Constitutional Assembly.

The Elections

Held after a long delay on May 26, 1946, the elections contained both promising and ominous omens. Outwardly, they did not constitute a clear-cut struggle between ideological values. All the competing parties were in the National Front and campaigned on the basis of the assumption that a coalition government of all parties would continue with a generally agreed-upon program: a policy combining social and economic reform with the maintenance of personal and political freedom. The elections were more a battle for positions and power than a confrontation over issues.

In contrast to the elections in all other countries of the area, which were managed by the respective Communist parties under the guise of national unity and in the presence of the Red Army, the elections in Czechoslovakia were free from outside pressure and one-party manipulation. Not that the Soviet Union did not attempt pressure; indeed, it planned to transport its troops across Czechoslovak territory during the height of the election campaign, but the democratic parties in the government protested and thwarted this threat. Generally, then, the elections were a democratic, though fierce, competition. This atmosphere tended to obscure the real nature of the contest—it was a crucial struggle between the values of a pluralistic society and the goals of a one-party system.

It was characteristic of the political mood in the various provinces that the traditionally progressive Czechs tended to discount the potential dangers inherent in a strong Communist Party, while the Moravians took a more cautious attitude, and the Slovaks, basically conservative, proved to be extremely suspicious of the democratic slogans and promises advanced by the Communists. However, the Communist Party enjoyed the advantage of controlling, through the Ministry of Information, the radio networks and the allocation of newsprint. The Party attracted voters with promises that avoided radical solutions, using rhetoric that resounded with such phrases as "democracy" and "personal liberty." The Party did put pressure on anonymous individuals whose wartime record had been less than spotless, branding them collaborators on the one hand, while on the other subtly suggesting that joining the Communist Party would automatically acquit them of suspicion. In many cases, when that tactic failed to be effective, the local Communist-controlled National Committees simply accused citizens of collaboration and denied them the right to vote. Upon appeal, their rights were often restored—but by that time, the elections were over. Many former members of the parties that were collectively accused of collaboration, particularly those from the Agrarian Party, did take advantage of the refuge offered in the CPC. Moreover, Julius Ďuriš, the Communist minister of agriculture, toured the country and assured gatherings of farmers that the Party's land reform plan would permit holdings up to the reasonable size of fifty hectares and that these holdings would not be collectivized. In addition, the thousands of families that had moved into the Sudeten lands owed a debt of gratitude—inevitably collected—to the Communist minister of the interior, Václav Nosek, who had arranged their settlement at the small price of loyalty to the Party.

The results of the elections sent some shock waves, as well as some pleasant surprises, through the ranks of the competing parties. In the Czech lands, the Communist Party received 40.17 percent of the vote and 93 seats in the National Assembly, reaping the harvest of a shrewd campaign, an efficient organization, and well-entrenched positions from which to distribute favors. Strangely enough, it garnered many votes from the most conservative and disgruntled element of the society—the peasants. In Slovakia, on the other hand, the Party fared poorly, gaining only 30.37 percent of the vote and 21 seats. There, the Democratic

Party won a resounding victory, with 62 percent of the vote and 43 seats. It received strong support from the predominantly agrarian population and the Catholic clergy, who did not hesitate to agitate against the "communist atheists." Two minor parties in Slovakia, the Labor Party and the Freedom Party, gathered 6.84 percent of the vote and 5 seats. Taken together, the democratic parties in the Czech lands surpassed the Communist Party's strength, totalling 59.48 percent of the vote and 138 seats in the National Assembly, but they were not united, either in program or in organization.

Suffering from a policy that vacillated between identification with the Communists or the democrats, the Social Democratic Party, once the second largest party in the nation, slipped to last place, receiving only 15.58 percent of the vote and 37 seats. Its wavering position in the decisive days that were to follow facilitated the Communist seizure of power in February 1948 and finally led to its absorption into the Communist Party. The National Socialist Party, the most persistent defender of democracy over the years, gained 23.66 percent of the vote and 55 seats. Analyzing the causes of this disappointing result, Prokop Drtina, minister of justice and a member of the party's Executive Committee, pointed to the inadequate organization of his party, but added painfully that the election had been won much earlier; it, "was won in Moscow and Košice." [6] The Catholic Party, less dynamic and propounding a program of Christian socialism, acquired 20.24 percent of the votes and 46 seats, faring particularly well in Moravia, where it gained 27.57 percent of the vote.

All in all, the elections were testimony to the tenacious vitality of democratic processes. Considering the varied pressures and the peculiarly unsettled postwar conditions, the elections were remarkably free, and they presented an accurate profile of political power. In the National Assembly, the democratic parties held a majority of 186 seats over 114 Communist seats. Theoretically, the Parliament was ready to discharge its responsibilities in a democratic manner. In practice, however, there were problems. Legis-

6. Václav Král, *Cestou k únoru: Dokumenty* (Prague: Svobodné slovo, 1963), p. 162.

lative authority was undermined by the "National Front" concept, which required that decisions be approved by the leaders of the political parties, rather than by elected representatives. Moreover, under the same cloak of national unity, one essential ingredient of a pluralistic system was lacking—an opposition party.

As a result of the elections, the government was reshuffled, with Gottwald installed as prime minister and with five deputy prime ministers representing the coalition parties; the rest of the portfolios were distributed among the parties as equitably as was practicable. In the twenty-six-member government, the democratic parties together held a majority of fifteen, over nine Communist and two nonpartisan members. This numerical ratio was misleading, however, because two Social Democrats leaned toward the Communist Party and General Svoboda, supposedly a nonpolitical expert, invariably sided with the Communists. To add to its strength, the Party also retained the key Ministries of Interior, Information, and Agriculture, and (to watch over the nonpartisan Masaryk) the secretaryship in the Ministry of Foreign Affairs. However, as in the National Assembly, the situation in the government appeared stabilized, and the administration could now devote its energy to the task of implementing its programs of economic reform and social equity.

Economic and
Social Challenges

As discussed earlier, Czechoslovakia was not a country of unbridgeable social cleavages. Within a system of free enterprise with a fairly healthy balance of agriculture and industry, the government had worked diligently, by way of numerous social welfare measures, toward alleviating blatant inequities among classes. After the war, however, it faced an unprecedented challenge in the newly aroused radical spirit of the workers; and it also had to effect a radical change in the ownership of national wealth. Properties belonging to the German minority and to collaborators were confiscated; thousands of Jews had died in the gas chambers, and

their possessions had never been reclaimed. Calls for the nationalization of key industries found a sympathetic response from the
general populace, few of whom had enjoyed much of the "concentration" of capital. The impact of the Soviet victory added
more fuel to the desire to restructure the economy and redistribute
the national wealth. In the light of Czechoslovak tradition, it appeared entirely natural to struggle ahead toward greater and
greater social and economic justice. As it turned out, however, the
crucial question was then, as it is today, whether, or to what extent,
a socialized economy is capable of improving the general standards of living and social relationships without jeopardizing personal and political freedoms. For three years, Czechoslovakia was
on trial, and political and social analysts watched, with hope and
anxiety, her experiment in social democracy.

The government faced two problems simultaneously: the
immediate need to rehabilitate the economy and the long-range
need to restructure the economic and social systems. The first
need was imperative. The cost of the war in lives, in health ruined
by years of concentration camps and privations, in the crippled
labor market, in destroyed property, and in shattered productivity
and foreign trade, was appalling. National losses were equal to the
whole of the national income from the years 1932–33 to
1937–38.

Despite the magnitude of the task, however, the short-term
recovery of the economy was effected rapidly. Partly through state
planning, and partly through foreign assistance (UNRRA), noteworthy progress was made. After one year of peace, industrial
production, which at the war's end had been down to 50 percent
of the 1937 level, had risen to 71 percent; agricultural production
rose by somewhat less, around 27 percent. Simultaneously—and
with both good and bad effects—significant changes were introduced into the structure of the economy.

In a few short months after the war, 16 percent of all industry had been nationalized, and 61 percent of all workers were
employed in these nationalized industries. A nationalization law,
proclaimed in October 1945, carried the process further; by 1948,
almost two-thirds of the labor force were employed in nationalized

industry. The banking and insurance industries were totally nation-alized. Compensation to former owners was guaranteed by law, but due to the subsequent Communist takeover, it was never paid.

Land holdings underwent similar drastic changes. A total of 3 million hectares was confiscated from former collaborators and the Sudeten German and Hungarian minorities, representing 36.5 percent of the total acreage in the Czech lands and 11.4 percent in Slovakia. The arable land, close to 2 million hectares, was distrib-uted (not to exceed 13 hectares per family) among 303,380 peas-ants and workers. Close to 1 million hectares of forest land were assigned to the state, communities, and cooperatives. These vast land resources were further enlarged when a law, passed in 1947, permitted expropriations of property exceeding 50 hectares, which led to the additional redistribution of nearly 1 million hectares of arable and forest lands. Further, farmers moving into these lands were materially assisted by access to free implements and con-sumer goods, as well as by ready access to favorable credit.

Changes in the overall distribution of national income inevi-tably followed. Wages and salaries moved from 59 percent of the total national income in 1937 to 68.5 percent in 1948. Con-versely, entrepreneurial income dropped from 32.2 percent in 1937 to 28.4 percent in 1948, and income from property declined from nearly 9 percent to only 3 percent in the same period. The government's wage policy also alleviated discrimination between men and women and between industrial and agricultural workers. Equally dramatic changes were effected within the labor ranks. In 1939, for example, an average white-collar worker in the Czech lands earned 162 percent more money than a blue-collar worker, while by 1948, the difference had narrowed to only some 34 per-cent. In the period between 1946 and 1948, the total volume of salaries and wages increased by one-third, and pensions increased by almost one-half, while prices remained relatively stable.

The result of all these changes, however, was not as uni-formly beneficial as had been hoped. Despite incentives, wage ad-justments, the redistribution of income, and land and property shifts, there were problems. Consumer goods were in short supply, and the inevitable black market of a controlled economy flourished. The general standard of living, which was well below the level of economic improvement, was not wholly satisfying—"average," rather than "equitable." In fact, this development was uneven: while the living conditions of the previously underprivileged classes exceeded the level of the most prosperous prewar years, those of the middle class fell behind.

Communist sources fail to mention or are reluctant to record other factors that negatively affected a healthy economic and social development, though these factors are fundamental to the question of the success or failure of a socializing economy. With increasing numbers of nationalized industrial enterprises, the problem of how to cope with a politicized administration and industrial and state bureaucracy—the familiar hydra of establishments in modern society—arose. The drive to achieve the planned production target appreciably lowered the quality of the products and thereby the reputation of Czechoslovak goods, which had been generally recognized abroad before the war. Further, the idea that the workers were now laboring in "their own" factories resulted, oddly enough, in widespread absenteeism and low working morale.

Inescapably, the process of nationalization was politicized. Matters of economics were subjected to politics. The Slovak Democratic Party and the Catholic Party both had reservations about the extent of nationalization and would have preferred the route of social reform. The National Socialist Party, left of center and certainly an exponent of nationalization, nevertheless insisted that personal freedom must not be endangered in the process. As its leading spokesman, Hubert Ripka, stated, "Men must not be exploited either by other men or by the State." The Social Democratic Party took Marx as the author of their text and in matters of nationalization leaned toward the Communist line, but propounded strictly democratic methods of achieving these socialist goals. The Communist Party took the Marxist-Leninist position on nationalization, but with a unique (and purely tactical) emphasis on the "special Czechoslovak road to socialism." This was supposed to mean a gradual nationalization, but to the Communists, consciously or unconsciously, it meant swift progress toward the goal Gottwald had confidentially enunciated in 1945—"socialism and the Soviets." President Beneš, who continued to enjoy great respect, expressed concern about the rapidity of the nationalization process, but was in favor of "Czechoslovak socialist principles" which could be implemented "in a democratic manner, without civil wars, without the dictatorship of the proletariat, without applying certain theories of Marxism and Leninism."

From this mishmash of opinion, no economic experts could hope to construct a model that might produce a viable mixed economy with balanced public and private sectors. Inevitably, the situation resulted in a pragmatism which carried some of the strength of flexibility, but more of the weakness, under political pressures, of irresolution. Still, even this strange mixture of principles and politics need not have doomed the Czechoslovak experiment in democratic socialism. On the contrary, in spite of formidable obstacles, it offered a potential, open to further improvement. At any rate, Czechoslovakia's economy, its stability and growth, were already ahead of other comparable countries. But the three-year period of trial was too short. In February 1948, it was brought to an abrupt end.

Toward a Cataclysm

For a time political freedoms were preserved in Czechoslovakia. Soon after the May 1946 elections, however, ominous events flashed warnings of serious problems. The Cold War had mounted in intensity, affecting every aspect of international relations: the workings of the United Nations, the Paris Peace Conference, the policies of economic assistance, the making of treaties, the questions of Berlin and Germany, the economic recovery of Western Europe, and, most significantly for Czechoslovakia, the political orientation of the Central and East European countries. The world was irresistibly dividing into two camps: East and West.

Inevitably, Czechoslovakia became a Cold War battleground. Allied with the Soviet Union, with all its neighbors in the process of communization, but at the same time, with a tradition of democratic philosophy, firmly aligned with Western values, Czechoslovakia set her course to avoid both Scylla and Charybdis. The task was not facilitated by the quarreling of her own leaders.

I was a member of the Czechoslovak delegation to the Paris Peace Conference in the summer of 1946 and served as chairman of the Economic Commission for Hungary, Rumania, Bulgaria, and Finland. Practically every issue debated, whether it was the restitution of property, reparations, or the status of the Danube, was viewed in the perspective of the Cold War. Objective criteria and claims consistently gave way to ideological exercises or the maneuverings of power politics.

On one occasion, for example, two Communist members of the ten-man Czechoslovak delegation applauded Andrei Vyshinsky when he accused the United States of "dollar diplomacy" and "trying to dominate the world with 'hand-outs.' " The reaction of the United States was swift—and counterproductive. On the instruction of the secretary of state, James Byrnes, $50 million of credits to Czechoslovakia for the purchase of surplus materials were immediately suspended and negotiations for a loan from the Export-Import Bank were adjourned. Byrnes's spiteful action was encouraged by the reports and recommendations of the American ambassador in Prague, Laurence A. Steinhardt, who had opposed any economic assistance ". . . unless and until the people of Czechoslovakia evidence a desire to rid themselves of the very real threat that now exists of virtually complete domination by the Communists" and until the Czechoslovak government paid in dollars for nationalized United States property.

Steinhardt failed to understand the nature of the struggle between the forces of democracy and communism and clearly mistook the vilification of American policy by Communist newspapers and speakers as government policy, ignoring the fact that democratic politicians and media resolutely parried all such Communist thrusts. President Beneš explained the delicate position of Czechoslovakia to Steinhardt, referring to Soviet pressures and regretting the friction. Nevertheless, Secretary Byrnes insisted that American-Czechoslovak relations could only be improved if the government avoided "inept actions" in dealings with the United

States, demonstrated an independent posture in international affairs, and handled equitably the matter of compensation for nationalized American property. Requests for future loans, he added, should be addressed to the World Bank.[7] Imposing such conditions as these, to control the "inept actions" of Communists and to assume an "independent" role in the world forum betrayed an incredible disregard for the precarious domestic and international situation of Czechoslovakia. Such blundering only strengthened the hands of the Communists and weakened the position of the democrats who were trying to establish some balance between Soviet and American influence in Czechoslovak affairs.

The events surrounding the question of Czechoslovak-French treaty of alliance provided another example of the tenuousness of the balance between East and West and how, in this case, France inadvertently tipped it in favor of the Soviet Union. For many months, the leadership of the democratic parties had worked on a treaty with Paris, and neither the Czechoslovak Communists nor Stalin had opposed the idea. A draft was prepared and sent to Paris, but it took the French government eleven months to send an amended version back to Prague. Whether the motives of the Czechoslovak democrats in promoting the treaty of alliance with France were to "open the window" to the West and counter-balance, at least to some extent, the winds blowing from the East; whether Moscow and the Czechoslovak Communists perceived the treaty as an instrument for further penetration of the West; whether France saw in the treaty a vehicle for reestablishing her position in Central Europe or feared it as a possible means of Soviet expansion—all such questions became moot as the Cold War accelerated. For during the eleven months that France procrastinated, a series of events rapidly deepened the divisions between East and West: the Truman Doctrine, the ouster of the Communists from the French government, and the Soviet government's rejection of the Marshall Plan and its interdiction to Czechoslovakia's participation in the plan. President Beneš (according to the "Notes about our foreign policy," dictated in the

7. National Archives, 860F .51/7-347; 860F .51/9-1746; 860F .00/12-2346.

summer of 1947 and in my possession) had been most anxious to sign the treaty with France, as he believed it would "once again tie France to Czechoslovakia" and, at the same time, "prevent the creation of an exclusively Western bloc." Nor did he fear that the treaty would give the West a chance to drive a wedge between the Soviet Union and Czechoslovakia, since "this no one can ever achieve." With the advance of the Cold War, however, both sides abandoned the idea of the treaty, and with its demise, the cause of democracy in Czechoslovakia suffered another setback.

The handwriting on the wall was becoming clearer and clearer, and its color was red. The Cominform, founded in September 1947, revived the Leninist concept of class struggle and international class solidarity. Rudolf Slánský, secretary-general of the CPC, speaking at the inaugural meeting, explained the steps by which the Party was planning to "throw the reactionary forces out of the National Front." [8] Against this backdrop, the struggle in Czechoslovakia grew more and more intense. Even as the Communists' tactics were being unmasked, the democratic forces were gathering strength and courage.

In November 1947, the university students' elections, always a reliable indicator of the political mood of the country, resulted in a telling 74 percent victory for democratic candidates, while the Communists garnered only 20 percent. Another and more significant sign of the political temper of the nation occurred when the Congress of the Social Democratic Party (also meeting in November) ousted Fierlinger from its leadership and pledged to pursue an independent policy. Moreover, as its true face began to be seen, the Communist Party was losing ground in general popularity, and public opinion polls as well as Party surveys predicted losses in the elections that were to take place in May 1948. It became clear that there was little hope that the Party could achieve the "51 percent" its slogan called for in the future Parliament. To the Communists, another strategy was always available, and it was soon set in motion.

The course of events leading to February 1948 is well

8. *Zasedání devíti komunistických stran: O založení informační kanceláře komunistických stran v Bělehradě* (Prague: Svoboda, n.d.), p. 113.

known. Implementing the Cominform call for class struggle, the CPC induced a series of political paroxysms. It proposed to solve the crisis in agriculture, caused by a severe drought, by imposing a levy, demagogically called the "millionaire tax," on all property exceeding the value of 1 million koruny. In fact, this tax would have affected not only the wealthy, but also the middle class in the already inflated economy. Another Communist tactic was the proposal to extend health insurance to every citizen, though the Party knew that the State treasury could not possibly carry such a burden at that time. The Party also agitated for a new, radical land reform and opened a campaign of vilification against the Slovak Democratic Party, accusing some of its leaders of treason. On the more violent side, Party functionaries sent packages containing explosives to three democratic ministers, Jan Masaryk, Petr Zenkl, and Prokop Drtina. The Communist minister of the interior intensified the process of taking over the police forces with reliable Party members. To "protect" the country against external enemies, the Party planted plots against national security and then "discovered" acts of espionage and "contacts of reactionaries with Western imperialists."

The courageous minister of justice, Prokop Drtina, unmasked the Communist police methods and traced the bomb packages to their source. Democratic leaders insisted on reinstating non-Communist police officers, branded the Communist policy irresponsible and demagogic, and rejected those Communist proposals they considered economically unfeasible. The government of national "unity," the National Front, was breaking up. Quoting from a "reliable source," Ambassador Steinhardt reported that, in a conversation with Beneš, Gottwald pointed to the increasing difficulties in assuring cooperation within the government and warned that "it might be necessary to purge non-communist parties." The president reportedly replied, "Then, I guess you will have to begin with me." [9] One wonders if Beneš remembered his earlier conversation in Moscow, when he assured Gottwald that if the Communists played their cards right, they were "sure to win."

9. National Archives, 860F. 00/11-2047.

I was in Prague during these crisis-laden days. On January 12, I spoke with President Beneš for two hours in the morning and two hours in the late afternoon. Beneš was obviously a sick man; after two strokes, he spoke with difficulty, but he was mentally alert. Though worried about international developments, he was "calm about the internal situation." "The elections will be held in the spring," he said, "Communists will lose, and rightly so. People understand their policy and will not be duped as they were in May 1946. They will lose something like 10 percent and the National Socialists and Social Democrats will gain. That will bring a just balance." He brushed aside my concern that the Communists might stage a coup to prevent an election loss, saying, "They thought of a coup in September 1947, but they abandoned the idea and will not try any more. They have found out for themselves that I enjoy a certain authority in the nation. . . . They know I have numerous supporters among the working class, even among many Communist workers. They have come to realize that they cannot go against me." He assured me that the Communists could not afford to attack him and continued, "I shall not move from my place and I shall defend our democracy till my last breath. They know it, and therefore there will be no coup. Besides that, the police are not fully in their hands. Half of them stand behind me, and the army, on the whole, is fully behind me." His parting words were, "Don't be worried. The danger of a Communist coup has passed. Return to Belgrade and carry on." These were his last words to me, at this, my last audience.

The fast-moving events during the first two months of 1948 centered around the fundamental problem of defending freedom by democratic methods against the combined forces of cajolery, threat, and violence. The democratic leaders decided to concentrate on the police issue, believing that an attack on Communist police practices would find a sympathetic response among the population and that on this question they would also be supported by the Social Democrats. At a meeting of the Council of Ministers, Drtina submitted a detailed report on police abuses. It was decided to establish an investigation commission and, meanwhile, have the minister of the interior reinstate the ousted police officers.

These decisions were never implemented. The Communists moved immediately to the well-tested strategy of intimidation and violence. In a massive counteroffensive, democratic leaders were branded as reactionaries; weapons were secretly distributed among former militia men; and the trade unions, unified and under Communist control, were mobilized for a meeting that would demand immediate, radical socialization. Antonín Zápotocký, the chairman, threatened, "If the Parliament does not fulfill the program of the trade unions, away with it!" [10] The confrontation was on.

Facing an implacable foe, the democratic leaders still put their trust in constitutional procedures. With the government paralyzed and the Cabinet unable even to convene, twelve democratic ministers submitted their resignations. Their expectation was, of course, that the resignations would not be accepted, that the president would ask the government to continue in office in a caretaker capacity, that the National Assembly would be dissolved, and that elections would forthwith be held. They also expected the democratic parties to gain in votes as the polls had predicted. It was the decent procedure of decent men in such a situation, but the tragic weakness of such a process is that the enemy often is not burdened with any such regard for decency.

To this day, the role of President Beneš in this crisis is not entirely known. According to most sources, he approved the plan, including the resignation of the ministers, and further, had urged the democratic leaders to stay firm, assuring them of his own resolute stand against Communist pressures. But the pressures mounted. Thousands of prearranged telegrams were sent to Beneš by local trade unions, urging him to oust the reactionaries from the government. Scores of workers' delegations called on him at his official residence. Gottwald saw him on several occasions and proposed the formation of a new government consisting of a reconstituted National Front. The Trade Unions Congress of 8,000 hand-picked delegates carried a threatening resolution

10. "Recollections and Reconstruction of the Czechoslovak February Crisis by a Group of Democratic Leaders" (in Czech; unpublished and untitled), stenographic report, London, 1949–1950; meeting, November 26, 1949.

with only ten lonely dissenting votes. Two and a half million workers staged a one-hour strike. The printers of some democratic papers stayed away from their jobs, and workers in the paper mills declined to deliver newsprint to these same papers.

Then, the militia was concentrated in Prague and sent to occupy key positions around the city. In his capacity as prime minister, Gottwald sent an order to the police, the national security guard, and the army, declaring a state of emergency. Public buildings were occupied; the headquarters of the National Socialist Party were searched; and numerous people were arrested. Democratic ministers were forbidden to enter their offices. A few military units, which were under the command of reliable officers, were put on alert. Action committees were set up all over the country, in factories and offices, in villages and towns, locally and nationally. The Communist Party was ready for action.

Threats were directed against democratic leaders who, for the most part, sat quietly in their private residences in the expectation that the president of the Republic would proceed, as agreed, along constitutional lines. Then, an ominous international dimension was added to the crisis. Valerian Zorin, the Soviet deputy foreign minister and a former ambassador to Czechoslovakia, appeared suddenly in Prague and contacted several democratic ministers. He tailored his remarks carefully to fit the individual listener, but on at least two occasions, he characterized the government crisis as "intolerable." He made it clear that the Soviet Union, indeed, would "not tolerate it," and added that "this time, Moscow will remain firm." A *Pravda* article gave indirect public support to Zorin's confidential statement by condemning "foreign reactionaries," at the same time praising the irresistible authority of the Communist Party of Czechoslovakia.

The Crisis:
Beneš in Focus

The focus of the drama, however, was President Beneš. As it had been at the time of Munich ten years before, his was the decision whether to resist—this time, the Communists—and possibly plunge his country into a civil war, or to submit, and open the gates to the dictatorship of one party. Gottwald then tightened the noose around Beneš's political neck. With mob activity increasing, Gottwald assured himself of the cooperation of one defector from the National Socialist Party and one from the Catholic Party. Most importantly, the Social Democratic Party, torn to shreds by intraparty conflict, joined forces with the Communists after Gottwald delivered a threat to them, "If you do not march with us, you will be liquidated the same as the others." With this alignment, Gottwald was in a position to impress Beneš with the demand that he accept the resignations of the twelve democratic ministers and nominate a new government of the National Front which, he assured Beneš, the Parliament would approve.

The president still resisted. In a conversation with four ministers, all members of the National Socialist Party and all his devoted political friends, Beneš declared, "I shall not give up. I said to Gottwald clearly, 'What you are doing is a state coup, a *putsch,* but I will not be pushed around'; I told him flatly, 'What you prepare is a second Munich.' " In rejecting Gottwald's proposal for an ersatz government, he told the visitors that he had refused to "accept this kind of majority, achieved artificially by intimidation and by the deliberate disintegration of the present political parties," and had charged Gottwald with the task of proceeding "in a strictly constitutional and democratic manner." His last words to the democratic leaders were, "I repeat what I have told you. I will act as I did in September 1938. I shall not give up, be sure of that." [11] The day was February 23; it was the ministers' last meeting with Beneš. They did not see him again.

The president's words in that final interview, his references to "constitutional" procedures, to Munich, had a strange quality of contradiction, of unreality. He knew that the Communists would not proceed in a "strictly constitutional and democratic manner" in their thrust for exclusive power. Perhaps—and his bewildering invocation of the ghost of Munich even as he stressed his determina-

11. Korbel, *Communist Subversion,* pp. 229, 230.

tion not to give up signals the possibility—he still believed himself to be (as he insisted he had been at Munich) the master of the situation, that his authority and his ability would be enough.

The life-long humanist did continue the struggle. During the night of February 24, he wrote to Gottwald, "You know my deep democratic convictions. I cannot but remain faithful to them at this moment, since, in my opinion, democracy is the only solid and permanent basis for human life and honesty and dignity." Believing that socialism and liberty must always march together, he appealed to Gottwald to seek a durable cooperation with all other parties. At the end, he expressed his belief that a "reasonable agreement" must be possible because it was "absolutely necessary." The Politburo flatly rejected Beneš's appeal and, once again, the battle was lost.

On the morning of February 25, Gottwald presented a list of members for a new government to the president. One-half of its members were Communists; three belonged to the Social Democratic Party (all Fierlinger-made fellow travelers); four had betrayed their own National Socialist or Catholic parties; and in Slovakia, one each had defected from the Democratic and Freedom parties. And one was—Jan Masaryk. One can speculate that this democrat, westerner, and by the Communists' own assessment, a reactionary, joined the government only at Beneš's personal request. At 4:00 P.M. on February 25, the president confirmed the new government. One sentence, addressed to the newly appointed ministers, said it all, "The state must be administered and led." Values, ideals, conscience, decency, history were to be replaced by an apparatus, by workable machinery.

Gottwald announced the victory to a wild crowd gathered in the historic square of St. Wenceslaus. The temperature was below zero; heavy clouds hung over the city; dusk enveloped the shivering multitudes. Nature provided an atmosphere reminiscent of the German occupation of Prague. There was one depressing difference: this time, the enemy came from within, not from without. More depressing, perhaps, were the similarities. One man, trusting too much in his own abilities, trusting too little in the historical values of his nation—values that still lived in the hearts of great multitudes of the people—more determined to ensure the nation's physical than its spiritual survival, was the instrument of both deaths. But he alone was not to blame. Many a Czech and Slovak leader must share the responsibility for the ignoble events of Munich, but in 1948, many Czechs and Slovaks, fascinated by the Communist propaganda, participated actively in the liquidation of democracy in their country.

It is not, however, the motives of the enemies of democracy that are bewildering, but rather, those of its friends (and Beneš was certainly one of these). The Gottwalds of the world are as easy to understand as the Hitlers, but it is difficult to comprehend the behavior of democratic men and women in the presence of such figures.

Except that democracy is founded upon trust, why are assurances by men such as Gottwald trusted so much and for so long?

Except that democracy is based on the principles of tolerance and respect, why are these qualities extended to men who represent the very negation of these principles?

Except that violence and force are corrosive to every system of peaceful order and justice, why are such weapons so often and for so long the exclusive property of the totalitarian?

Until there are compelling answers to those questions, there can never be any satisfying explanation to the riddle of Beneš's behavior at Munich or during the Communist coup of 1948.

For indeed, if democratic leadership—which, after all, is representative of the wish of the majority of the populace—cannot devise the weapons necessary to withstand the unscrupulous, the uncivil methods of the minority, then the democratic cause is forever lost.

To T. G. Masaryk there was in such defense, including—when it was required—resort to violence, the very practice of ethics. In the presence of malevolent evil, intent on the violation of human freedom, his "old hands" would take up the brick and hurl it at the aggressor.

Admittedly, in 1948 the situation was not simple, and the dividing line between acceptable and unacceptable behavior was exceedingly thin. The entrance of the Communist Party into the postwar coalition government was the seemingly inevitable result of the overpowering presence of Soviet armed forces in the area and Moscow's equally overpowering political influence. In addition, the coalition had already been agreed to by Beneš in Moscow, since he was rightly aware of the significance of the role the Communists would play in the postwar reconstruction of his country.

There is then no moral justification to oppose, save in the arena of politics, the presence of the Communist Party in this postwar government. But it should have been evident from the beginning that at some moment the Communist Party would inevitably move from the legitimate processes of democratic behavior into those that by infiltration and subversion would make possible the "takeover" that the ballot, the legitimate expressions of the public will, denied to them.

The cardinal problem then was to identify that moment, to sense the watershed of action that divides democratic from totalitarian behavior, and to move at once with whatever resolution, whatever force is required, to stem the gathering violence that as Lenin himself put it, is "unrestricted by law."

In retrospect, that moment is probably more apparent than it was at the time. But when the systematic infiltration of the critical government areas—the police and the army—began and with the Communists seizing control of the trade unions—the storm warnings were up, the deluge was on its way. Beneš was not naive. He must have seen these warnings, and he as well as the other democratic leaders should have moved with resolution and with whatever weaponry was needed.

But they did not. On one hand their democratic decency was paralyzing; on the other, the risks of Soviet response were once again more real to Beneš than were the democratic values for the sake of which the risks should have been taken.

Chapter Ten

Years of Shame, The Stalinist Years 1948-1962

If by now any sort of thesis has emerged from what has been written here, it should go something like this:

———that there remains in the national tradition of Czechoslovaks a kind of ethnic memory of a former idealism and heroism which, like seeds, lie dormant in the soil, but which, given a bit of the sun of tranquillity, flowers into a passion for freedom and social justice unusual in kind and degree in all of Eastern Europe;

———that there also remains a conditioned reflex for survival, nurtured carefully during 300 years of oppression, in which every trick of cautious advance and hasty retreat has been carefully explored and well learned;

———that when this passion for freedom and social justice, and the will to survive are suddenly opposed in separate and conflicting orbits of events, survival becomes the first law.

No period of time in history of twentieth-century Czechoslovakia so dramatically and shamefully proclaims the truth of that

last statement than do the "Stalinist years," from 1948 to 1962—
fourteen years during which, with a few exceptions, there was a
total negation of personal freedom and social justice.

Politics

After the Communist takeover in February 1948, events followed
a path predictable from the experience of other countries in Eastern and Central Europe. Thousands of people were thrown out of
their jobs; hundreds were arrested; and thousands more fled the
country, among them many politicians of the democratic parties.
According to indices that came to light during investigations carried
on in 1968, Jan Masaryk was murdered by Soviet agents. The
elections, held in May 1948, with, of course, only one slate offered—that of the National Front, by then under the complete
control of the Communist Party of Czechoslovakia—resulted in the
faimiliar "victory" (86.01 percent). In subsequent elections, the
Party's "popularity" grew to an incredible 99.9 percent of the
vote.

President Beneš retired to his private residence in southern
Bohemia and made only one public appearance, on the occasion
of the six-hundredth anniversary of Charles University. There, he
evoked the old themes of "truth, freedom, and morality." Declin-
ing to sign the new Constitution, he resigned in June, and he died
three months later.

The new Constitution bore a faint resemblance to Western
constitutional principles. Separation of powers was recognized,
human rights guaranteed, a limited private ownership assured.
However, one important qualification constrained these rights and
freedoms: every citizen had the obligation to "observe in all of his
actions the interests of the state." The definition of those interests
was left to the Communist Party.

By May 1949, the Party had 2.3 million members and
embraced one-third of the adult population—most of them opportunists and careerists—a sad commentary on the moral fiber of the
nation. Had the Party principle of "democratic centralism" been

allowed any pragmatic meaning, the mass membership could have exercised at least some influence over its policies. In fact, the delegates to Party Congresses were hand-picked, and the members of the Central Committee were chosen by the Politburo, consisting in 1949 of twenty-two members. The leadership proudly proclaimed that all decisions of the Party were carried unanimously, failing somehow to understand that this very fact signified an utter degradation of the human mind. The country was not a "people's democracy," as it continued to be officially designated, nor was it even a "dictatorship of the proletariat"; rather, it was a self-perpetuating oligarchy.

The special "Czechoslovak road to socialism" was soon forgotten, replaced by the Soviet model publicly proclaimed by the Party. A vigorous campaign against religion obliterated Zápotocký's apotheosis of "the mystical magic, the secrets, and miracles, enobling the whole Christian mind." The Stalin "cult" was pushed to extremes and even extended (on a minor scale, of course) to Gottwald himself. The terrorism of the police knew no barriers, not even that of Party membership. During the early 1950s, a massive wave of purges swept across Party ranks, engulfing even its principals, such as the Party secretary-general, Rudolf Slánský, and Vlado Clementis, the minister of foreign affairs. As in Moscow, the purge took the Nazi character of anti-Semitism, as many of the accused were branded zionists. Later, in the spring of 1968, Karol Bacílek, minister of security, who had been in charge of the trials, stated, in trying to defend himself, that he acted on Moscows orders. Most shamefully, the decapitation of some accused "traitors" was preceded by massive demands for their execution, including even an appeal from a son asking for a death sentence for his father!

In February 1956, the Twentieth Congress of the Communist Party of the Soviet Union proclaimed the equality of all Communist parties and the right of each country to follow its own path to socialism; it also announced, in a secret session, the official denigration of Stalin. Strangely, neither of these momentous pronouncements created a ripple in Czechoslovakia, except among lower levels of the Party. In the spring of 1956, the first rumblings among the intelligentsia, noticeable in all Communist states, found an echo among university students and writers in Czechoslovakia, but the culminating explosions in Poland and Hungary in the fall of that year only convinced the CPC of the correctness of its Stalinist policy. Every repressive step was taken in the name of "socialist legality."

Four dreary years later, in July 1960, a new Constitution ushered the country into an era of "higher" socialist development. Accordingly, since "socialism had won," its victory was reflected in the country's new official name: the Czechoslovak Socialist Republic. In the Constitution, the Communist Party was designated the "vanguard of the working class"; the sections of the 1948 document guaranteeing the rights to private ownership, freedom of association, and creative work and scientific research were omitted; political rights and the judicial process were subjugated to the "interests of the state and working people" and the protection of the "socialist state." In fact, what had been in practice since 1948 was legalized in 1960, under the banner of gathering forces for the "transition to communism." In fact, the transition took the country in a direction entirely opposite to Marx's goal of a classless, self-administering society of truly free men. However, even those Party members who had read (or heard of) Marx did not seem much concerned.

The press was to lead the people along the socialist path, and all citizens were to be educated in "loyalty to the cause of socialism." It was a cruel twist. A country which for a century had sought in education not only a realization of its inherent values, but had also used it as an instrument of national salvation, now found, in the socialization of that same education, cultural insult added to political injury. After a slow start at reform in the late 1940s, the Soviet school system was slavishly copied. With it, the quality of education, loaded as it was with obligatory courses in Marxism-Leninism, suffered greatly, but even this violation of an almost sacred Czechoslovak institution—the schools—created no significant outcry. Freedom lay deep in the earth now. Nothing stirred. The need for rapid industrialization led to particular emphasis on the technical sciences, while social sciences and the humanities were neglected or, as in the case of sociology, entirely eliminated. As it was officially proclaimed, the working class was to produce its own intelligentsia.

Culture

By 1950, the concept of "socialist realism" had been established in literature and the fine arts, and men of arts and letters were given the opportunity to create according to its dictates. Contact with the literature and science of Western countries was entirely suppressed. On the other hand, Soviet newspapers and books (especially translations of works by Lenin and Stalin) were available in great quantities and for low prices. In spite of some brief relaxations in 1953 and 1956, a dismal cultural uniformity prevailed throughout the "Stalinist" years.

History was sacrificed on the altar of Stalinist interpretation, which was redundant with ideology and burdened with blatant falsehood. The origin of Czechoslovakia was no longer attributed to the machinations of Western imperialism, nor was it the product of Versailles capitalism, as Communist agitators and writers had asserted after World War I. The "legend" that the country's independence resulted from the efforts of Wilson and Masaryk was unmasked, since, in fact, Western imperialists were against the idea of freedom for Czechoslovakia, and Wilson served the war goals of Wall Street. In the 1950s, the "truth" was, according to the Party's principal ideologist, Václav Kopecký, that "without the Soviet October of 1917, there would have been no Czechoslovak October of 1918." He admitted with brutal frankness that, since historical events were interpreted "according to who writes the history," Communists now possessed the pen and were writing the nation's history "from the point of view of . . . class truth." [1]

As we shall see, the "class truth" of the 1950s not only differed from that of the 1920s, it changed again in the 1960s. Since the young generations of the Stalinist period had no access to

1. Václav Kopecký, *Tridsať rokov ČSR* (Bratislava: Poverenictvo informacií, 1948), p. 6.

sources of information other than those approved by the Party, the consequences of such scholarship in the field of education were nothing short of catastrophic, and the Party, aware of the power of indoctrination, made full use of these channels.

At a superficial glance, Communist sources offer an impressive picture of the quantitative growth of education and culture in Czechoslovakia. One of them supplies comparisons between the years 1936 and 1955: for example, the number of classes in general education increased by 2,000; the number of students in vocational schools doubled and at universities, tripled; of these, less than one-third in 1936, but more than-one half in 1955, were in technical-training programs—a sign of the forced decline in liberal arts. Therefore, the number of institutions of higher learning specializing in technical subjects more than doubled, and the number of students in technical programs more than quadrupled between 1936 and 1955. By 1955, there were 370.8 university students for every 100,000 citizens, a ratio that substantially surpassed that of many West European countries. In cultural terms, over the twenty-year period, the number of repertory theaters increased by eighteen, and the number of plays presented and their audiences both doubled. The number of cinema houses also doubled, as did the number of their performances and audiences. However, the number of books published declined: in 1937, 6,490 books of a wide variety were published, while in 1955, there were only 4,399 new titles, of which 656 were classified as fiction, 527 were in the technical sciences, and 105 were Marxist-Leninist works; at the same time, the number of volumes and patrons in public libraries almost doubled. These glittering statistics cannot conceal the leaden core of the purpose of the educational and cultural effort: an ideological *Gleichschaltung.*

How could this nation sink to such a depth of spiritual degradation? To say that the country was under Soviet control, that the Communist leadership effectively emulated Stalin's iron politics of suppression, even after his death, suggests only a partial answer. Some other, not altogether reprehensible, reasons may be offered. It should be remembered that Masaryk himself was fearful of the Czechoslovak reaction to adversity unless time for growth and maturation, a "changing of the generations," could take place in an atmosphere of peace. Anything but peace had been the Czechoslovaks' fate, as they suffered first, betrayal, invasion, occupation, persecution and death in time of war, and then, oppression, subversion, domination and death in time of "peace." There may have been something of a catatonic retreat from reality, from old values and former passions under the weight of this final fear of Czech betraying Czech, Slovak betraying Slovak, in communism's familiar exercise of "the higher good." Still, to understand is not to excuse, and with the exception of a few intellectuals, the Czechoslovak people cannot freely escape their own portion of accountability. Their facility at adjustment, though frequently dictated by the necessity of sheer survival, was often motivated by self-interest. This time, they more than "bent their moral spines"; they seemed to give tacit but servile approval to freedom's blight, while subsequent events testified to their widespread discontent. They joined the Party in unprecedented numbers and gave it an overwhelming mandate at the polls. Not by the leadership alone, this time, but by far too many of the people, freedom was passed over for subsistence, and social justice became a dimly remembered phrase.

The Situation
in Slovakia

Slovakia did not escape the erosion of the Stalinist years. Indeed, she experienced, in addition, the gradual abolition of her autonomy. The overwhelming victory of the Democratic Party in the 1946 elections served as a signal to the Communist Party that the "reactionary" Slovaks were to be watched, that real autonomy might enable them to elude Party control and subvert Soviet-modeled socialist goals. After all, in August 1948, Slovaks—warier by far of Communist snares than were the Czechs—constituted only 12.3 percent of the total membership of the CPC, and even as late as 1958, only 14 percent. Step by step, the rights invested in the Slovak National Council and Board of Commissioners during the period between 1945 and 1948 were taken away. The Constitution of 1948 reduced the National Council, originally endowed with considerable legislative power, to being a formal body that met rarely, usually only to commemorate historical events. The Board of Commissioners, originally an influential executive organ appointed by the National Council, was made a mere transmission belt for the directives of the central government and was appointed by Prague.

Even the Slovak Communist Party failed the test of reliability. Though preserved as a regional tool, it was united with the Communist Party of Czechoslovakia in September 1948 and subjected to its policy and discipline. Sharing with the Czechs the bitterness of general oppression, the Slovaks had additional cause for discontent. They were deprived not only of an autonomous status, but even of the very symbols of their national identity—and by none other than the centralist Communist Party, once a pillar of Slovak national rights.

In matters of economy, however, Slovakia received preferential treatment. In the expectation that the nation would find compensation for its political losses in substantial economic growth, the CPC channelled considerable industrial investment into Slovakia. According to official sources, while industrial growth in the Czech lands in 1964 was four times higher than in 1948, in Slovakia it had increased more than six times. In 1937, Slovaks shared only 13.4 percent of the total national income; in 1950, the percentage was 21.9, and per capita income had more than doubled, approaching the level of the Czech lands, while in 1937, it had been lower by half. This encouraging economic experience produced a political backlash. The industrialization of Slovakia only intensified the nationalistic feelings of its people. The Marxist formula, that a people can be freed from bourgeois nationalism by making them a nation of free producers, went somewhat wrong: socialist production only heightened Slovak nationalism.

Socioeconomic
Changes

If, then, political uniformity and repression deprive a people of personal freedom one has a right to know the price—whether this loss is to be compensated by an equitable distribution of national wealth. Before the socialization of its economy began, Czechoslovakia had been an industrialized nation, and some interested Western social scientists and politicians followed her new, socialist economic development closely. In contrast to the Soviet Union and other economically backward countries, Czechoslovakia provided a testing ground for a command economy system in a country with a high level of development. The results of the new system were mixed.

Though the 1948 Constitution guaranteed private ownership of land up to fifty hectares and of industries up to fifty employees, these legal assurances were quickly disposed of. Besides the 10 percent of arable land organized by 1953 into state farms, the government created four types of cooperatives, of which the two "higher" types resembled collective farms. By 1960, over 90 percent of the land had been collectivized. This result was achieved by persecuting the kulaks and a not-so-subtle "persuading" small farmers. Individual farmers were subjected to discrimination in the allocation of machinery, in orders to produce less profitable crops, in delivery quotas about 10 percent higher than those for cooperatives, and in the reduction of rations. If they failed to follow any of these directives, their land was turned into cooperatives, or they joined them "voluntarily."

Similar methods were applied to industry. After a brief spell of experimentation (1948–50), during which a mixed economy still required market determinants and some flexibility, a rigid command economy was introduced, featuring centralized planning, controls, and pricing. Heavy industry was given preference over light industry and agriculture, without adequate regard for the country's limited supply of raw materials. The process of nationalization was so rapid that, by 1949, all but 4 percent of the labor force was employed in state enterprises; wholesale business and foreign trade were wholly nationalized; and retail businesses in private hands were reduced to a negligible proportion (.03 percent by 1959) of the total retail trade. Foreign trade, the lifeblood of the Czechoslovak economy, was reoriented from West to East; in 1937, only 16.3 percent of the foreign trade was with the East, while in 1953, it had reached 78.5 percent—with all the attendant consequences of difficult adjustments, the loss of highly developed Western technology, and an unbalanced economy. As a publication by a Communist scholar in the subsequent period of liberalization characterized the situation, the economy was marked by a lack of "critical evaluation of individual measures of economic policy," by "subjectivism . . . a conviction of the omnipotence of directives and authoritarian decisions from the center," and by a "sectarian attitude toward the intelligentsia. . . ."

The structural changes in every sector of the economy were of such revolutionary magnitude that losses in values were inevitable. These losses were compounded by rigid centralized instructions, unrealistic targets in most heavy industries, overbureaucratization, and a lack of competence in key positions. During the mid-1960s, for example, almost one-half of all industrial directors and deputy directors down to foremen were not qualified for their positions, though this situation improved as time went on. Membership in the Party, not knowledge or experience, was the decisive criterion for appointment.

Agricultural production suffered even more than industrial production. Though the planned agricultural targets were set at a lower level than industrial goals, in 1959 the real achievement was still below the prewar level; it began to rise in 1963. The causes of this discouraging picture lay in the substantial decrease in the labor force and the lack of personal interest in production on the part of collectivized farmers.

In spite of all these difficulties, the rate of Czechoslovak economic growth was remarkable. Interpreting masses of figures that are either not reliable or are computed according to different theoretical constructs is a risky business, but the general consensus of economists supports this conclusion. Taking 1948 as a base year, the GNP had doubled by 1957 and tripled by 1966; industrial production was 2.7 percent higher in 1957 and 5.1 percent higher in 1966. Personal consumption, however, rose by only 1.7 percent and 2.4 percent respectively. This disparity between the rate of growth in the GNP and in personal consumption is indicative of a high labor effort on one hand and low labor reward on the other—a depressing phenomenon in an economy that advocates just compensation. By 1958, the discrepancy was alleviated, and then it leveled off.

The restructuring of the economic system along the lines briefly described implied, of course, profound changes in employment categories. A few figures tell the story. In 1930, 64.1 percent of the population lived on salaries and wages; in 1950, the percentage had risen to 72.8; in 1961, to 84.2; and in 1969, to 87.9. The peasantry, which in 1930 represented 22.2 percent of the population, dropped in 1950 to 20.3 percent; in 1961, to 3.5 percent; and in 1969, to 2.2 percent. The percentage of collective farmers (members of cooperatives) rose from zero in 1930 to 10.6 percent in 1961 and dropped slightly in 1969 to 8.3 percent. The category of capitalists (as defined by the Communists) included in 1930 only 5.5 percent of the population; in 1950 it dropped to 3.1 percent, and from 1960 on was altogether eliminated. These figures indicate a tremendous shift from self-employment to salary and wage dependency—a radical social change indeed, and from a socialist point of view, logical.

Whether or not this social change also brought social justice is an entirely different question. From the outset this goal was tainted by compulsion and drastic measures. Farmers, tradesmen, and other self-employed individuals were exposed to discriminatory policies; if they resisted, they were accused of being reactionaries and enemies of the people; their property was confiscated, and they were denied health services. Pensioners who held important positions in the old bourgeois regime were denied pensions and ration cards. Children of bourgeois families suffered from the guilt of their parentage and were denied admission to university studies. On the other hand, students with worker family backgrounds were given preferential treatment, sometimes without regard for their qualifications, and children of Party members sat on top of this pyramid of "social justice" in education.

In June 1953, a currency reform contributed materially to the process of equalizing the nation's material existence, and it affected all strata of the population, in a complete misinterpretation of any concept of social justice. All savings from the pre-1945 period, already diminished by measures taken in November 1945, were now entirely wiped out, and post-1945 savings were converted into the new currency, reducing them progressively according to their amount. This measure affected not only the remnants of the bourgeoisie, but also a large segment of the skilled labor force, and it became the main cause of workers' demonstrations in Plzeň and elsewhere. In these protests, the working class, influenced by Marxist propaganda about its privileged position in a socialist society and enjoying relatively high wages, signaled its first disaffection with such a policy of "social justice."

National insurance practice comprised another discrepancy between social change and social justice. Theoretically, national insurance was based on the principles of universality and equality, providing all citizens with protection from the cradle to the grave. During the first years of the socialist order, it became a political weapon. Insurance benefits differed according to type of employment, whether in agriculture, industry, services, or self-employment. In the last category, many were excluded from any benefits at all.

Though the science of medicine achieved respectable levels in numerous research institutes, the practice of medicine suffered, sharing with industry the experience of low-quality output. In 1958, according to Communist sources, since a doctor saw 50 to 100 patients a day, frequently in groups, the average time devoted to each patient was five to seven minutes. On the other hand, the number of physicians grew: in 1937, there was one doctor for every 1,236 persons; by 1955, the ratio was around one doctor for every 600 persons. About the same improvement was recorded for the number of hospital beds—from 3.3 to 7.7 per 1,000 inhabitants—during the same period. Socialized medicine was considered a significant step forward in social justice, but its quality suffered greatly from weakened social and professional ethics. Moreover, the national insurance encouraged absenteeism. In 1954, for example, 80 million working days were missed, as an average of 220,000 workers failed daily to report to work because of illness. In 1956, the figure for disabled workers had risen to 228,000 daily, and in 1958, to 270,000. This experience necessitated an amendment to the National Insurance Act, whereby the benefits for the first three days of illness were lowered.

The new policies brought substantial progress in the status and employment of women, though women remained short of equality with men. The initial step forward was related to enlarged educational opportunities. In 1961, for example, in the age category between twenty and twenty-four, the numbers of women and men with a university education were almost equal, whereas in the age group between twenty-five and thirty-four, the ratio was one to three. As to employment of women with higher education, the number of women in the labor force increased between 1948 and 1963 more than four times, representing in 1963 more than two-thirds of all employees, while the proportion in 1948 had been only one-sixth. In positions that required a secondary school education, women comprised an overwhelming majority at all times. Their earnings, however, indicated there was not more equality under socialist than under capitalist practices: women earned only two-thirds of the salaries of men in equivalent positions.

Another aspect of the process of socialization was concerned with narrowing the gap between the incomes of white-collar and blue-collar workers. While the salaries of the latter were, on the average, two and one-half times lower before the war, the difference was reduced by 1948 to one and one-third. However, industrial workers' wages varied considerably, with miners and metal industry workers at the top and food industry workers at the bottom. By the middle 1950s, the government's effort toward equalizing individual incomes proved economically and socially counterproductive, a situation which compelled the policy planners to reform the scales and differentials of income. The salaries of technical personnel went up, but those of administrators dropped below the level of workers' wages. By 1965, leading managers in the engineering field topped the list of categories in earnings, followed by skilled miners and head doctors in regional hospitals. A doctor-practitioner was about halfway down the list; a lawyer twenty points below the physician, and a secondary school teacher slightly below him. A hospital nurse earned about one-fourth of the leading engineer's salary, and a practical nurse was at the bottom of the scale, making about one-sixth of the top category salary.

The scale was obviously far removed from the earlier attempt to level off individual income; it reflected the Party's position on the relative usefulness of various professions to a socialist society, and it reveals some striking discrepancies. These were only deepened by the high earnings of military officers, members of the secret police, and Party functionaries. Though these salaries were not made public, they were generally thought to reach or surpass the top levels of the scale. The same was true of the salaries of intellectuals and artists who were willing to serve the Party's ideological interests.

The horizontal change, from self-employment to salary-wage positions, was complemented by a vertical movement, from lower to higher categories of employment, with an increasing number of technical and public service personnel. This trend, triggered by technological progress and the bureaucratization of the economy, gave the Party an opportunity to put its reliable members into positions of responsibility. As a consequence of this policy, close to 500,000 positions that should have required either secondary or college education (one-third of this work category) were occupied by people who lacked adequate schooling.

The upward trend in employment, combined with the differentials in earnings, increased the number of people who stepped from the proletariat into the "middle class" in terms of earnings. In 1937, only 20 percent of all income recipients were considered to have middle incomes, while the majority of the population was in the low income bracket. By 1967, the middle income category had risen to 47 percent, and in 1968, to 62 percent of income recipients. This was a praiseworthy accomplishment in terms of raising the standard of living and narrowing social discrepancies. Considering the ideologically motivated advances in income and position, however, it also encouraged the creation of a "new class," endowed with extraordinary power and great material privileges. It is thought that in a country of 14 million inhabitants, the positions of power in direct control of production were in the hands of less than 1.5 percent of the population.

One category of the society requires special mention: the pensioners, who by 1968 represented one-fifth of the population, as women were obliged to retire at the age of fifty-five and men at the age of sixty. Apparently, social justice was not applicable to the aging, who were of no further use to socialist production. While in 1937, retirement benefits amounted to 32.3 percent of average earnings, they had dropped in 1948 to 28.1 percent, and remained in 1968 at 2.1 percent below the prewar level. In terms of real income, workers' pensions had almost doubled in 1946 (in comparison to 1937), but the pensions of all other employees dropped by one-half. Twenty years later, 93.5 percent of pensioners' households belonged to the two lowest categories of income, while 6.5 percent enjoyed incomes in the two highest categories of earnings.[2]

Such, then, was the Czechoslovak experience during the "Stalinist" years. If social justice can be defined as the evening out of national wealth among all members of the population, then it might be argued that the Czechoslovak passion for social justice had never burned brighter than during these dismal years. But such nonsense will not do.

An equitable distribution (which is a far cry from an "averaging out") of a nation's wealth is possible, not only by definition, but by experiential evidence, only in a democratic society in which the people share the responsibility for that equity. Even then, an equitable distribution is of little value if it is viewed as an end in itself, rather than as a means of achieving social justice in its true sense: the opportunity for each citizen to find the satisfaction of self-fulfillment, to make choices among real alternatives, to develop voluntarily his social consciousness, to make willingly an ethical commitment to his society and to himself, and to discover and be able to act in a personally rewarding life style.

None of these attributes can develop in a closed society; none can be "made to order" by the fiat of any economic or political system. The reality of social justice can only grow—and then

2. This analysis is based primarily on a careful scholarly study by Jaroslav Krejčí, *Social Change and Stratification in Postwar Czechoslovakia* (New York: Columbia University Press, 1972), pp. 39–156.

slowly—in an environment of personal freedom. When such changes are accomplished by fiat, there is not only the inevitable sacrifice of the ultimate end of social justice—personal freedom—but also the development of an inescapable rigidity, a kind of hardening of the social arteries, that soon affects the very efficiency of the system itself. Such rigidity, as was noted, for example, in the case of rewards for labor without regard for the degree of responsibility, began to play havoc with the relatively sophisticated Czechoslovak economy.

By 1962, individuals in the scholarly community had come to realize that the country's economic growth depended on flexibility in planning, production, and marketing. This realization, in turn, generated new thinking about the true meaning of social justice and led ultimately to the conclusion that economic reform could succeed only with a parallel development in political relaxation. These thoughts ushered in a new era of liberalization of Communist Czechoslovakia.

Chapter Eleven

The Sisyphean Years
1962–1968

Despite the terrifying manipulative power of a totalitarian system, some men caught up in these systems somehow, some way, cling with a kind of desperation to enough of their moral sensibilities as to know, suddenly, that if they would remain men they have now reached the very end of compromise and surrender, that they stand now on the brink of the abyss. Such a man may have given up all but the last of his ideas, his sense of society, his meaningful work, his vision of himself, driven as he has been by his animal instinct to stay alive within this system in which one's life is daily bought with the price of one's soul.

But a spark of his humanity is still alive, and because it is he realizes that he has reached the point of no return. No longer can he anesthetize the pain of his daily surrender by movies or music or liquor or the laughter of friends. Now he must face it—the awful reality of the truth. But he must face as well the prospect of penalty and loss if his own truth is to replace that of the state as the object of his principal concern.

Perhaps it is because they know the price may well be high that it is precisely at such a moment that those who turn to the truth as an act of salvation do so with a fierce affection. It is both the tragedy and the beauty of life that suffering is so often the finest source of regeneration; that near despair may itself be the seedbed of hope.

Thus it was that in the early 1960s, the promises that once were Masaryk's Czechoslovakia lay in ashes. But beneath them glimmered the proverbial spark, the spark of ever-restless minds and of unextinguishable conscience. Now the people who had welcomed the victory of the Party in 1948 as the dawn of a new era, had to face themselves and the truth.

"Scientific socialism" was to have been the guarantee of success. Revolutionary changes in ownership of sources and means of production were to have created the basis for social equality. A planned economy was to have assured prosperity. Socialist realism was to depict the true meaning of life. A "gentle" excision of the remnants of the bourgeoisie was to have assured the safety and freedom of the socialist spirit. The Party had promised and the Party knew the truth—the single truth that was to be permitted.

During the fourteen years between 1948 and 1962, the once-enthusiastic Czechoslovak proponents of communism saw their visions fade away and were forced to realize that all they had believed in was an illusion. Nationalization had become an end in itself instead of an instrument of social justice. The rigid centralization of the economy and its consequent bureaucracy in critical areas of industrial administration and production had brought economic growth to a halt. Moreover, the dismal situation had been aggravated by the schizophrenic attitude of the Party itself. Inherent in the Communist system is a pathological distrust of everything, which produces widespread alienation within the society, and mutual estrangement between the masses and the leadership, between individuals in and outside of the Party, and between people within the Party itself. This situation existed in Czechoslovakia. As a prominent writer, Milan Kundera, subsequently put it, "Official slogans were full of joy, yet we dared not play even the slightest prank." Jean-Paul Sartre, who certainly cannot be accused of any lack of sympathy with communism, elaborated Kundera's thought when he wrote, "In the name of realism, we were forbidden to depict reality; in the name of the cult of youth, we were prevented from being young; in the name of socialist joy, joyousness was suppressed." [1] Sartre added, "The socialist idea seemed to have gone mad." The communism that was to have freed man from the fetters of capitalism, shackled him instead with the multiple chains of personal frustration, cultural starvation, economic insecurity, and social repression. It was a particularly bitter irony for Party members; they fell victim to the captivity of their own planning.

The Economy

During this dreary period of general demoralization (and perhaps born of it), thoughts of reform began to emerge. Slowly, they grew and embraced all spheres of activity. Criticisms of the Communist past generated new propositions which, in turn, grew into programs. The eventual acceptance and implementation of these programs culminated in the Czechoslovak Spring of 1968. Once again, the mind of man asserted itself over the "system," and the nation rediscovered its spirit. This is not to say, alas, that great spiritual concerns triggered the initial ripples that eventually led to the Spring.

Understandably, the necessities of daily life caused these first stirrings, which were calls for a reform in the economy. To paraphrase Lenin, the chain of proletarian solidarity broke at its weakest link. By the early 1960s, the economic situation had deteriorated to the point of crisis. Industrial growth was lower than in any other East European country; in 1963, it was below one percent. Agricultural production dropped to the 1938 level. In 1962, the third Five Year Plan, which had already been revised several times, was abandoned altogether. Exports to other Communist

---

1. Antonín J. Liehm, *The Politics of Culture* (New York: Grove Press, 1972), pp. 16, 17.

countries declined, due to the limiting regulations on trade, their own industrialization, and the growth of their trade with the West. Agricultural imports, however, increased, due to the poor performance of the domestic sector. It became clear that the rigidity of centralized planning and its controls system lay at the root of the problem.

In 1963, a few economists advanced certain carefully worded propositions to change the planning and management of the economy. Indeed, as early as 1959, some courageous but isolated scholarly studies had appeared calling for "decentralization and perfection" of the planned economy. They all began with the assumption that while the fundamentals of the socialist economy must be preserved, Stalin's model must be radically revised, if not discarded. It should be noted that these economists were all Party members (necessarily, since non-Communist economists had no opportunity to express their views), some of them in highly responsible positions. They theorized about ways and means of making the economy efficient: the creation and implementation of an economic plan more responsive to the demands of the market; the transferral of some responsibilities for industrial management from central offices to the directors of individual enterprises; the development of new methods for operating industries in a businesslike, income-expenditure related manner; and the adjustment of the rewards policy and the introduction of incentive motives in production. They wanted these reforms even at the price of eliminating dogmatism.

These criticisms and propositions were viewed with suspicion by the Communist leaders, whose rigid, Stalin-modeled minds were unreceptive to any innovative ideas, perceiving in them a threat to their entrenched positions. Nevertheless, the growing bankruptcy of continuing experiences compelled even the most reluctant Party leaders to consider alternative solutions.

In September 1964, the Party Presidium accepted a plan for a reformed economic system presented by Ota Šik, who had respectable credentials as chairman of the Scientists' Collegium of Economics at the Czechoslovak Academy of Sciences and, equally important, as a member of the Party's Central Committee. The new economic policy was to be implemented progressively, to be fully in effect by January 1966. As the reform plan was being implemented, the lingering reservations of the leadership surfaced. Antonín Novotný, the Party's secretary-general and president of the Republic, stated that the Party "certainly does not intend to let the introduction of a new system open the way to anarchy and an uncontrolled development, or weaken the role of the Plan."

The economic reformers soon realized that opposition to change was motivated not only by narrow economic concepts, but also by political considerations. As early as 1964, when the economists were formulating their theories, they were aware of the great need to effect, as Šik so very cautiously put it, "certain changes in the sphere of the organization of the superstructure of the state." His colleague, Radoslav Selucký, went even further when he wrote that the "national economy cannot do without considerable change in its political and economic organization." In 1966, the reformers knew in fact what they had only feared two years earlier— that the whole experiment in the economy would fail if it were not allowed to develop in a similarly reformed political framework. Flexibility in a socialist economy demanded at least some freedom of the socialist spirit.

Politics

Advocates of such freedom were not lacking, either in numbers or in quality. As one would expect, they came from the ranks of philosophers, sociologists, and writers. They revived the great tradition of the scholarly community, pointing new directions for the nation in a time of profound distress. Once again, humanism was the touchstone of their ideas.

The process of intellectual and political regeneration which they led was organic. They hoped to rebuild the socialist society in the image of social humanism, to create, as Alexander Dubček beautifully summed it up later, "socialism with a human face." Its strength was in its endurance, extending over a period of six years as its protagonists, in an environment of official hostility, slowly marshaled their forces, fending off the Party's periodic interventions and interdictions.

The obstacles that the reformers faced were formidable: to transform the ideology of communism as it was practiced into what they considered to be a true Marxism; to replace the Party of appointed *aparatchiki* with a democratized (not democratic) political organization; and, in the process, to overcome the opposition of a wide variety of vested interests. The proposed reforms were many and significant. Freedom of expression was not to be bestowed as a limited privilege, but guaranteed as an inalienable right; changes in the system were not to be granted as temporizing concessions, but established as respected institutions. At first, it was necessary to present these positions in the Aesopian language that a suppressed people learn to use. By 1968, however, the veil was lifted and the central ideas of what was called "democratic socialism" were expressed in the plain language of a new political, economic, cultural, and social program.

Again, less than idealistic motivations initiated the first moves by the reformers. By the end of the 1950s, the society was at a standstill. A deep chasm yawned between the people and the Party. The heavy bureaucracy thwarted constructive initiatives. A sense of purposelessness was everywhere, and over the whole scene hung the unbearable cloud of police omnipresence and omnipotence. Even after Stalin had been denigrated at the Twentieth Congress of the CPSU, and after Poland and Hungary had experienced periods of liberalization, Novotný, the CPC supreme leader, continued to pursue Stalinist policies. The people of Czechoslovakia became conscious of the fact that their painful situation was not the result of the mistakes of a few individuals, but the inevitable product of a faulty system. Change in the system itself was overdue.

At first, changes were initiated on an individual basis, in timid efforts dictated by obvious circumstances. Then, they slowly gained momentum, broadening in scope and changing in nature. What began as carefully worded propositions propounded by a few intellectuals developed into national programs. Then, it really began to happen. Under mounting pressure, the Twelfth Party Congress in December 1962 voted to investigate the political trials of the early 1950s and, as a result, the Supreme Court concluded that in many cases the proceedings had been illegal, based on forged documents and coercion.

These findings not only shook the whole societal structure, they also shattered the long-proclaimed principle of "socialist legality." They had a particularly profound effect in Slovakia, which had its own martyrs in Vlado Clementis, former minister of foreign affairs, Laco Novomeský, a popular poet and publicist, and Gustáv Husák, one of the leaders of the Slovak national uprising in August 1944. All had been accused of narrow Slovak nationalism. Clementis paid the full price for his mistakes, though Novomeský and Husák were permitted "reeducation" in a prison cell. Such "rehabilitation" triggered a wave of Slovak indignation and intensified the activities of the intellectuals.

Even though reluctantly undertaken, the processes of reform released long-suppressed intellectual forces which began to probe into all sectors of life. Open attacks on the personality cult, so far directed only against Stalin, now included Czechoslovak personalities in the Party's pantheon and came finally to encompass even the principle of the Party's infallibility. Dogmatism became another object of critical analysis; sociology and psychology were reinstated as respectable disciplines; and education underwent a vigorous reform that stressed such outrageous postulates as training in independnt thought. In May 1963, Eduard Goldstücker, newly released from political imprisonment, organized a conference on Franz Kafka who, though acclaimed throughout the world, had been on the index of his own country. Theater, films, and literature were freed from the shackles of socialist realism. Western existentialist plays were introduced, avant-garde experimentation was revived, and imports of Western literature doubled in the seven years between 1958 and 1965. Some of the best Czechoslovak films, carrying the message of humanity and the simple joy of life, found their way into Western cinema houses and received much acclaim. Novels addressing the problems of totalitarian systems, which had been hidden for years, saw the light of day at last and were published, first abroad and then in their original language.

Cultural and educational contacts with Western Europe increased rapidly. Translations of English, French, and German books grew from 1964 to 1967 by fifty-five works, while translations of Russian works dropped by sixty-five volumes. The number of foreign students attending Czechoslovak universities rose from about 1,000 in 1955 to nearly 3,500 in 1967. International cultural and scientific conferences in Prague and elsewhere were arranged, and Czechoslovak writers, scholars, and artists were permitted to attend similar events in Western Europe. Czechoslovak television stations began to broadcast some popular Western programs. Travel to Western Europe, limited in the 1950s to officials, expanded from 1958 to 1966 by more than three times and in two more years by more than seven times. Travel to Czechoslovakia rose twenty-five times between 1961 and 1966 and reached a peak in 1968. To look at the travel picture another way, in 1937, 106 out of each 1,000 Czechoslovak citizens traveled abroad; in 1949, the number had dropped to 4.5 but rose to some 40 persons per 1,000 in the early 1960s and to 148 per 1,000 by 1967, and of these, about one-fourth traveled west.

All these activities found their philosophical justification in a fresh analysis of Marxist theory. First, Stalinism was sharply criticized as a negation of true Marxism; second, Lenin's theory was stringently, though subtly, questioned; and finally, Marx himself was revised by studies that focused on his humanism, on a simplified version of the "young Marx" (which conveniently overlooked his writings on violent revolution and the dictatorship of the proletariat). The growing problem of alienation, which according to Marx was an inevitable product of a capitalism that should have disappeared in a classless society, attracted the critical attention of the neo-Marxist philosophers. They dared to point to the profound and pervasive nature of alienation in the Czechoslovak socialist society and to the obvious fact that social conflicts had not disappeared. Even in a classless society, they maintained, interest groups continue to flourish and to clash in social confrontations.

Scholarly journals in history, jurisprudence, and philosophy returned to the old concepts of the Czechoslovak philosophy of history, seeking in them the justification of their position on current problems of the country. Subtly bypassing the theory of historical materialism, they focused on ethics and intellectual attitudes as the important formative components of the nation's heritage. Studies appeared that reexamined the concept of the single party in the light of Marx's theory; they indicated the advantages of a pluralistic society and a representative government and also suggested the need to reflect on Western political developments. A jurisprudence journal defended the idea of choice among several candidates for political office, and a philosophical periodical warned against a drastic effort to "finish off" religion "quickly and easily" with threats and punitive measures. The same source was critical of the whole life ethos of communism, asserting that it was not adequate to the psychic needs of the people who, while "rationally Communists, emotionally and morally are increasingly living in the past" out of a sense of current helplessness.

This thrust for the reformulation of the underlying concepts of the Czechoslovak society gained a concentrated impetus in the Congress of the Union of Czechoslovak Writers in June 1967. Reading the speeches of the participants in that congress is a fascinating experience. The language, which had been mutilated by russisms during the Stalinist years, shines in all its richness and beauty; the themes, formulated up to then only in journals in scholarly terms, are expressed in a scintillating variety of literary styles. The lectures addressed the familiar problems of Stalinism, censorship, dehumanization, and the writer's responsibility to society, and some of them went far beyond previous criticism to accuse the Party of abuse of power.

Ludvík Vaculík, a Party member, delivered a searing analysis of the relationship between power and the rights of free citizens and, delineating the descent of the people into a state of fear, apathy, despair, and fretful concern with petty worries and futile wishes, he concluded, "I think there are no longer any free citizens left in Czechoslovakia." He attacked "the boss" (Novotný), who, while wielding unlimited power, surrounded himself with

vulgarians, whereas people who possess a "quiet and unostentatious standard of decency . . . have disappeared from public life."
In this way, he said, a link had been established between dejected
men, who are "tied together by the most miserable bonds one can
think of—common disgust." Vaculík reminded his audience of the
interwar Czechoslovakia, which "after all . . . achieved a high
level of democracy," and of the early postwar years, when there
was progress under socialism. He contrasted these periods with the
years of Stalinist communism, when "not one single human problem was solved," neither the mundane problems of housing, education, and the economy, nor the spiritual and ethical problems of
finding one's own self-fulfillment.[2] To him, these were not questions of socialism or any economic system, but of power versus
human rights and freedom.

Milan Kundera spoke of the transcendental value of literature, which under socialism must not succumb to pressure to cir-
cumscribe its content or its style. He condemned Stalinism, which
had corrupted "a great humane movement" and had turned "love
for humanity into cruelty toward people" and "love for truth into
denunciations." Still, since the "miraculous soil of art can turn suffering into spiritual wealth," Czechoslovak literature must provide,
now as in the past, through its "greatness or meanness, its courage
or cowardice, its provincialism or universality, the answer to the
question of the existence of the nation: is its survival worthwhile?" [3]

Other writers focused on a special strength in their country's history and pointed to a continuity between its unique meaning and the teachings of socialism. Jan Procházka, a member of
the Party's Central Committee, wrote most significantly, "We have
something in our tradition which, I think, our socialist brethren in
other countries have had no opportunity to experience: democracy." He continued:

I do not have in mind only those twenty years of the pre-Munich Republic, when precisely this democracy made possible—and for even the

2. Andrew Oxley et al., eds., *Czechoslovakia: The Party and the People* (New York: St.
Martin's Press, 1973), pp. 31, 33.

3. Dušan Hamšík, *Writers against Rulers* (London: Hutchinson, 1971), pp. 175, 176.

Communist Party of Czechoslovakia—a fantastic and, for the Central European situation, unprecedented growth. I have in mind also the whole period of the reawakening when the struggle for the language, for national values, was being waged hand in hand with our efforts for social progress and true civil liberty.[4]

Contrary to Communist dogma, Procházka asserted that "man has a value above revolutions and counter-revolutions."

These remarkable admissions from a Communist official testified to the intensity of the effort to think through the problems of communism in the light of the ideals of humanity. Logically and inevitably, the life and philosophy of Thomas G. Masaryk came up for reconsideration. The "back to the young Marx" idea was supplemented by a "back to the old Masaryk" movement. In 1967, Procházka considered Masaryk's work "gigantic" and found it encouraging that "nobody anymore excludes T. G. Masaryk from the nation's patriots . . . nobody alleges anymore that Edvard Beneš was an agent of imperialism. . . . T. G. Masaryk has much to say to the socialist man of today."[5] Such thoughts were by no means uncommon in this period. Two leading philosophical journals, *Filosofický časopis* and *Nová mysl,* published thought-provoking studies on socialism and humanism, neo-Marxism, Stalin's Soviet Union, and a "new concept of man"—the man of the "twentieth, not the nineteenth, century." Masaryk's rehabilitation culminated in 1968, when Communist philosophers at last accepted the basic tenet of his philosophy that "man is valuable for himself alone."

The intellectual ferment of these years was characteristic of the role of intellectuals throughout Czechoslovak history. This time, however, special significance lay in the fact that the dialogue was carried on by Communist scholars and writers whose origins, mostly of the working class, could not possibly expose them to charges of "bourgeois" mentality or counterrevolutionary intentions. On the contrary, it was their newly aroused ethical and social conscience, awakened perhaps by the cruel experience of the Sta-

4. Jan Procházka, *Politika pro každého* (Prague: Mladá fronta, n.d.), p. 190.
5. Ibid.

linist dogma—an experience that some of them had actively promoted—which impelled their humanistic thinking. Nevertheless,
the demand for reform had not yet reached the point of general
outcry. The population at large followed the developments in fascinated passivity, and from their privileged position in a socialist
society, many workers watched them with suspicion and concern.

There was one exception to the general passivity: the university students. Through their newspapers and organizations they
gave significant support to the campaign of the intellectuals. As
students, they were perhaps more aware than others of the oppressive nature of Stalinism and were also more estranged from
the official environment. When the students were polled in 1965
on the question of how many student-members had joined the
Party out of conviction, their devastating answer was only 11.3
percent. This testimony to the failure of the regime is even more
significant when one considers that it was expressed by that young
generation which had grown up in a Communist society, which
sprang from the working class, and in which Lenin had put all his
hopes. With a great deal of humor as well as clarity, Prague students, on the occasion of the traditional festival, *Majales,* carried
such provocative posters as, "Whoever cannot read or write can
always quote" and "Dare to criticize only the dead." [6] Whatever
the ultimate impact of the student movement, there is no doubt
that it contributed materially to the whole atmosphere of critical
reevaluation of the society.

Slovakia Again

At its initial stage, Slovak intellectuals stood in the forefront of the
struggle for liberation. In addition to their general concern for reform, they had their own special cause: the Slovak right to equality
with the Czechs. During the early 1960s, many Slovak voices were
raised, demanding not only the rehabilitation of the victims of
Stalinism, but also recognition of the merits of the Slovak uprising

6. Galia Golan, *The Czechoslovak Reform Movement: Communism in Crisis, 1962–1968*
(London: Cambridge University Press, 1971), p. 101, n. 2.

in 1944 and of Slovak national institutions. A law passed in May 1964 restored some authority to the Slovak National Council and to the Board of Commissioners—a mild concession intended to serve as a "maximum contribution toward strengthening the united Czechoslovak economy and further rapprochement of these brotherly nations." However, the Marxist notion that the economic progress of Slovakia was the answer to Slovak grievances was entirely false, since Slovak leaders insisted on equality in every respect. A provocative theoretical and pragmatic conflict developed between the legitimate degree of centralism in the state economy and the proper accommodation of the claims of national individuality. The fundamental question was how to reconcile the apparent contradiction of allowing an independent national entity to exist within a centrally directed economic system. Ironically, when decentralization measures were introduced in the economic reform of 1965, the Slovak economy was adversely affected. A "separate but equal" partnership in an economy in which investment, management, and marketing were based on national arguments depressed the weaker partner, since Slovakia lacked investment sources while it possessed a surplus of labor and natural resources. Even Alexander Dubček, first secretary of the Communist Party of Slovakia, voiced mild criticism of the decentralization measures.

The most significant aspect of the Slovak reformers' appeal was that, for the first time in Slovakia's struggle for national identity, recognition of these specific demands was sought within a broader context—the democratization of the whole country. In fact, the Slovaks preceded the Czechs in stressing the need for freedom of expression and for the humanization of the system. It was only in 1968 that the Slovak ranks split on the issue of whether to relate their drive for a lasting solution to the Slovak problem—federation—to overall national goals or to exploit the current favorable conditions to achieve their specific, immediate Slovak aims.

As early as May 1964, however, the editorial board of *Kulturný život,* the leading journal in Slovakia issued a statement which deplored its past uncritical position and promised a regenerated policy, an alliance with "everything that is really new, progressive, and humane." Laco Novomeský, the chairman of the editorial board, whose popularity as a poet and writer had been greatly enhanced by his imprisonment during the Stalinist period, pleaded for complete freedom of artistic and critical expression and, on one occasion in April 1966, put to the public the searching question, "What can be done with a society which is suffocating in its self-satisfaction? This is the tragedy of Soviet literature. Problems cannot be solved just by quoting Lenin instead of Stalin." [7]

Indeed, there was now no escape by such easy routes as turning from Stalin to Lenin, or by mindless memorization of lines from Marx, or by rigid dogmatism of whatever stripe. The struggle for reform had leaped the boundaries between the Slovak and Czech lands. Step by step, it had gathered strength, and the Party found itself in a state of siege.

The Party's
Counter-Reformation

Deprived of the nation's support, exposed to ideological assault, and facing the collapse of the economy, the Party—isolated from the mainstream of thought—still refused to face the reality of the crisis. Economic reforms were introduced halfheartedly and were even sabotaged at times by conservative Party stalwarts. Emphatic warnings by scholars of the inevitable failure of economic measures if they were not imbedded in political reformation were ignored. Nevertheless, the Party leadership (though it had not yet been attacked) was conscious of the potential danger to its position and to the system itself.

Novotný and his associates reacted as dictators invariably do when driven into a corner: they tried to "blow hot and cold," to retreat one way and advance another. In November 1963, during the first wave of demands for liberalization, Novotný relaxed some

---

7. Antonín J. Liehm [AJL], "Two Days with Novomeský," *Kultúmý život* (April 22, 1966), in *Research Departments of Radio Free Europe*, 1777–1811 (May 2, 1966): 4.

controls over the mass media. At the same time, he repeatedly stressed that no one was permitted to put himself above the Party or to criticize the socialist society. In the spring of 1965, the editor of the scholarly journal *Dějiny a současnost* was dismissed for ideological deviation, and the majority of the journal's editorial board resigned in protest. At the Thirteenth Congress of the CPC in the spring of 1966, Novotný lashed out at students and "liberals" who, he alleged, were influenced by foreign philosophies and were acting against socialist principles. The flood of criticism released at the writers' Congress of June 1967 was answered by the Party's ideologist, Jiří Hendrych, who accused the participants of acting against the interests of the Party and the state and ended with a threat: "We shall not leave matches in the hands of irresponsible elements and anarchists!" [8] Shortly thereafter, the "matches" were indeed removed from the writers' hands. The most outspoken literary journal, *Literární noviny,* was brought under the direct control of the Ministry of Culture and Information, whereupon most authors refused to write for it.

The Party
in Turmoil

In this atmosphere of growing tension, pressures began to mount within the Party itself, threatening its monolithic structure. Waves of purges began in April 1963, when two former members of the Politburo were deprived of Party membership and two others were dismissed from office. The revelations about the savage miscarriages of justice in the trials of the 1950s called for further dismissals. Two Slovak members of the Politburo, V. Široký and J. Ďuriš, were ejected from it in September 1963 and, together with three other high functionaries, were dismissed from their government posts as well. The fact that Novotný himself, as a member of the Politburo since 1951, had condoned the trials and, as the Party's first secretary after September 1953 and president of the

8. Hamšík, *Writers against Rulers,* p. 66.

Republic after November 1957, had been, at best, lukewarm toward efforts to investigate them, was not mentioned.

Failures in the economy caused interminable wrangling in the sessions of the Central Committee. At the Thirteenth Congress, Ota Šik criticized the Party for its dogmatism in both economics and politics and pleaded for economic flexibility and political liberalization.

On the most sensitive issue, Slovakia, Novotný responded to the Slovak leaders' calls for extended rights by accusing them of narrow nationalism. Dubček was his principal target. Though the Party leadership was obviously paralyzed and in total disarray, Novotný tried to control the situation by imposing censorship and strict Party discipline. All criticism was prohibited, and some intellectuals were reprimanded or expelled from the Party.

Inevitably, the malaise at the top levels infected the local *aparatchiki* and the rank and file membership; the first were isolated and insecure; the latter were apathetic and withdrawn. It was reported that only 30 to 40 percent of the Party members attended local meetings and that in one district in Moravia, over two-thirds of the local organization's members were over twenty-four years of age—a sign that young people preferred to stay out of the Party.

The conflicts within the Party erupted at the October 1967 session of the Central Committee, and there was no way Novotný could silence the criticism. The economy was in a shambles; the reformers were accelerating their drive for liberalization; the youth of the nation had demonstrated its dissatisfaction; the people in general were hostile to the system; and the Party itself was in the throes of a cutthroat crisis. Novotný was considered the chief culprit, and other Party leaders sought to avert disaster by stripping him of at least one of the two functions he combined as first secretary of the Party and president of the Republic. This effort proved to be only the first in a series of moves that opened the floodgates of reform.

The internecine struggle continued until the end of 1967. Fearful that their conversations might be bugged, the leaders of the opposition met in small groups in private houses, knowing that

Novotný had already prepared a list of persons who were to be arrested. As the Central Committee met toward the end of the year, it became clear to Novotný that he could no longer hold to his position. Even Leonid Brezhnev, who visited Prague in December, abstained from intervention and summed up the Soviet position in one sentence: *"Eto vashe delo* [It is your problem].*"* On January 5, 1968, Novotný resigned as .first secretary of the CPC and, under pressure, proposed as his successor none other than Alexander Dubček.

Socialism with a Human Face

Dubček's brilliant phrase, "socialism with a human face," rang throughout the free world. Eloquent in its simplicity and succinct in its meaning, it summed up the program of the Marxist reformers: to preserve the egalitarian principles of socialism and, at the same time, to imbue the society with the values of humanism. The phrase must have been immediately offensive to Moscow and the other Communist capitals, with its implication of contradistinction from their "dehumanized" socialism.

Dubček possessed all the credentials of a dedicated Communist. Born in 1921 of a worker's family which, after a brief stay in the United States, had returned to its native Slovakia after World War I, Dubček moved with his father to the Soviet Union in the following year. He received a Soviet education and returned to Slovakia in 1938. He joined the ranks of the workers and of the Party and took part in the Slovak uprising in which his brother, Julius, was killed. During the postwar period, he held various positions of local Party responsibility. His potential to gain power in the Party was enhanced when he was selected to attend the Soviet Party's political institute in Moscow in 1955.

Dubček was a man eminently qualified for Party leadership—a former worker and an experienced functionary, educated and trained in the leading Communist system, ideologically reliable, dedicated to the cause, and devoted to the Soviet Union.

Also, he was a Slovak, who could speak personally of his people's justifiable grievances. It was this last attribute that brought him to the center of power, initially as first secretary of the Communist Party of Slovakia in May 1966, and then, in January 1968, as the principal officer of the entire Communist Party of Czechoslovakia.

Nothing in Dubček's earlier career had indicated either the desire or the temperament for leadership. Except for occasional skirmishes with Novotný over the state economy and the Slovak question (which were not known to the public at that time), he abstained from participation in the public debate about reform and liberalization. He tended quietly to Slovak Party affairs and was hardly known in wider circles. His unpretentious way of life, his neat attire (including the rather old-fashioned, formal vest), his modest and quiet manner—all conveyed the impression of an accountant in a solid, conservative bank, not the image of a revolutionary.

Nevertheless, though outwardly cautious, he cultivated contacts with Slovak intellectuals and slowly absorbed their reformist thought. He was sufficiently sensitive to be conscious of the cruelty of dogmatism and was ready, therefore, to accept the idea of a pragmatic and more humane socialism. He was catapulted into a position of central power without struggling for it, emerging as the leader by the choice of others and, in fact, as a compromise candidate. Little did he know on that day in January how far the dynamics of the events would take him—that he would come to be both the symbol and the principal defender of his own "socialism with a human face." Once impelled into national power, Dubček did not hesitate to contribute his own ideas to new programs and to provide inspiring leadership.

The Spring

The dramatic changes in national leadership had a fundamental impact on the nature and scope of the reform activities. During the preceding years, writings had been limited to scholarly and political-literary journals and primarily criticized Stalinist practices. In the main, all such ideas were expressed in carefully veiled language, for the censors sifting the output of editorial offices still guarded the purity of the ideology (as it was understood by the Party) and of Party interests. But after January 1968, daily papers, including the Party organ, *Rudé právo*, joined the battle. Sales of some periodicals reached the unprecedented level of 300,000 copies. Similarly, the dailies of the National Socialist Party and the Catholic People's Party (which still functioned nominally) became increasingly popular. Radio and television, once plagued with officially imposed dullness, were turned on again with eagerness and curiosity. All mass media were entirely freed, and they played a leading role in the process of revival.

All these "technical" manifestations were, of course, the consequences of a basic and substantive change. Language became outspoken; acting under the pressures of the reformers and public opinion, the censors one day simply quit their jobs. Criticism of the past turned into constructive demands for the correction of the present. Not only were the failings of the system attacked, but its principles and premises (and even some basic theoretical tenets of Marxism) were called into question. The old dogmas fell victim to new, creative propositions. The word "democracy," abused for decades by Communist propagandists, regained its true meaning—not a single-party "people's government," but a pluralistic "government by the people." Economic socialism was to be accompanied by personal and political freedom. The nation was to find in its own history a fountain of moral inspiration. Slovakia was to have full satisfaction of her claim to equality with the Czech lands in a constitutional federation. The advocates of these momentous changes, all of them Communists, were convinced that, ideologically speaking, they were writing a new and glorious chapter in the history of Marxism.

The reformers' ideas were embodied in a number of documents, drafted by prominent individuals and various interest groups, including the Party itself. Most important of all was the voluminous and comprehensive Action Program, adopted in April 1968 by the Central Committee. The document opened with a telling sentence: "The social movement in the Czech lands and in

Slovakia during the twentieth century has been carried along by two great currents—the national liberation movement and socialism." The program rehabilitated the "policy of Czechoslovakia's road to socialism" during the three postwar years and, mixing severe criticism of the past with constructive proposals for the future, it stressed the importance of recognizing the "various needs and interests of individual people and social groups." Not content with this Marxian heresy, the Action Program called for such pragmatic measures as putting an end to income equalization and for applying the "principles of remuneration according to quantity, quality, and social usefulness of work." The economy of the country must be democratized, the program continued, and the economic policy must not be blunted by "taking from those who work well and giving to those who work badly." Enterprises must become independent and their management accountable to democratically elected bodies. Trade unions must serve the interests of the workers, not the Party. The socialist economy must introduce flexible market mechanisms. Agricultural production and cooperatives must become more efficient. In general, the standard of living throughout the society must improve.

The Action Program further stipulated that the entire political system, guaranteed by a new constitution, must be reformed to "permit a new, dynamic development of socialist social relations," to ensure "freedoms of assembly and association," and to make certain that "legal norms . . . provide a more precise guarantee of the freedom of speech for minority interests and opinions" and protect in a "better and more consistent way the personal rights and property of citizens." The National Assembly was to be a "socialist parliament with all the scope for action the parliament of a democratic republic must have" and the Party must take steps to make the government responsible to the National Assembly. The executive, legislative, and judicial responsibilities were to be delineated and separated from each other. Courts, the program stated, must be "independent of political factors and . . . bound only by law." Political power must be diffused and the Ministry of the Interior, in particular, which had assumed "an undue concentration" of powers, must be reduced to become only a "department for internal state administration," returning to the tradition of its security force "advancing side by side with our people." Rehabilitation of the victims of illegal or unjustified denunciations, trials, and purges must be carried out "in all its political and civic consequences."

The Action Program met fully the demands of the Slovak nation. After all other ideas—centralization, autonomy, and even secession—had been explored and rejected or proven unsuccessful, the relations between Czechs and Slovaks were at last to be based on the principle of complete equality in the form of a federation. Both nations would have their own legislative and executive bodies, and only matters of state interest would be handled by common federal organs. A new constitution would preclude, in particular, the "possibility of outvoting the Slovak nation in legal issues concerning relations between Czechs and Slovaks and the constitutional status of Slovakia."

Even as these guarantees were being extended, however, the ever-suspicious Slovaks addressed the old warning to the Czechs: should inequality be perpetuated, the Slovaks would find their own way to meet their goals, "even if this means separation and the foundation of an independent socialist state," as one paper put it. In August, *Kulturný život* added that the Slovaks could not afford to neglect to examine other "alternatives in the solution of the perspectives of a small nation." After all, though discredited, the Slovak Republic existed as "the national State of Slovaks, the only one in our history. . . . Let us not turn away from it; it is part of our national tradition." [9] It was strange that a Communist journal should invoke with some pride the memory of a fascist state. In reality, however, it was only another variation on the theme expressed so often by leaders of the extreme Right and Left, reminding the Czech partner that the Slovak spouse could dissolve the marriage at any time—a sad and depressing note in

9. Galia Golan, *Reform Rule in Czechoslovakia: The Dubček Era* (London: Cambridge University Press, 1973), p. 194; Robert W. Dean, *Nationalism and Political Change in Eastern Europe: The Slovak Question and the Czechoslovak Reform Movement* (Denver: Monograph Series in World Affairs, 1973), p. 31.

this Spring of general rejoicing. Nevertheless, all that seemed to matter at the moment were the encouraging promises of the Action Program.

A convincing proof that the Party was seeking the old springs of Czechoslovak tradition was the long section of the Action Program devoted to education and culture. It asked for basic reforms in education, improvements in educational standards, the self-management of universities, academic freedom and access to foreign literature, equal opportunities for education, and assurances of the recognition of the "prestige, authority, and social importance of the educators." The program considered "care for culture, material and spiritual, . . . not only the concern of the cultural front," but of the "entire society." Rejecting "bureaucratic and administrative methods of implementing cultural policy," it called for complete freedom of cultural expression and a return to culture's traditionally humanistic tasks. While recognizing that the Communist Party could not relinquish its "inspiring role . . . in the struggle for the transformation of the world," the document suggested that humanist values need not diminish, indeed, could only enhance, the socialist philosophy.[10]

In the past, many Communist statements had been festooned with noble words—freedom, democracy, equality, progress, justice—all for show, empty of meaning, and the people had grown deaf to them. This time, however, within an atmosphere which Masaryk might have called a "revolution of hearts and minds," the words of the Action Program had a genuine ring, and the people once again believed and hoped. Without underestimating the problem of intra-Party opposition, silent for the moment, and without ignoring the potential international repercussions, there was indeed cause for hope.

The Action Program was the work of combined forces: the intellectuals and some top Party officials. The first group made some compromises, and the latter moved a long way from their dogmatic position of a few months earlier. The essential concepts,

10. For the text of the Action Program, see Robin A. Remington, ed., *Winter in Prague: Documents on Czechoslovak Communism in Crisis* (Cambridge, Mass.: M.I.T. Press, 1969), pp. 88–137.

however, were produced by the ever-growing ranks of writers, scholars, journalists, commentators, and artists who, even after the publication of the Action Program, continued to propound ideas that went even beyond its intent. These ideas dealt with fundamental but highly sensitive problems.

Václav Slavík, the director of the Party's Institute of Political Science and a member of the Central Committee, stated that in the field of political science, "there must be nothing that is taboo." When asked if a single-party system was compatible with democratic values, Slavík answered in the affirmative, but qualified his position by stating that the Communist Party did not consider "its political and ideological leading role as its natural right in perpetuity, but as something it must constantly deserve." Above all else, he said, "there must be democratic values within the Party" which "must be controlled by the public" and with the sources of information "open to every citizen." Further, he continued, "the opinion of the majority must be respected, but the opinion of the minority must be taken into account. . . . It is a question of real freedom, for only the freedom of the individual is the freedom of all."

Jan Procházka, reacting to the attacks of conservative circles in the Party who, he said, "discredited socialism, deadened it and changed it into a religion, full of icons and saints' quotations," found it encouraging that the nation had not lost "the torment of conscience, nor the longing for truth" in all the years of struggle. He wanted a "Czechoslovak, democratic, and humane socialism." With reference to the country's relations with the Soviet Union, he rejected the notion that socialism meant subjection to any master; rather, he said, it meant "freedom among equal nations in a just world." Speaking to a group of young people gathered in a park, Procházka concluded, "We must prove that good goals can be realized only through good means." [11]

Eduard Goldstücker, referring frequently to the nation's traditional longing for freedom and social progress and citing many

11. Jiří Lederer, "O politice zcela otevřeně" [interview with Václav Slavík], *Reportér* 3, no. 7 (February 14–21, 1968), p. 6; Procházka, *Politika pro každého*, pp. 229–31.

examples in its history, paraphrased the old Hussite saying "In spite of everything, the truth prevails." It is now apparent, he said, that the country wants "desperately to realize the ideals of socialism—human brotherhood and freedom." [12]

Karel Kosík, a leading philosopher, saw in the current crisis "primarily a discussion about the meaning of national and human existence" and condemned "the system" as "that remarkable conglomeration of bureaucracy and Byzantinism . . . that monstrous symbiosis of the state with the pagan church, of hypocrisy with fanaticism, ideology with faith, bureaucratic greyness with mass hysteria." [13]

Zdeněk Mlynář, who occupied a key position as head of the Party's Committee for Political Reform, wrote about the need to recognize the existence of various strata of society, declaring that their specific interests must find expression in a "pluralistic socialist system," possibly even in the eventual admission of two political parties. Since this development would be premature, however, he proposed that the CPC monopoly should be replaced by a pluralistic National Front, with free elections. On another occasion, he presented the idea that Czechoslovak socialism must preserve some of the old values, such as Christianity and the independence of the individual.

Ivan Sviták, another leading Marxist philosopher and a prolific writer and speaker, was mercilessly critical of the Party, of bureaucracy, and of totalitarian methods. He summed up his demands saying, "We want democracy, not democratization." What concerned him was the danger that even minor concessions in a still one-party system could perpetuate the Party's exclusive role. Radoslav Selucký saw in the Czechoslovak reform program a "European, democratic, and humanistic interpretation of Marxism" which would contribute to the strengthening of socialism throughout the world.

The discipline of history, too, witnessed a radical revision. A new group of historians emerged from an enforced obscurity and began refuting every argument of their Stalinist predecessors. The

---

12. Oxley, *Czechoslovakia*, p. 231.   13. Ibid., p. 48.

origins of Czechoslovakia were once again subjected to a new interpretation, one which did not differ materially from the "legend" attributed to liberal historians. Further, the quality of their research proved to be remarkable. The new writers ascribed the process of liberation of the country during World War I to a combination of factors. One was the political and cultural growth of the nation which brought it to full maturity and which logically culminated in the popular demand for independence. In addition, there was the inevitable impact of new ideas that would shape a future Europe in which Czechoslovakia would find its rightful place. And finally, there was the programmatic leadership that Masaryk provided, equipped as he was with a political philosophy of democracy and progress which corresponded to the thinking of the nation and the political direction of the West. These scholars, therefore, rejected not only the charge made during the 1920s that Czechoslovakia was the product of the Versailles Peace Treaty and of Western imperialism, but they also, amazingly (they were all young Communists), destroyed the notion held during the 1950s that the October Revolution was the sole cause of their nation's existence. They found the inspiring force in the February Revolution and, while not ignoring the limited role that the October Revolution played in the Czechoslovak events, they expressed criticism of its consequence—the Brest-Litovsk Treaty. Recognizing the necessity for the Soviet Union to sign the treaty, they maintained that it probably had an injurious effect on the future of Czechoslovakia since it explicitly left the fate of Central Europe to Germany. Therefore, "the Russian Revolution has lost enormously in the eyes of Czech and Slovak socialists." Furthermore, the Brest-Litovsk Treaty permitted the German and Austrian high commands to transfer divisions from the Russian to the French and Italian fronts, facilitating their resumption of offensive operations. Had it not been for the Allied counteroffensive and the break-through on the fatal "Black August" which finally led to the the Allied victory, there would have been no Czechoslovakia.

In the light of this evaluation, the reformist authors condemned their dogmatist predecessors' writings about Masaryk as "lacking any objective historical perspective." To these new writers, Masaryk was "the greatest thinker and politician of the preceding capitalist phase of Czechoslovak history . . . a founder of the Czechoslovak Republic." [14] These writings undoubtedly created a sense of intellectual freedom from the past. They encouraged individuals in all walks of life to make their positions known.

Then, in June, came a statement called "2,000 Words" which became the most eloquent document of that period. It shook the top echelon of the Party, even among the supporters of the reform movement, and it created a furor in Moscow. The statement was addressed to "workers, farmers, scientists, artists and all people" and was signed by some 150 persons, including prominent scholars, writers, and artists, three Olympic champions, and, most importantly, perhaps, many workers and farmers. It contained a scathing attack on the past practices of the Party, which had caused it to become a "power organization . . . attractive to egotists, avid for rule, to calculating cowards and to people with bad consciences." In this situation, it continued, "Parliament forgot how to proceed; the government forgot how to govern and the directors how to direct. . . . Still worse was that we all but lost our trust in one another. Personal and collective honor declined."

Then, pointing to the many officials who still opposed change, the appeal insisted that there must be no slackening of effort, that the "aim of humanizing this regime" must be fulfilled. "Let us demand the resignation of those who have misused their power . . . who have acted brutally or dishonestly. . . . Let us establish committees for the defense of freedom of expression." As to fears of outside intervention, "2,000 Words" stated, "Faced with all these superior forces, all we can do is to start nothing but attempt to hold our own. We can assure our government that we will back it—with weapons if necessary—as long as it does what we give it the mandate to do, and we can assure our allies that we will observe our alliances, friendships, and trade agreements." The statement concluded with what was to prove an ironic prophecy:

14. J. Mlynárik, "Vznik československého státu," Reportér 3, no. 41 (October 23–30, 1968): 4; Oldřich Janeček, "Tomáš G. Masaryk," Nová mysl 22, no. 6 (1968): 681, 682.

"The Spring has now ended and will never return. By winter, we will know everything." [15]

In treating matters of foreign policy, the spokesmen of reform, while always emphasizing the necessity of a loyal alliance with the Soviet Union, added a new connotation to this relationship and sought a greater role for Czechoslovakia in world affairs. Jiří Hanák pointedly recognized that the country had, at the time of the formation of the Republic, "two real statesmen, Masaryk and Beneš" at the helm and that the nation then had "something we have seriously missed in the last twenty years: its own diplomacy, its own foreign policy, and a solid international influence." As an example, Hanák pointed to the Little Entente, which was a "great and useful idea . . . at the least, an expression of an independent, active foreign policy." Significantly, this favorable opinion of the Little Entente was written toward the end of July, when Czechoslovakia was being subjected to severe criticism by all the nations of the Warsaw Pact Organization except Rumania and the nonaligned Yugoslavia who had been its partners in the earlier alliance and who now gave open support to the reform developments.

In a broader context, Hanák further suggested that the slogan "with the Soviet Union for eternity" should not be "used in an entirely automatic way, without considering the specific conditions of our country." While recognizing that a permanent alliance with the Soviet Union was decisive for the well-being of the country, Hanák said Czechoslovakia should not behave like "a carefree child who is protected from all evil by a strong and reliable brother." He was also critical of the official policy toward Israel and stated that "suspension of diplomatic relations with Israel is not one of the actions of which we should boast." He further advocated a change in the country's policy toward West Germany and expressed support for the progressive forces of West Germany's Social Democratic Party. [16]

15. For the text of "2,000 Words," see Remington, *Winter in Prague*, pp. 196–202.

16. Jiří Hanák, "Malá dohoda—Zdravá myšlenka," *Reportér* 3, no. 13 (March 27–April 3, 1968): 22–23, and no. 30 (July 24–31, 1968): 24–25.

Another analyst, Alexander Ort, revived the old idea that Czechoslovakia was "the heart of Europe" and pleaded for an active role in an all-European policy, for an initiative, a new diplomacy that could "relate itself with pride to all progressive and democratic traditions." [17] Still other writers asked for equality for all the members of the Warsaw Pact Organization, obviously criticizing the Soviet Union's controlling role. General Václav Prchlík, who was in charge of the most important Party function, security, even suggested a revision of the Warsaw Pact to guarantee the equality of its members. The Action Program went so far as to state that Czechoslovakia would take its own stand on basic issues of world policy, participate actively in all European affairs, and improve its relations with Western Europe while, at the same time, maintaining its alliance with the Soviet Union and other members of the Warsaw Pact Organization on a basis of equality.

In this electrifying atmosphere, the reins of the Party changed hands. Novotný was dismissed from the presidency of the Republic in March (and expelled from the Central Committee of the Party two months later) and replaced by the simple-minded Ludvík Svoboda, who enjoyed the political advantage of holding the Order of Hero of the Soviet Union, the highest Soviet award, bestowed on him for his subservient services to Stalin during the war. The Party's chief ideologist, Jiří Hendrych, a determined dogmatist, was also dismissed, and the Party was now led, without any physical liquidation of the opposition, by the "liberals" — Dubček, Josef Smrkovský, František Kriegel, Oldřich Černík, Čestmír Císař, and Josef Špaček. These men spoke on many occasions, before a wide variety of audiences, and the themes of their addresses were the same as those of the originators of the reform movement: the Czechoslovak tradition of democracy and progress, the Czechoslovak road to socialism, the necessity of freedom of expression, intra-Party democracy, the need for a reformed socialist economy, and humanism and the dignity of man.

They exercised caution on one delicate issue: the position of

17. Alexander Ort, "Konstanty a kontinuita zahraniční politiky," *Reportér* 3, no. 22 (May 29–June 4, 1968): 17–18.

the Party in the reformed society. Partly because of pressure from Moscow, partly because of their own concern about the Party's future, the leaders were against any idea of permitting, at least as yet, a genuinely pluralistic system that would allow political parties outside the National Front to function. Conceding the need to make the Party popular and responsive to the people's wishes, they proposed to abandon the past policy of concentrating all power in the Party and envisioned its function as an ideological leader and guide that would persuade, not dictate to, the masses. Still, the CPC would remain the single governing party. The leaders attempted to influence the mass media, which were giving all-out support to the reform movement, to exercise restraint. The government even publicly expressed its regret for the "2,000 Words" statement and the Politburo disassociated itself from General Prchlík's stand on the Warsaw Pact (and he was given another military assignment).

Those antireformists who remained in the Party leadership waged a bitter counterattack. Vasil Bilák warned openly against giving freedom to the press, and Drahomír Kolder attacked the "anti-Communist" forces, singling out Ivan Sviták, who advocated, Kolder claimed, "a new political structure, similar to the bourgeois-democratic type" and detachment from the alliance with the Soviet Union.

In spite of such flurries of retreat and reaction, however, the hurricane of reform continued to sweep the nation and its most important effect—the transformation of the Party—continued. Faced with the necessity of responsive action to the demands of the reformers or ruin, the Party chose to reform. In August 1968, new Party statutes were published, to be submitted to the Fourteenth Congress, planned for September. It is a refreshing document and differs in many aspects from the statutes of any other governing Communist Party. Its introductory section pledges allegiance to the "international communist and revolutionary movement," to the "principle of proletarian internationalism and socialist patriotism," and to the "fraternal relations and collaboration of the Czechoslovak people with the Soviet people. . . ." However, it also linked the CPC with the "national, democratic, and revolu-

tionary traditions" of the Czechoslovak people, stating further that
the Party was a "deeply humanistic party," one which wanted "to
preserve its vanguard mission in the struggle . . . for socialism,
democracy, human justice, freedom, and the humanistic ideals of
communism in our country."

The Party's internal life was to be governed by a new interpretation of the principle of democratic centralism, which would
provide for a "confrontation of views" and an equal opportunity
for every Party member to express his own viewpoint. Though
"the minority is subordinate to the majority," the document stipu-
lates that the minority has the right "to persist in its view" and to
ask for a "re-evaluation of policy" on the basis of new information. All Party organs were to be elected by secret ballot. To remove the problem of the assymetrical model, with the CPC controlling Party affairs over the whole country while the Communist
Party of Slovakia was subordinated and limited to Slovakia, the
new draft established two separate territorial organizations with
considerable independent authority, which together formed a
"united international Communist Party of Czechoslovakia." [18] This
arrangement satisfied, at long last, the demands of the Slovak
Communists.

These spectacular innovations would probably never have
been undertaken had the Party been under pressure not only from
the mass media, but from the public as well. Talk of reform was
everywhere, and the whole country became enveloped in an atmosphere of real liberation. New associations and clubs were
formed and issued statements, all carrying messages of freedom
and socialist humanism. The National Socialist Party and the Catholic People's Party, vegetating for years with the "generous" permission of the CPC within the National Front, ousted their utterly
compromised leadership and showed signs of vitality. Efforts were
underway to revive the old Social Democratic Party which had
been absorbed in 1948 into the Communist Party. Farmers arranged meetings and asked for free elections of officers of collective farms. Workers, at first influenced by Novotný's harangues,

18. For the text of the statutes, see Remington, *Winter in Prague*, pp. 265–87.

soon understood the full meaning and value of reform and, in some instances, established committees for the defense of freedom of the press. The Circle of Independent Writers published a declaration reminding the nation of the values of "humanity, cultural freedom, and independence" and made it clear that the country could not "even approach the ideals of socialism" as long as that was interpreted as the "antithesis of democracy."

Celebrations on May 1, the traditional Labor Day, turned into mass demonstrations for freedom. In the past, they had been managed by the Party as a glorification of the working class; in 1968, the May Day parades became spontaneous celebrations in cities and towns throughout the country, in which the young and the old, the workers and farmers, the intelligentsia and the thinning ranks of the World War I Legionaries marched as one people. Placards demanded the immediate dissolution of the secret police, free elections, the suspension of interference with foreign broadcasts, and the like, and some even carried such religious slogans as "Jesus—not Caesar" and "We demand a Christian Republic." Portraits of T. G. Masaryk were everywhere, but no mention was made of the Soviet Union, though one witty poster amplified Lenin's popular dictum to "Learn, learn, learn—from Masaryk!" On the lighter side, there were such student witticisms as

Let them kill me, as long as they lead me.

Signed: A Sheep

or,

I would be glad to
add to
the population—
But I lack an apartment
and the streets lack privacy
for copulation

and the satiric, "We demand instant prosperity!"

It is difficult to evaluate the results of polls which were conducted during "the Spring," since the psychological consequences of the twenty years during which people were forbidden to speak their minds freely cannot be ascertained. Nevertheless, the polls convincingly revealed the preferences of the people. In general, their responses expressed an overwhelming desire for political change, as well as for the preservation of the socialist economy. In a poll conducted in the Czech lands in July concerning the formation of an opposition party, no respondent favored a party with a nonsocialist program; on the other hand, the people evidently did favor a pluralistic system, since only 21 percent were opposed to the formation of parties other than the Communist Party. A high number of respondents (48 percent) favored a socialist program that would correspond to Communist philosophy but would differ in its processes of realization.

In a survey conducted in Slovakia in July, 61.5 percent of respondents recognized the advantages of collective farms and believed that the standard of living and the cultural level in the countryside were improved by collectivization; 16.7 percent expressed the opinion that the improvement could be achieved without collectivization; and only 7.7 percent felt that collectives were detrimental.

Still another survey covering the whole country, indicated the Party's standing in the eyes of the public. Before January 1968, only 23 percent of the respondents had trust (determined by combining the categories "trust" and "complete trust") in the Party, while 48 percent had no trust (determined by combining "distrust" and "complete distrust") in it, and 29 percent had cautiously "neither trust nor distrust." In June, undoubtedly reflecting public awareness of the Party's response to the reform movement, 51 percent of the people polled trusted the Party and only 16 percent did not; but 33 percent were still cautious enough to respond, "neither trust, nor distrust." A few weeks later, 89 percent of those polled favored the continuation of the socialist economic system and only 5 percent favored a return to capitalism and 6 percent had "no opinion." However, a poll conducted in the Czech lands revealed that only 43 percent would vote for the Communist Party in free elections, while a large number (27 percent) cautiously answered, "Don't know." Interestingly, among the non-Communist respondents, a high percentage (28 percent) said they would vote for the Communist Party and an even higher percentage (34) said, "Don't know." In short, it seems clear that in 1968 the reformed CPC enjoyed greater prestige throughout Czechoslovakia than it had ever before achieved.

Most significantly, an overwhelming 96 percent of responding members of the Party agreed with the statement, "The construction of socialism . . . is our internal affair, based definitely on the supreme will of our people." [19] That response was the one that was heard in Moscow. Tito had been enough. There would be no construction of any socialist society, free, or humane, or anything else, based on "the will and traditions of the Czechoslovak people." The Spring was condemned to death. By winter, the people of Czechoslovakia would "know everything."

Sisyphus's Ordeal

From the moment the revolt of the intellectuals began to attack the Party itself, at around the turn of the year 1967–68, the Communist parties of the Warsaw Pact Organization—with the exception of Rumania's Communists, who gave full political and moral support to their comrades in Prague—watched the developments in Czechoslovakia with increasing suspicion. They mounted a carefully orchestrated campaign of criticism, starting with admonitions veiled in familiar Communist phraseology, progressing to open accusations and threats, and culminating in a military invasion. It should be mentioned that the Hungarian Communists, were reluctant to pursue this course, but eventually followed the Moscow line.

In March 1968, the leaders of the Communist parties in the Soviet Union, Bulgaria, Hungary, East Germany, Poland, and Czechoslovakia (with Rumania conspicuously absent) met in Dresden. The meeting's communiqué asked for increased vigi-

19. Based on J. A. Piekalkiewicz, *Public Opinion Polling in Czechoslovakia, 1968–69* (New York: Praeger, 1972), pp. 10–11, 37, 45, 227, 229, 310–11.

THE SISYPHEAN YEARS

lance against the "aggressive intentions and subversive actions of the imperialist forces," emphasized the necessity for "further consolidation of the socialist countries," and expressed confidence that "the working class and all the working people of the Czechoslovak Republic, under the leadership of the Communist Party of Czechoslovakia, will ensure the further development of socialist construction in the country." [20] Even if they had not taken part in the meeting that prompted this still-gentle expression of misgivings, the Czechoslovak delegates could not possibly have misread its meaning.

This was only the beginning. In April, a resolution of the CPSU, asking for an "implacable struggle against enemy ideology," demanded a "vigorous and united action by all the forces of socialism, democracy, and national liberation." The following month, *Izvestia* went a step further, branding the concept of noninterference in a socialist country by other Communist states "bourgeois ideology". It condemned the "artful slogan of 'democratization' or 'liberalization,'" which the ruling circles in the United States called "liberalization ideas," and lastly pointed to the need "to make skillful use of those existing means of ideological steadfastness and understanding: Soviet patriotism and proletarian internationalism." This criticism was supplemented by Brezhnev's private conversations with Dubček and Smrkovský on their visit to Moscow at about that same time, in which his dissatisfaction with developments in Czechoslovakia was made apparent.

With the publication of the Action Program and, in particular, of the "2,000 Words," criticism abroad turned into open attacks, published in various Party organs in East Germany, Poland, Hungary, Bulgaria, and, of course, the Soviet Union. *Pravda* wrote about "forces in Czechoslovakia hostile to socialism," about the dangers of "counterrevolution," and stressed in conclusion that the people of the Soviet Union and other socialist countries were aware of the danger that "certain anti-socialist forces" would impede the "further successful development of frater-

20. Remington, *Winter in Prague*, pp. 55–57.

nal Czechoslovakia." However, the article ended, ". . . Czechoslovak working people can always count on the understanding and
complete support of the people of the Soviet land." [21] Twenty
years earlier, *Pravda* had promised similar understanding and support on the eve of the Communist takeover in Czechoslovakia.

Prague still did not respond to the message. These Czechs
and Slovaks who had again, for a few moments, tasted a considerable degree of their former freedom, could not or would not heed
the rumblings of the coming storm.

On July 15, representatives of five Communist parties met
in Warsaw (the Rumanians again refused to attend the meeting)
and sent a letter to the Czechoslovak Central Committee, making
their position and demands unmistakably clear. The letter expressed "profound anxiety" over the "reactionaries' offensive,
supported by imperialism" against the Party and Czechoslovakia's
"social system," thus endangering "the interests of the entire socialist system." While professing that they did not wish to interfere
in the planning of a socialist economy, they could not allow "hostile forces" to create the "threat that Czechoslovakia may break
away from the socialist commonwealth." The letter stated unequivocally, "This is no longer your own internal affair."

To avoid any doubt about the meaning of its plain language, the letter elaborated on this issue, pointing to the commitment of all Communist countries to defend socialism and "the collective security of the socialist countries," since every party bore
"the responsibility not only to its own working class . . . but also
to the international working class." Therefore, the cause required a
"bold offensive against rightist and anti-socialist forces, a cessation
of the activities of all political organizations that oppose socialism"
and the Party's "assumption of control over the mass news
media." In short, the cause required complete and utter solidarity
in the Party ranks in the face of the now-obvious threat of
"counterrevolution." And then came the essence of the entire
warning, "In this struggle, you may count on the solidarity and

21. Ibid., pp. 137–38, 158–61, 203–7.

comprehensive assistance of the fraternal socialist countries." [22] No one could say Prague had not been warned of the consequences of its drive toward freedom.

The military maneuvers of the Warsaw Pact countries, conducted in Czechoslovakia in June, were prolonged, and the last Soviet units remained until the end of July. The most extensive maneuvers of the Soviet forces since 1945 were carried on in Poland, Hungary, and East Germany, and extended through the days when the Soviet and Czechoslovak Politburo members finally met at a little railroad station at Čierná-nad-Tisou on the Czechoslovak-Soviet border.

The atmosphere of the occasion was clearly that of ultimatum. Dubček and his associates refused to give in. At one point, Dubček, weeping, talked about his personal catastrophe, the grief of a man who had dedicated his whole life to the cause of communism, who had loved the Soviet Union, and was now accused of betrayal. The four-day meeting produced a meagre communiqué, filled largely with the usual phrases about an "atmosphere of complete frankness, sincerity, and mutual understanding." It ended, however, with the significant announcement that the leaders of the six parties would meet in Bratislava two days later, on August 3. The proponents of communism "with a human face" were to confront finally the ugly realities of the ideology which they, and those who had come before, had long ago set loose in their land. There could be only one result.

Lasting one day, the Bratislava meeting was outwardly remarkable in one respect: its long and detailed communiqué did not mention the situation in Czechoslovakia at all. It could have been taken from the notes of any Communist gathering in recent years. It spoke of imperialist threats to socialism, revanchism, militarism, and neo-Nazism in West Germany; of imperialist forces in the United States and the NATO bloc; of the war in Vietnam and the aggressive policy of Israel. All these dangers demanded unity among the socialist countries and an intensification of the anti-

22. Ibid., pp. 225–31.

imperialist struggle. There was also the usual reference to cooperation of the socialist countries on the basis of "the principles of
equality, respect for sovereignty and national independence, territorial integrity, and fraternal mutual aid and solidarity." [23] There
was an almost unbelievable cynicism about that last statement, for
at that very moment the five other parties to the communiqué
were violating all of these principles.

As Smrkovský later testified, after the meeting in Čierná,
Brezhnev called Dubček daily, urging him to comply with the
demands to dismiss the "liberal" leaders from the government and
the Party, to introduce censorship, and to dissolve any "reactionary" organizations. Whether or not he wished to comply, it was
too late for Dubček, or anyone, to rechannel the national will. Indeed, Soviet pressure only intensified the nation's thirst for independence and freedom and hardened its resolution. People
seized upon the visits of Marshal Tito and President Nicolae
Ceauşescu to Czechoslovakia in August as opportunities to demonstrate their sentiments and strengthen Dubček's determination
to carry out his program of "socialism with a human face."

But it was, of course, all a charade. The pagan gods cannot
permit Sisyphus to conquer. The stone must always be hurled
back to the bottom of the hill. The great irony of this version of the
myth is that Sisyphus himself had created these implacable gods!
The actual event will go down in the annals of the Communist
movement as a regrettable episode; in the annals of world history
it will go down as an act of supreme perfidy.

"Fraternal" Invasion

At 11 P.M. on August 20, 1968, the troops of five members of the
Warsaw Pact invaded Czechoslovakia. Soviet airborne forces, including tank and artillery units, were landed in Prague and Bratislava. As the "allied" armies poured into the country, the Soviet

23. Ibid., pp. 255, 256–61.

ambassadors called at the chancelleries of the Western governments to advise them that the invasion was a "domestic" affair
among socialist states undertaken in the interest of peace.

At the time of the invasion, the Politburo of the Communist
Party of Czechoslovakia was in session, making preparations for
the forthcoming Fourteenth Congress. Totally unprepared for a
military move against the nation, it quickly passed a resolution
condemning the occupation (though, significantly, the vote was
only seven to four in favor of the resolution), but also appealed to
the people to "keep the peace and not to resist the advancing armies." To millions of Czechs and Slovaks there must have been
a nightmarish quality to both the act of invasion and the appeal to
keep calm—they had seen the march of the German army into
Czechoslovakia in 1938; they had heard General Syrový's admo-
nition to "keep calm."

It could not be happening again—but it was. This time it
was not the invasion of a known enemy, but of allied, fraternal nations, and the appeal did not come from a "bourgeois traitor," but
from Communist comrades. Similar contradictory statements of
defiance and appeals for submissive behavior were issued by President Svoboda and the National Assembly.

The Party Presidium never finished its deliberations. Within
a few minutes after the troops landed, telephone lines were cut,
and soldiers, armed with machine guns, entered the building.
Every person present was put up against the wall, and the ring-
leaders of the "counterrevolution"—Dubček, Smrkovský,
Černík, and Kriegel, all lifelong, dedicated Communists—were
taken away. The Soviet ambassador, Stepan Vasilievich Cher-
vonenko, performing an unusual mission for a diplomat and in the
highly significant company of the commander of the occupying
forces, General Ivan Pavlovsky, called on President Svoboda to in-
form him officially of the invasion and to demand that he appoint
a new government, composed of conservative, "true" Communists who had opposed the reforms. In a moment of *lucidum inter-
vallum* that was to last for a few critical days, Svoboda refused and
declared himself aligned with the four arrested leaders.

Two days later, *Pravda* published a long proclamation, purportedly originating in Czechoslovakia, which severely criticized the Czechoslovak Party leaders for their support of reactionary forces and asked "the Soviet Union and other fraternal socialist countries for assistance." The proclamation lacked one essential detail: it carried no signatures. Popular wit had it that this enormous number of soldiers—some 500,000—had been ordered into Czechoslovakia to find the person who invited them to come!

Czechoslovak comrades offered no friendship to these visitors from the other "fraternal" nations. The invading army was received with scorn and indignation. People painted swastikas on their tanks, spat at them, turned around street signs to confuse them, isolated them in a devastating silence when a noon hour strike was ordered, and otherwise harrassed them. Some did speak to them, but only to try to convince them of the immorality and utter foolishness of the invasion. It was an exercise in mass passive resistance which spoke eloquently of Czech and Slovak feelings.

The atmosphere crackled with tension. Generally reluctant to use arms, the invading army nevertheless resorted to some bloody retaliation, and an unknown number of protestors, entirely unarmed, were killed. The museum in St. Wenceslaus Square was shelled, pockmarked with holes which the people called "El Grechko reliefs," punning on the name of the Soviet minister of defense.

Meanwhile, the invasion proceeded with precision. Following carefully laid plans, the armed forces occupied central buildings, including the "most strategic" loci of power, the Academy of Sciences and the Writers' Union. For a time, the radio and television stations escaped occupation and broadcast official defiance. After they were seized, the technicians and announcers escaped and went underground to continue their patriotic efforts. The Party's Congress was hastily convened in a factory on the outskirts of the capital. Its delegates, over 1,200 of them, passed undetected through the lines of Soviet tanks, dressed as workers, joining an incoming "regular" shift. This "underground" Party Congress passed a program that went even beyond the Action Program in its demands for national and Party integrity, reform, and freedom. Expressing full confidence in Dubček, it reelected him first secretary of the Party, unaware that he and his closest associates were prisoners in Soviet hands.

"Fraternal" Capitulation

After being moved from one place to another, mistreated, dirty and hungry, Dubček and the other prisoners were taken to Moscow. President Svoboda was also there, but on his own initiative and accompanied by a group of Communist leaders of both conservative and liberal convictions. Svoboda, still in a defiant mood, refused to talk with Soviet representatives without the participation of his detained comrades. Painful and frustrating "negotiations" ensued. The Czechoslovaks were presented with a document of capitulation. Frantic consultations and arguments, both between the two sides and within the Czechoslovak group itself, which was now split, followed. As Smrkovský subsequently wrote, most of them wept at one time or another, some fell ill, and Dubček suffered recurring heart trouble. At first, with both passion and disdain, they resisted signing the infamous document, but the intense, emotional struggle was exhausting. Boris N. Ponomarev, one of the Soviet negotiators and a candidate for the Politburo, told the anguished dissenters, with all the cynical patience of a certain winner, "If you don't sign now, you will sign next week; if not next week, then in two weeks; if not in two weeks, then in one month."

Smrkovský and others tried to make the Soviet representatives realize the horrendous consequences of submission, not only for Czechoslovakia, but for the Communist movement throughout the world. "Comrades," Smrkovský told them, "you have destroyed the centuries-old friendship that existed between our nations . . . you had in our people the most faithful friends, and you destroyed it all in one night." Such appeals, of course, meant nothing to the Soviets. At the end of six days of grilling, the statement of capitulation was signed. Only Kriegel remained adamant.

On August 28, *Pravda* published a communiqué reporting on the negotiations. In innocuous language that concealed the real import of the crisis, it expressed the Soviet understanding for Czechoslovakia's effort to perfect "the methods of guiding society" and to develop "a socialist democracy." Since an agreement had been reached on her differences with the Soviet Union, the communiqué continued, Czechoslovakia would request that her case be withdrawn from the agenda of the United Nations. The inevitable reference to the principles of "mutual respect, equality, territorial integrity, independence, and socialist solidarity," glossing over the invasion of a sister nation, was now not only a cynical concealment of intentions, but also a blasphemous outrage against truth.

The key sentence of the communiqué stated that "an understanding was reached on the measures aimed at the swiftest possible normalization of the situation." A secret protocol spelled out what measures of "normalization" meant—the conditions for the withdrawal of Soviet troops, the "corrections" accepted by its representatives, to which Czechoslovakia must submit. The conditions were not entirely "fraternal." The Fourteenth Congress of the Communist Party of Czechoslovakia was declared invalid. Individuals who were considered subversive, who hampered the process of consolidating the Party's absolute authority, were to be purged. Once again, the mass media were to be put under strict control and, accordingly, personnel changes were to be made in responsible positions. "Anti-socialist" organizations were to be banned. The Party would not permit the dismissal of its functionaries who had "struggled for the consolidation of socialist positions against anti-socialist forces and for friendly relations with the U.S.S.R." Czechoslovakia would actively participate in a consolidated defense system of the Warsaw Pact nations to face "the treacherous activities of imperialism." Last, the Ministry of the Interior was to be consolidated. The Soviet troops would be withdrawn in stages, "as soon as the threat to socialism" was removed.

The last measure of the total infamy was the agreement that the Moscow negotiations were to be "strictly confidential." [24]

24. Ibid., 376–78, 379–82.

The facts of a total capitulation, the dishonor of an aggression and the disgrace of a submission that were, in fact, Munich and the German occupation all over again, were to be carefully concealed. The Party that had heaped vituperation on the "bourgeois" Beneš and Hácha, now followed in their footsteps. The actors in the drama in 1968 were different, but the scenario was basically identical, even to the ironic detail that the Czechoslovak Party leaders, though supposedly hardened by years of resistance and revolutionary struggle, wept grievously, as had the Czechoslovak generals at the time of Munich. In the end, they all signed the documents of capitulation.

Once again, the leaders of the nation were apparently unable to perceive any alternatives to submission. Subsequently and privately, Smrkovský reasoned that they should have opposed the invasion, even with arms. In 1968, a refusal at least to sign the papers of submission would have fully exposed the Soviet betrayal to a watching world, forcing Moscow to impose a puppet government on the country and defend its aggression before the United Nations. Yet, they signed (all but František Kriegel, whom P. Ye. Shelest, a member of the Soviet Politburo, called "that Galician Jew"), though they must have realized that their valiant efforts to establish a " socialism with a human face" would come to nothing after they had submitted to tyranny. The one abstainer, Kriegel, became the cause of an ironic incident. At the moment of their departure from Moscow, the other delegates noticed his absence at the airport. In a last, desperate gesture, they threatened not to leave. Kriegel was produced, and the plane finally took off.

While they were in Moscow, the Czechoslovak representatives knew almost nothing of what was happening at home, since their contacts with Prague were being interrupted. When they returned, they found the nation in an uproar. One after another, Svoboda, Dubček, Černík, and Smrkovský appeared before the television cameras and tried to explain to the perplexed and frantic nation the trauma of their experience in Moscow and to justify their actions. Not unlike Beneš at the time of Munich, they had wanted to spare the nation bloodshed; again not unlike Beneš, they still believed that they could save something of value. But, they admitted, "certain measures" would have to be undertaken to "normalize" the situation before the fruits of the Spring could be harvested. On August 29, Smrkovský made a moving speech in which he pointed to the tragedy of a small nation, situated in a particularly sensitive area, the "tragedy of a people whose every effort has been aimed at great and noble goals" that had been repeatedly thwarted. He admitted that in Moscow the Czechoslovak delegation could have rejected any compromise and even chosen "recourse to bayonets" to "expel the troops . . . to safeguard the nation's character." They had accepted a compromise, he said, in the full realization that the "decision could be regarded by Czechoslovak people and by history as a wise solution or as treason." [25]

The people were not willing to accept the "compromise" or submit to its conditions. Demonstrations continued and riots flared up; resolutions passed by workers' organizations poured into Party headquarters; students barricaded themselves in the buildings of Charles University and food was supplied to them by the people; workers united with students in a solid front—a phenomenon unheard of in the history of communism; newspapers persisted in their campaign of defiance; the Academy of Sciences issued a "Black Book" to counteract the Soviet-authored "White Book"; public opinion polls expressed overwhelming confidence in Dubček. The Central Committee again confirmed his leadership, but with a kind of ambiguity tailor-made in Moscow. On October 28, the national Independence Day, massive anti-Soviet demonstrations took place and the government, the National Assembly, and the Party paid tribute to T. G. Masaryk, whose picture was displayed all over Prague.

The West followed the spectacle in Czechoslovakia with awe and indignation, but also with a deliberately visible awareness of its own impotence. Western statesmen condemned the Soviet invasion as a violation of international law and the Charter of the United Nations, but were caught in the web of their own policy of détente. President Lyndon Johnson, insensitive to the real meaning of the Soviet action, still toyed with the idea of a meeting with

25. Ibid., pp. 384, 385.

the Soviet leaders; Chancellor Kurt Georg Kiesinger declared that
West Germany would continue to "pursue a consistent *Ostpolitik*"
since there could not be "any fundamental change in the policy of
détente." General de Gaulle predictably found a justification for
French foreign policy in the events in Czechoslovakia and was,
therefore, determined to "continue to work for the independence
of nations and the liberty of men, and for détente, entente, and
cooperation." Prime Minister Harold Wilson was "chilled" and
drew an analogy between the Soviet invasion and that of Germany thirty years before, but he recognized that "whatever the
tragic disappointments of the last few days . . . we all know that
the only future for the world rests upon continuing to work for
détente between East and West."

The recitation of these pathetic statements does not imply
that the West should have opposed the Soviet invasion with military force, though it does suggest that an obvious chilling of their
ardor for détente might have informed the Soviets that the Western world and its conscience were still alive—and that it did care.
But whatever justification or lack thereof there may be for the
West's inoffensive reactions, the fact remains that, once again, as
at the time of Munich, Czechoslovakia stood alone, that it once
again succumbed to superior outside forces, unaided and, in an
even crueler sense, betrayed.

The West's reaction to the Soviet invasion invites another
analogy: as Hitler's invasion of Czechoslovakia in March 1939
served as a rude awakening to France and England, as the Communist putsch in February 1948 revealed the real thrust of Communist expansionism and triggered the West to sign the NATO
Pact in April 1949, so also did the Soviet agression in 1968 produce, at least temporarily, its repercussions. Most significantly, it
generated worldwide protests by scores of Communist parties and
accelerated the process of criticism of the CPSU and the "democratization" (real or pretended) of such important Communist parties as those of France and Italy.

The consequences of such "ill winds," accompanied always
by Czechoslovakia's unintended sacrifice, can hardly be expected
to bring to the Czechoslovak people even a perverse satisfaction.

In August 1968, moreover, the Soviet government cared little about or ignored altogether, the effects of its action upon the homogeneity of the international Communist movement.

Meanwhile, the Soviet mills were grinding, slowly but "exceeding small." The Soviet government first presented the invasion as a legally valid act: socialist international law was different from bourgeois law, and it was not only the right, but also the duty of Communist nations to intervene in a Communist country whose system was threatened by a counterrevolution which could endanger the whole commonwealth. This concept, contrary to the basic tenet of international law—nonintervention—enunciated a new principle—limited sovereignty, or, as it was dubbed, the Brezhnev Doctrine. From there, it was only a short step for the Soviet government to force on the Czechoslovak government, in October 1968, a treaty that "legalized" the "temporary stationing of Soviet troops on Czechoslovak territory."

Even in the shadow of Soviet guns, the people found ways to express their feelings. In a last convulsive effort to symbolize the nation's suffering, Jan Palach, a student, immolated himself, and hundreds of thousands of people publicly mourned his death. In March 1969, a defeat of the Soviets by the Czechoslovak hockey team in Stockholm was celebrated wildly in Prague as a political victory, and crowds demolished the office of the Soviet *Aeroflot*. This was the proverbial last straw.

When a tool is required, one can usually be found. So in this case, the Soviets found a person who was willing to serve their purpose. They did not enlist a subservient dogmatist; such a man would have been too compromised to be useful. Instead, they turned to Gustáv Husák, once a leader of the Slovak reformers and nationalists. His accommodating attitude during the Moscow negotiations had attracted the Soviets' attention, and he was ready to bring about a real "normalization" of the situation in Czechoslovakia. Speaking vehemently against "counterrevolutionary forces," he swiftly ascended the ladder of Party power. In April 1969, he replaced his old comrade, Dubček, as first secretary and immediately set out to liquidate the remnants of the Czechoslovak Spring. With the Party in safe hands, the bulk of the Soviet troops were removed, leaving behind some 50,000 soldiers for an indefinite period. Life was back to "normal" in Czechoslovakia.

One fruit of the Spring was preserved: the Czech lands and Slovakia became a federation. At last the Slovaks gained equality with the Czechs. Even this achievement, however, was jeopardized because pragmatic measures recentralizing the country's administration weakened the spirit of the federation. Most important, the Party preserved the assymetric model, investing its authority in Prague, where it was now represented by Gustáv Husák. On the other hand, there was backlash. Many Czechs questioned the wisdom of the union of the two nations, and their once warm feelings toward the Slovaks turned appreciably cold. The irony and incongruity of this situation were tellingly personified in Husák—at one time, a Slovak nationalist; at another, a potential advocate of a Soviet Slovakia; then again, a nationalist and a reformer; and finally, the occupant of highest seat of power, elected in 1975 by an obedient Parliament as president of the Republic.

Under Husák, the nation became an intellectual and spiritual cemetery where, once more, the ideals of humanity were buried deep. Inevitably, Dubček, Smrkovský, and other reformers were first deprived of their Party positions and then expelled from its ranks. Hundreds of intellectuals were arrested or assigned to manual or clerical jobs. Even more deadly was the damage to the people's morale. As in the Stalinist years, they became indifferent to public issues, attending apathetically to daily work and trying only to satisfy their material needs. The country fell once more into a deep, anesthetized sleep.

Some Perplexities
of the Spring

There remain many perplexities about this strange period of Czechoslovak history, those years of gradual thaw that led at last to the short-lived "Spring."

What was the ultimate goal of the reformers, and how

much change would have taken place had not the whole movement been obliterated by armed intervention?

The repeated statements of the new leaders of the CPC
and the theses developed by Communist theoreticians all point
toward a determination to achieve the establishment of personal
freedom, even within the Communist rubric. A belief in the rights
of the individual, a respect for his inalienable dignity, a sense of
the individual as the center of societal concern and not an object
of economic management—all of these were contained in the reformers' many manifestos.

It is clear, however, that the implementation of these goals
was to remain within the organization and structure of not just the
socialist system but also "the Party." Therein, perhaps, lay the
fatal flaw, one that would still have proved to be the undoing of
"socialism with a human face." For the fundamental question
must be raised as to whether personal freedom is ever really possible within a system that denies the possibility of political choice.

True, the Party's proposed statutes stipulated that its function would be confined to ideological guidance; its structures
would be democratized, and its procedures would respect and
guarantee the rights of the minority. Also, the Party was to be entirely separate from the executive powers and processes of the
government, which was to be responsible only to the National Assembly.

Even in concept, however, such is at best a spurious democracy. A single-party system, however liberal, is by definition incompatible with the inescapably pluralistic nature of political democracy. That is why such analysts as Ivan Sviták, the reformer's
reformer, pointedly and insistently asked for "democracy," not
"democratization." The argument that intra-Party democracy
would permit the expression and consideration of opposing views
is not convincing. Even this kind of democracy, if practiced hon-
estly and with full acceptance of its consequences, would have led
to factionalism, and this, in turn, to the public contestation of ideas
and the eventual recourse of the opposition to the electorate. The
artificial shell of one-party cohesion would have shattered from the

inside under the force of centrifugal tension, and other political parties would have emerged. For a time, perhaps, all of these new parties would have been essentially Marxist, and such a development certainly would not have endangered the socialist system guaranteed by the Constitution. Indeed, this introduction of a democratic political practice into the fabric of the socialist system would have created a truly "new society."

Such a democratic political practice would have threatened the autocracy of the Party, however—it is this fact that seemed impossible for even this leadership to tolerate—and no rationalization can dispose of the discrepancy between the professed democratic ideals of the reformers and the institutionalization of the single-party system. Hence the dilemma. At such a moment the society must either develop a real political pluralism and take its chances on how far and in what direction that choice will take it, or retrench through ever-increasing controls and limitations of personal freedom. The tantalizing question of which direction Czechoslovakia would have chosen, given additional time, must remain forever unanswered.

In a very real sense, the question is useless, for there would eventually have been a Soviet-led intervention, an understandable and justifiable intervention from a rigid Communist point of view. For Moscow, the threat was intolerable. The Czechoslovak Spring represented a whole new concept of communism, a new direction in economics, in human relations, and in politics—a dynamic communism, identified with humanistic Marxism and unquestionably attractive to the people of all other Communist countries. There were signs of growing sympathy everywhere, particularly among the intellectuals who followed the developments in Czechoslovakia with great interest. Ulbricht's East Germany and Gomulka's Poland appeared especially sensitive, as both countries were governed by rigid regimes with extensive controls, and as they were neighbors of the "reform-infested" Czechoslovakia. East Germany's position was doubly vulnerable, as that country was also exposed to the appealing democratic experience of West Germany, and Poland still remembered Gomulka's initial liberalizing measures after he came to power in 1956.

Even in the Soviet Union, the Czechoslovak Spring encouraged a new, outspoken dissent, and the example of a federalized Slovakia had a tremendous potential impact on the traditionally anti-Moscow Ukraine. Moscow, East Berlin, Warsaw, Sofia, and to a lesser extent, Budapest, perceived the poison of Czechoslovak freedom seeping into the bloodstream of their own establishments, made even more vulnerable by Prague's concept of a nonauthoritarian role for the Party.

In matters of sheer power, Moscow did not accept in good faith the CPC's assurances of fidelity to the Communist states' system of alliances—and perhaps with good reason in the light of its own understanding of loyalty. The Party's program did emphasize the close ties with the Warsaw Pact countries, but it spoke also of good relations with the West and Czechoslovakia's own contribution to the cause of peace. Such statements did not contradict Soviet official policy, except that they implied that Prague's foreign policy did not necessarily need Moscow's approval or coordination. Though, as a matter of principle, the Soviet government and the Party had for years repeatedly proclaimed their respect for the policy of noninterference in the domestic affairs of other countries, they viewed with deep suspicion the Czechoslovak reformers' enunciation of that same policy. Obviously, it made a difference who defined these generally proclaimed rules of international conduct and under what circumstances. Originating in Prague in the atmosphere of the Spring, such declarations had the scent of Ceauşescu and Tito about them and raised the spectre, for Moscow, of a Dubček with his own interpretation of sovereignty, equality, and independence. Though the years had seen great changes in certain measures, no Soviet leader, whether Stalin or Khrushchev or Brezhnev, had ever compromised Moscow's traditional efforts for dominance in the Communist world. The Czechoslovak experiment posed a potentially dangerous challenge to this role, one that might prove to be contagious.

Ideologically, the danger was equally serious. If Marxism permitted—as it did, in theory—"adjustment" according to the specific conditions pertaining to the historical cultural, social, and economic development of each or any individual country, there

would be no nation that could not take recourse to its own interpretation. Hence, the Czechoslovak Spring undermined the
CPSU's position of ideological supremacy as well as its political authority. With Maoism and Titoism already on the scene, each
claiming its own version of Moscow's claim, the CPSU could not
afford to have the heresy spread. In Moscow's view, invasion was
the necessary cure.

So the invasion took place, the heresy was crushed, the
"human face" was laid to rest.

A final, and in light of events, almost peripheral question
arises: why did the invasion come as such a total surprise, indeed a
shock, to the Communist leaders of the reform movement? Upon
his return from Moscow, Smrkovský had mused rather vaguely
that probably some "price" would be exacted, but never did he
imagine such an extreme one as occupation. This seems a strange
lack of foresight, for after all, the Communist parties of the Eastern
bloc (with the exception of Rumania) had collectively and individ-
ually sent a number of warnings to the Czechoslovak Party, and
their newspapers had parroted these accusations. Moreover, the
press accused the Western imperialists of preparing for active assistance to the "counter-revolution" in Czechoslovakia and, to prove
the point, a cache of arms—planted by Soviet agents—was "discovered" in Bohemia. The handwriting on the wall was there, but
the Communist leaders in Prague seemed not to see it.

Above all else, the brutal Soviet intervention in Hungary
and the obvious Soviet readiness to march into Poland in the fall
of 1956 were still fresh memories in the minds of everyone but
these Czechoslovak comrades. It is not surprising that the intelligence service lacked information about the actual preparations
for invasion by the "fraternal" armies, but it is astonishing that the
Hungarian precedent should have been overlooked.

Finally, the training of the Communist leaders in Prague
should be questioned. Did not the method of "scientific socialism"
teach them to analyze every situation objectively and to predict sci-
entifically, on the basis of "objective conditions," each course of
action and its outcome? Nor did the Party leaders follow Lenin's
rule on the importance of a political strategy of cool-headed, inex-

orable determination which suppresses emotional involvement. In the heady atmosphere of the Spring, they were carried away by the enthusiasm for change. Called to order by Moscow, their Communist will, which should have been steel after years of struggle, collapsed and, again swept away by emotion, they wept. There is surely something to be learned from the event, when disciplined Communists who had come to desire a "human face" for their socialism, under this pressure became themselves not Leninist—but human!

The only plausible explanation for their blindness is that they were completely sincere in their conviction that they were remaining faithful to the alliance with the Soviet Union, that their reforms were advancing the real cause of communism. They believed that they were "writing a new chapter in the history of Marxism-Leninism."

Or perhaps the answer is still simpler: the taste of some freedom created an insatiable appetite; during those moments in Czechoslovakia, the decades of Communist discipline gave way to the deeper meanings of its centuries-old history.

In the end, when the crisis was upon them, whether Communist discipline reasserted itself, or whether the age-old craft of survival snuffed out the will to be free, the inescapable invasion took place without the firing of a retaliatory shot.

Half a century earlier, Masaryk had called upon his nation to deaustrianize its spirit, to shake off the burden of the heritage of subservience, and to stand erect in full human dignity. During the Munich crisis, in spite of twenty years of remarkable effort, the burden still weighed too heavily on the minds and resolution of the Czechoslovak leadership. Then, in the late 1960s, the short few months of the Spring failed equally to destalinize the nation, that it might defend the freedom it had found again. Was it the burden of the twenty years of Stalin—or was it the burden of three centuries of dedication to human survival that led them to protest but not to resist?

The answer to that dreadful question lies beyond this moment. However, even now, as the nation lies prostrate, faint voices of dissent are dimly heard from time to time, through the Western press or in the quieter assemblies of academe. The spark is still there. One cannot doubt that it will flicker one day again into flame, and freedom will return to this land that is so essentially humane. And if again it dies, unprotected by the leaders and undefended by the people, then it will rise again and still again.

For whatever the answer to that fateful question may be, it is not the abdication of the ideal that is the meaning of Czechoslovak history. Rather, it is the unextinguishable spark. Given a leadership that itself so resolutely believes, as did "the Old Man," Thomas Garrique Masaryk, the nation will take up again its active role in mankind's never-ending struggle for freedom and social justice.

Bibliography

Documents

(It should be noted that original Czechoslovak documents are accessible for research purposes only to reliable Party members, and that those listed here and published during the Communist regime, were selected and possibly edited according to Party directives. It was only in the period of liberalization (1962–68) that Czechoslovak scholarship achieved, step by step, a remarkable level of quality, and produced what appears to be unedited primary sources. The date of publication is, therefore, of great importance in judging the authenticity of the documents.)

Československo-sovětské vztahy v době velké vlastenecké války 1941–1945: Dokumenty a materiály. Prague: Státní nakl. polit. literatury, 1960.
Cesta ke květnu: Dokumenty o vzniku a vývoji lidové demokracie v Československu do února 1948. Vol. I-1. Edited by M. Klimeš et al. Prague: Čs. akademie věd, 1965.
Chtěli nás vyhubit. Prague: Naše vojsko, 1961.

Dokumenty o vztazích československého lidu k národům SSSR v letech 1917–1945: Velká víra a naděje. Edited by Čestmír Amort. Prague: Státní pedagogické nakl., 1968.

Documenty z historie československe politiky 1939–1943: Acta Occupationis Bohemiae & Moraviae. 2 vols. Edited by L. Otáhalová and M. Červinková. Prague: Academia, 1966.

Doležal, Jiří and Křen, Jan, eds. *Czechoslovakia's Fight: Documents on the Resistance Movement of the Czechoslovak People, 1938–1945.* Prague: Čs. akademie věd, 1964.

Král, Václav. *Cestou k únoru: Dokumenty.* Prague: Svobodné slovo, 1963.

Král, Václav, ed. *Das Abkommen von München, 1938: Dokumente.* Prague: Academia, 1968.

————, ed. *Lesson from History: Documents Concerning Nazi Policies for Germanisation and Extermination in Czechoslovakia.* Prague: Orbis, 1962.

————. *Politické strany a Mnichov: Dokumenty.* Prague: Svobodné slovo, 1961.

Leták, Miroslav, ed. *V osidlech zrady: Dokumenty 1933–1938.* Prague: Svobodné slovo, 1965.

Mnichov v dokumentech. Prague: Státní nakl. polit. literatury, 1958.

National Archives. Diplomatic Branch, Record Group 59, General Records of the Department of State.

Pelikán, Jiří. *The Secret Vysočany Congress.* London: The Penguin Press, 1971.

Program nové československé vlády národní fronty Čechů a Slováků. Prague: Ministerstvo informací, 1945.

"Recollections and Reconstruction of the Czechoslovak February Crisis by a Group of Democratic Leaders" (in Czech; unpublished and untitled). Stenographic Report. London, 1949–50.

Remington, Robin A. *Winter in Prague: Documents on Czechoslovak Communism in Crisis.* Cambridge: MIT Press, 1969.

Rok šedesátýosmý v usneseních a dokumentech ÚV KSČ. Prague: Svoboda, 1969.

Ústav dějin Komunistické strany Československa. *Chtěli jsme bojovat: Dokumenty o boji KSČ a lidu na obranu Československa 1938.* 2 vols. Prague: Nakl. politické literatury, 1963.

Ústav pro mezinárodní politiku a ekonomii. *Dokumenty československé zahraniční politiky 1945–1960.* Prague: Státní nakl. politické literatury, 1960.

Založení komunistické strany Československa 1917–1924: Dokumenty. Prague: Státní nakladatelství politické literatury (n.d.).

Zasedání devíti komunistických stran: O založení informační kanceláře komunistických stran v Bělehradě. Prague: Svoboda (n.d.).

Za svobodu českého a slovenského národa: Sborník dokumentů k dějinám KSČ v 1938–1945. Prague: Státní nakl. polit. literatury, 1956.

Selected General Works

Albright, Madeleine Korbel. "The Role of the Press in Political Change: Czechoslovakia 1968." Ph.D. dissertation, Columbia University, 1976.

Amort, Čestmír. *Cesta ke svobodě: Historická fakta 1938–1945.* Prague: Ministerstvo školství (n.d.).

———. *Heydrichiáda.* Prague: Naše vojsko, 1965.

———. *SSSR a osvobození Československa.* Prague: Svoboda, 1970.

Bareš, Gustav. *Proti Mnichovu.* Prague: Státní nakl. politické literatury, 1958.

Barto, Jaroslav. *Riešenie vzťahu Čechov a Slovákov (1944–1948).* Bratislava: Epocha, 1968.

Barton, Paul. *Prague à l'heure de Moscou: Analyse d'une démocratie populaire.* Paris: Horay, 1954.

Bartoš, F. M. *Z dějin hesla Pravda vítězí* (n.p., n.d.).

Beckmann, Rudolf. *K diplomatickému pozadí Mnichova: Kapitoly o britské mnichovské politice.* Prague: Státní nakl. polit. literatury, 1954.

Beer, Ferdinand et al. *Dejinná križovatka: Slovenské národné povstanie—predpoklady a výsledky.* Bratislava: (n.p.), 1964.

Beneš, Edvard. *Czechoslovak Policy for Victory and Peace.* London: Czechoslovak Ministry of Foreign Affairs, 1944.

———. *Democracy Today and Tomorrow.* New York: The Macmillan Co., 1939.

———. *Masarykovo pojetí ideje národní a problém jednoty československé.* Bratislava: Učená společnost Šafaříkova, 1935.

———. *Mnichovské dny: Paměti.* Prague: Svoboda, 1968.

———. *Nová slovanská politika.* London: Čs. výbor pro slovanskou vzájemnost, 1943.

———. *Paměti: Od Mnichova k nové válce a novému vítězství.* Prague: Orbis, 1947.

———: *Světová válka a revoluce.* 3 vols. Prague: Čin and Orbis, 1928.

———. *Tři roky druhé světové války.* London: Čechoslovák (n.d.).

Bojový odkaz roku 1919: Spomienky bojovníkov za slovenskú Republiku rád a za maďarskú Republiku rád. Bratislava: Slov. vyd. polit. literatúry, 1960.

Bokeš, František. *Dejiny Slovenska a Slovákov od najstarších čias po oslobodenie.* Bratislava: Slovenská akadémia vied a umení, 1946.

Borovička, J. *Ten Years of Czechoslovak Politics.* Prague: Orbis, 1929.

Brabenec, Jiří. *ČSSR v kostce: Včera a dnes, doma a v cizině.* Prague: Lidová demokracie, 1960.

Brandes, Detlef. *Die Tschechen unter deutschem Protektorat.* Munich: Oldenbourg, 1969. Part I. *Besatzungspolitik, Kollaboration und Widerstand im Protektorat Böhmen und Mähren bis Heydrichs Tod (1939–1942).*

Bradley, J. F. N. *Czechoslovakia: A Short History.* Edinburgh: Edinburgh University Press, 1971.

Brock, Peter. *The Political and Social Doctrines of the Unity of Czech Brethren in the 15th and Early 16th Centuries.* The Hague: Mouton & Co., 1957.

Brock, Peter and Skilling. H. G., eds. *The Czech Renascence of the Nineteenth Century.* Toronto: University of Toronto Press, 1970.

Brod, Toman. *Na západní frontě.* Prague: Naše vojsko, 1965.

Bruegel, J. W. *Czechoslovakia before Munich: The German Minority Problem and British Appeasement.* London: Cambridge University Press, 1973.

———. *Tschechen und Deutsche, 1918–1938.* Munich: Nymphenburger Verlagshandlung, 1967.

Brzorád, Vilém J. *Economy of Czechoslovakia.* Washington, D.C.: Council for Economic and Industry Research, 1955.

Bušek, Vratislav and Spulber, Nicolas, eds. *Czechoslovakia.* New York: Praeger, 1957.

Butter, O. and Ruml, B. *La République Tchécoslovaque: Aperçu de la vie intellectuelle, politique, économique et sociale.* Prague: Orbis, 1921.

Čapek, Karel et al. *At the Cross-Roads of Europe: A Historical Outline of the Democratic Idea in Czechoslovakia.* Prague: P.E.N. Club, 1938.

———. *Hovory s T.G. Masarykem.* London: Allen & Unwin, 1941.

César, Jaroslav and Černý, Bohumil. *Politika německých buržoazních stran v Československu v letech 1918–1938.* 2 vols. Prague: Čs. akademie věd, 1962.

César, Jaroslav and Otáhal, Milan, eds. *Hnutí venkovského lidu v českých zemích v letech 1918–1922.* Prague: Čs. akademie věd, 1958.

Český národ soudí K. H. Franka. Prague: Ministerstvo informací, 1947.

Chaloupecký, V. *Zápas o Slovensko.* Prague: Čin, 1930.

Chalupný, E. *Národní filosofie československá.* 2 vols. Prague: (n.p.), 1932.

Chyba, Antonín. *Postavení dělnické třídy v kapitalistickém Československu.* Prague: Svoboda, 1972.

Císař, Čestmír. *S lety jsme rostli.* Prague: Státní nakl. polit. literatury, 1960.

Clementis, Vladimír. *Odkazy z Londýna.* Bratislava: Obroda, 1947.

———. *"Panslavizmus" kedysi a teraz.* London: Čs. výbor pre slovanskú vzájomnosť, 1943.

Czechoslovakia Fights Back. Washington, D.C.: American Council on Public Affairs, 1943.

Dean, Robert W. *Nationalism and Political Change in Eastern Europe: The Slovak Question and the Czechoslovak Reform Movement.* Denver: Monograph Series in World Affairs, 1973.

Dějiny Československa v datech. Prague: Svoboda, 1968.

Dějiny Komunistické strany Československa. Prague: Nakl. politické literatury, 1961.

Dérer, Ivan. *Slovenský vývoj a l'ud'ácká zrada.* Prague: Kvasnička a Hampl, 1946.

———. *The Unity of the Czechs and Slovaks.* Prague: Orbis, 1938.

Deset let lidově demokratického Československa 1945–1955. Prague: Čs. ústav zahraniční, 1955.

Deset let rozvoje národního hospodářství a kultury Čs. republiky, 1945–1955. Prague: Rudé právo, 1956.

Diamond, William. *Czechoslovakia between East and West.* London: Stevens, 1947.

Dobrý, Anatol. *Hospodářská krize československého průmyslu ve vztahu k Mnichovu.* Prague: Čs. akademie věd, 1959.

Doležal, Jiří. *Jediná cesta: Cesta ozbrojeného boje v českých zemích.* Prague: Naše vojsko, 1966.

Drtina, Prokop. *A nyní promluví Pavel Svatý.* Prague: V. Žikeš, 1945.

Dvacet let rozvoje československé socialistické republiky. Prague: Nakl. polit. lit., 1965.

Eisner, Pavel. *Chrám i turz: Kniha o češtině.* Prague: Podroužek, 1946.

Eubank, Keith. *Munich.* Norman, Okla.: University of Oklahoma Press, 1963.

Falťan, Samo. *Slovenská otázka v Československu.* Bratislava: Vydav. politickej literatúry, 1968.

Faltus, Jozef. *Stručný hospodářský vývoj Československa do roku 1955.* Prague: Svoboda, 1969.

Fierlinger, Zdeněk. *Ve službách ČSR.* 2 vols. Prague: Svoboda, 1951.

Filo, Milan. *Boj KSČ na Slovensku za obranu republiky v rokoch 1937–1938.* Bratislava: Slovenské vyd. pol. literatúry, 1960.

Firt, Julius. *Knihy a osudy.* Köln: Index, 1972.

Four Fighting Years. London: Hutchinson, 1943.

Friedman, Otto. *The Break-Up of Czech Democracy.* London: Golancz, 1950.

Friš, Edo. *Myšlienka a čin: Úvahy o Československu 1938–1948.* Bratislava: Vydavatelstvo politickej literatúry, 1968.

Gadourek, Ivan. *The Political Control of Czechoslovakia: A Study in Social Control of a Soviet Communist State.* Leiden: Stenfert Kroese, 1953.

Gajan, Koloman. *Německý imperialismus a československo-německé vztahy v letech 1918–1921.* Prague: Čs. akademie věd, 1962.

Gajanová, Alena. *ČSR a středoevropská politika velmocí.* Prague: Academia, 1967.

Golan, Galia. *The Czechoslovak Reform Movement: Communism in Crisis, 1962–1968.* London: Cambridge University Press, 1971.

———. *Reform Rule in Czechoslovakia. The Dubček Era, 1968–1969.* London: Cambridge University Press, 1973.

———. "The Democratic-Liberal Tradition in the Czech Land." A Paper. Hebrew University of Jerusalem (n.d.).

Gottwald, Klement. *Se Sovětským svazem na věčné časy.* Prague: Svět sovětů, 1955.

———. *Spisy.* Prague: Státní nakl. polit. literatury, 1953–61.

Grant Duff, Sheila. *Europe and the Czechs.* Harmondsworth, Middlesex: Penguin Books, 1938.

Graus, František et al. *Naše živá i mrtvá minulost.* Prague: Svoboda, 1968.

Gruber, Dr. Josef. *Czechoslovakia: A Survey of Economic and Social Conditions.* New York: The Macmillan Co., 1924.

Hajda, Jan, ed. *A Study of Contemporary Czechoslovakia.* Chicago: University of Chicago, for Human Relations Area Files, 1955.

Hájek, J. S. *Wilsonovská legenda v dějinách ČSR.* Prague: Státní nakl. politické literatury, 1953.

Hájek, Miloš. *Od Mnichova k 15. březnu.* Prague: Státní nakl. politické literatury, 1959.

Hamšík, Dušan. *Writers against Rulers.* London: Hutchinson, 1971.

Harkins, William and Šimončič, Klement. *Czech and Slovak Literature.* New York: Columbia University Press, 1950.

Hitchcock, Edward B. *I Built a Temple for Peace: The Life of Eduard Beneš.* New York: Harper, 1940.

Hoch, Karel. *The Political Parties in Czechoslovakia.* Prague: Orbis, 1936.

Hodža, Milan. *Federation in Central Europe: Reflections and Reminiscences.* London: Jarrolds, 1942.

Holá, Věra, Menclová, Jarmila, and Zumanová Božena, eds. *Vzpomínky na vznik KSČ.* Prague: Nakladateství polit. literatury, 1962.

Holesovsky, Vaclav. *Planning and Market in the Czechoslovak Reform.* New Haven, Conn.: Yale University Press, 1972.

Holotík, L'udovit. *Štefánikovská legenda a vznik ČSR.* Bratislava: Slovenská akadémie vied, 1960.

Hořec, Jaromír. *Cesty, ktoré viedli k Mníchovu.* Bratislava: ÚV KSS, 1955.

Husa, Václav. *Dějiny Československa.* Prague: Orbis, 1961.

Husák, Gustáv. *Svedectvo o Slovenskom národnom povstaní.* Bratislava: Vydavat. politickej literatúry, 1964.

Idea československého státu a lidová kultura. Prague: Státní nakladatelství, 1938.

Jablonický, Jozef. *Z ilegality do povstania.* Bratislava: Epocha, 1969.

Jancar, Barbara Wolfe. *Czechoslovakia and the Absolute Monopoly of Power: A Study of Political Power in a Communist System.* New York: Praeger, 1971.

Janeček, Oldřich. *Odboj a revoluce 1938–1945.* Prague: Naše vojsko, 1965.

Janeček, Oldřich et al., eds. *Z počátků odboje.* Prague: Naše vojsko, 1969.

Janin, Pierre T. *Milan Rastislav Štefánik.* Prague: Orbis, 1932.

Jelínek, Jaroslav. *Politické ústředí domácího odboje.* Prague: Kvasnička, Hampl, 1947.

Jelinek, Yeshayahu. "Slovakia and its Minorities 1935–1945—People with and without National Protection." Mimeographed. Haifa: University of Haifa, 1973.

———. "The Vatican, the Catholic Church, the Catholics, and the Persecution of the Jews during World War II: The Case of Slovakia." In *Jews and non-Jews in Eastern Europe,* edited by B. Vago and G. L. Mosse. New York: John Wiley, 1974.

Jindra, V. *Rudolf Beran: Dokumenty zrady.* Prague: Svoboda, 1946.

Kaplan, Karel. *Znárodnění a socialismus.* Prague: Práce, 1968.

Kapras, Jan, ed. *Idea československého státu.* 2 vols. Prague: Národní rada československá, 1936.

Kárník, Zdeněk. *Socialisté na rozcestí: Habsburk, Masaryk či Šmeral?* Prague: Svoboda, 1968.

Kennan, George F. *From Prague after Munich: Diplomatic Papers, 1938–1940.* Princeton, N.J.: Princeton University Press, 1968.

Kerner, Robert J., ed. *Czechoslovakia, Twenty Years of Independence.* Berkeley: University of California Press, 1940.

Ke vzniku ČSR: Sborník statí k ohlasu Říjnové revoluce a ke vzniku ČSR. Prague: Naše vojsko, 1958.

Kladiva, Jaroslav. *Kultura a politika (1945–1948).* Prague: Svoboda, 1968.

Kopecký, Václav. *ČSR a KSČ.* Prague: Státní nakl. polit. literatury, 1960.

———. *Tridsať rokov ČSR.* Bratislava: Poverenictvo informacií, 1948.

Korbel, Josef. *The Communist Subversion of Czechoslovakia, 1938–1948: The Failure of Coexistence.* Princeton, N.J.: Princeton University Press, 1959.

Kotrlý, Josef et al. *Pražské povstání 1945.* Washington, D.C.: Rada svobodného Československa, 1965.

Kozák, J. B. et al. eds. *Masarykova práce: Sborník ze spisů, řečí a projevů prvního presidenta Československé republiky.* Prague: Státní nakladatelství, 1930.

Král, Václav. *Pravda o okupaci.* Prague: Naše vojsko, 1962.

———. *Spojenectví československo-sovětskéí v evropské politice, 1935–1939.* Prague: Academia, 1970.

Kramer, Juraj. *Slovenské autonomistické hnutie v rokoch 1918–1919.* Bratislava: Slovenská akadémie vied, 1962.

Krejčí, Jaroslav. *Social Change and Stratification in Postwar Czechoslovakia.* New York: Columbia University Press, 1972.

Křen, Jan. *Do emigrace: Západní zahraniční odboj 1938–1939.* Prague: Naše vojsko, 1967.

———. *Mnichovská zrada.* Prague: Státní nakl. polit. literatury, 1958.

———. *V emigraci: Západní zahraniční odboj 1939–1940.* Prague: Naše vojsko, 1969.

Krofta, Kamil. *Bílá Hora.* Prague: Otto, 1913.

———. *Čechové a Slováci před svým státním sjednocením.* Prague: Orbis, 1932.

———. *Z dob naší první republiky.* Prague: Laichter, 1939.

———. *Žižka a husitská revoluce.* Prague: Laichter, 1936.

Kusin, Vladimir V. *The Intellectual Origins of the Prague Spring.* London: Cambridge University Press, 1971.

———. *Political Groupings in the Czechoslovak Reform Movement.* New York: Columbia University Press, 1972.

Kvaček, Robert. *Nad Evropou zataženo.* Prague: Svoboda, 1966.

Lettrich, Jozef. *History of Modern Slovakia.* New York: Praeger, 1955.

Liehm, Antonin J. *The Politics of Culture.* New York: Grove Press, 1972.

Littell, Robert. *The Czech Black Book.* New York: Praeger, 1969.

Lockhart, Sir Robert H. Bruce. *Jan Masaryk: A Personal Memoir*. New York: Philosophical Library, 1951.

———. *Retreat from Glory*. New York: Putnam's, 1934.

Loevenheim, Francis L. *Peace or Appeasement? Hitler, Chamberlain, and the Munich Crisis*. Boston: Houghton Mifflin, 1965.

Ludwig, Emil. *Defender of Democracy. Masaryk of Czechoslovakia*. New York: R. M. McBride, 1936.

Lukeš, František. *Podivný mír*. Prague: Svoboda, 1968.

Luža, Radomír. *The Transfer of the Sudeten Germans: A Study of Czech-German Relations, 1933–1963*. New York: New York University Press, 1964.

Lvová, Míla. *Mnichov a Edvard Beneš*. Prague: Svoboda, 1968.

Macek, J. *The Hussite Movement in Bohemia*. Prague: Orbis, 1965.

Machovec, Milan. *Husovo učení*. Prague: Československá akademie věd, 1953.

———. *Tomáš G. Masaryk*. Prague: Svobodné slovo, 1968.

Mainus, František. *Totální nasazení: Češi na pracích v Německu, 1939–1945*. Brno: Universita J. E. Purkyně, 1970.

Mamatey, Victor S. *The United States and East Central Europe: A Study of Wilsonian Diplomacy and Propaganda*. Princeton, N.J.: Princeton University Press, 1957.

Mamatey, Victor S. and Luža, R., eds. *A History of the Czechoslovak Republic 1918–1948*. Princeton: Princeton University Press, 1973.

Masaryk, Jan. *Ani Opona ani Most*. Prague: Vl. Žikeš, 1947.

———. *Volá Londýn*. Prague: Práce, 1947.

Masaryk, Tomáš Garrigue. *Česká otázka: Snahy a tužby národního obrození*. Prague: Pokrok, 1908.

———. *Cesta democracie*. 2 vols. Prague: Čin, 1933.

———. *Karel Havlíček: Snahy a tužby politického probuzení*. Prague: Laichter, 1896.

———. *Masaryk on Marx*. Edited and translated by Erazim V. Kohák. Lewisburg, Pa.: Bucknell University Press, 1972.

———. *The Meaning of Czech History*. Edited and with an introduction by René Wellek. Translated by Peter Kussi. Chapel Hill N.C.: University of North Carolina Press, 1974.

———. *The New Europe*. Lewisburg, Pa.: Bucknell University Press, 1972.

———. *Palackého idea národa českého*. Prague: Čin (n.d.).

———. *Problém malého národa*. Prague: Čin (n.d.).

———. *Světová revoluce za války a ve válce, 1914–1918*. Prague: Čin, 1925.

Mastny, Vojtech. *The Czechs under Nazi Rule: The Failure of National Resistance 1939–1942*. New York: Columbia University Press, 1971.

Michal, Jan M. *Central Planning in Czechoslovakia*. Stanford: Stanford University Press, 1960.

Mikus, Joseph A. *Slovakia: A Political History, 1918–1950*. Milwaukee, Wisc.: Marquette University Press, 1963.

Mlynář, Zdeněk. *Československý pokus o reformu 1968: Analýza jeho teorie a praxe*. Köln: Index, 1975.

Mlynárik, Ján. *Nezamestnanosť na Slovensku (1918–1938)*. Bratislava: Osveta, 1964.

Moravec, Frantisek. *Master of Spies: The Memoirs of General Frantisek Moravec*. New York: Doubleday, 1975.

Nedvěd, Jaroslav. *Cesta ke sloučení sociální demokracie s komunistickou stranou v roce 1948*. Prague: Academia, 1968.

Nejedlý, Zdeněk. *O smyslu českých dějin*. Prague: Svoboda, 1952.

──────. *T. G. Masaryk ve vývoji české společnosti a čs. státu*. Prague: Ministerstvo informací a osvěty, 1950.

Němec, František. *Social Security in Czechoslovakia*. London: Czechoslovak Ministry of Foreign Affairs, 1943.

Němec, František and Moudrý, Vladimír. *The Soviet Seizure of Subcarpatian Ruthenia*. Toronto: W. B. Anderson, 1955.

Německý imperialismus proti ČSR (1918–1939). Prague: Nakladatelství politické literatury, 1962.

Nové dokumenty k historii Mnichova. Prague: Státní nakladatelství politické literatury, 1958.

O československé zahraniční politice 1918–1939. Prague: Státní nakladateství politické literatury, 1956.

Olivová, Věra. *The Doomed Democracy: Czechoslovakia in a Disrupted Europe, 1914–1938*. London: Sidwick & Jackson, 1972.

──────. *Politika československé buržoasie v letech 1921–1923*. Prague: Čs. akademie věd, 1961.

Olivová-Pávová, Věra. *Československo-sovětské vztahy v letech 1918–1922*. Prague: Naše vojsko, 1957.

Olšovský, Rudolf et al. *Přehled hospodářského rozvoje Československa v letech 1918–1945*. Prague: Státní nakladateství politické literatury, 1961.

Olšovský, Rudolf et al. *Stručný hospodářský vývoj Československa do roku 1955*. Prague: Svoboda, 1969.

Opat, Jaroslav. *O novou demokracii, 1945–1948*. Prague: Čs. akademie věd, 1966.

Otáhal, Milan. *Zápas o pozemkovou reformu v ČSR*. Prague: Čs. akademie věd, 1963.

O vzájomných vzťahoch Čechov a Slovákov. Bratislava: Slovenská akadémie vied, 1956.

Oxley, Andrew et al., eds. *Czechoslovakia; The Party and the People*. New York: St. Martin's Press, 1973.

Paleček, Antonín. *Antonín Švehla. Selský vůdce a budovatel státu*. Prague: Státní nakladatelství, 1934.

──────. "Formative Years of the First Republic of Czechoslovakia. The Statemanship of Antonín Švehla." In *Czechoslovakia Past and Present*, edited by Miloslav Rechcigl, Jr. The Hague: Mouton, 1964.

Paul, David Warren. "Nationalism, Pluralism and Schweikism in Czechoslovakia's Political Culture." Ph. d. dissertation, Princeton University, 1973.

Pavlík, B., ed. KSČ v boji za svobodu. Prague: Svoboda, 1949.

Pekař, Josef. Masarykova česká filosofie. Prague: Historický klub, 1927.

⸻. O smysl našich dějin. Prague: Historický klub, 1929.

Peroutka, Ferdinand. Budování státu: Československá politika v letech popřevratových. 4 vols. Prague: Borový, 1934–36.

⸻. Jací jsme. Prague: Borový, 1934.

Piekalkiewicz, Jaroslav A. Public Opinion Polling in Czechoslovakia, 1968–1969: Results and Analysis of Survey Conducted During the Dubček Era. New York: Praeger, 1972.

Plevza, V. et al. eds. Prehlad dejín KSČ na Slovensku. Bratislava: Pravda, 1971.

Pomaizl, Karel. Vznik ČSR 1918: Problém marxistické vědecké interpretace. Prague: Čs. akademie věd, 1965.

Pražák, Albert. Smysl dvou revolucí. Prague: Herman, 1945.

Příspěvek k dějinám KSČ: Potlačená zpráva. Vienna: Europa-Verlag, 1970.

Procházka, Jan. Politika pro každého. Prague: Mladá fronta, (n.d.).

Prokeš, J. Základní problémy českých dějin. Prague: Svoboda, 1925.

První československý plán. Prague: Ministerstvo informací, 1946.

Rádl, Emanuel. O smysl našich dějin. Prague: Čin, 1925.

⸻. Válka Čechů s Němci. Prague: Čin 1928.

Rašín, Alois. Financial Policy of Czechoslovakia during the First Years of its History. Oxford: Clarendon Press, 1923.

Rechcigl, Miloslav, Jr., ed. Czechoslovak Contribution to World Culture. The Hague: Mouton, 1964.

Reimann, P. Geschichte der Kommunistischen Partei der Tschechoslovakei. Berlin: Hoym, 1929.

Reisky de Dubnic, Vladimir. Communist Propaganda Methods: A Case Study on Czechoslovakia. New York: Praeger, 1960.

Ripka, Hubert. Czechoslovakia Enslaved: The Story of the Communist Coup d'Etat. London: Gollancz, 1950.

⸻. Munich: Before and After. London: Gollancz, 1939.

Rozehnal, Alois. Unfulfilled Promises: Social Insurance in Czechoslovakia. Rome: Accademia cristiana cecoslovacca, 1961.

Salomon, Michel. Prague Notebook: The Strangled Revolution. Boston: Little, Brown, 1971.

Selucky, Radoslav. Czechoslovakia: The Plan that Failed. London: Thomas Nelson, 1970.

⸻. Economic Reforms in Eastern Europe: Political Background and Economic Significance. New York: Praeger, 1972.

Seton-Watson, Hugh. Eastern Europe Between the Wars 1918–1941. London: Cambridge University Press, 1946.

Seton-Watson, Robert W. History of the Czechs and Slovaks. London: Hutchinson, 1943.

Seton-Watson, Robert, ed. *Slovakia Then and Now*. London: Allen & Unwin, 1931.

Selver, Paul. *A Century of Czech and Slovak Poetry*. London: The New Europe, 1946.

Shawcross, William. *Dubcek*. New York: Simon and Schuster, 1970.

Sidor, Karol. *Andrej Hlinka*. Bratislava: Sv. Andrej, 1934.

Skilling, H. Gordon. *Communism National and International: Eastern Europe after Stalin*. Toronto: University of Toronto Press, 1964.

Slovenské národné povstanie: Nemci a Slovensko 1944. Dokumenty. Bratislava: Epocha, 1970.

Slovenské národné povstanie roku 1944: Sborník príspevkov z národno-oslovodzovacieho boja 1938–1945. Bratislava: Slovenská akadémie vied, 1965.

Smutný, Jaromír. *Únorový převrat 1948*. London: Ústav Dr. Edvarda Beneše pro politické a sociální studium, 1953.

Social Institute of the Czechoslovak Republic, ed. *Social Policy in the Czechoslovak Republic*. Prague: Orbis, 1924.

Soják, Vladimír, ed. *O československé zahraniční politice 1918–1939*. Prague: Státní nakl. polit. literatury, 1956.

Součková, Milada. *A Literature in Crisis: Czech Literature 1938–1950*. New York: National Committee for a Free Europe, 1954.

Steiner, Eugen, *The Slovak Dilemma*. London: Cambridge University Press, 1973.

Sterling, Claire. *The Masaryk Case*. New York: Harper, 1969.

Stloukal, Karel. *Československý stát v představách T. G. Masaryka za války*. Prague: Politický klub čs. narodní demokracie, 1930.

Štoll, Ladislav. *Umění a ideologický boj*. Prague: Svoboda, 1972.

Stránský, Jaroslav. *Hovory k domovu*. Prague: Borový, 1946.

Stránský, R. *The Educational and Cultural System of the Czechoslovak Republic*. Prague: Žikeš (n.d.).

Suda, Zdenek. *The Czechoslovak Socialist Republic*. Baltimore: The Johns Hopkins Press, 1969.

Šulc, Zdislav. *Ideály, iluze a skutečnost*. Prague: Svoboda, 1968.

Sviták, Ivan. *The Czechoslovak Experiment*. New York: Columbia University Press, 1971.

Svoboda, Ludvík. *Cestami života*. Vol. 1. Prague: Naše vojsko, 1971.

Szulc, Tad. *Czechoslovakia Since World War II*. New York: The Viking Press, 1971.

Táborský, Edward. *Communism in Czechoslovakia, 1948–1960*. Princeton, N.J.: Princeton University Press, 1961.

Tatu, Michel. *L'Hérésie impossible: Chronique du drame tchécoslovaque*. Paris: Grasset, 1968.

Thompson, Laurence V. *The Greatest Treason; the Untold Story of Munich*. New York: Morrow, 1968.

Thomson, S. Harrison: *Czechoslovakia in European History.* Princeton, N.J.: Princeton University Press, 1953.

Tigrid, Pavel. *Why Dubcek Fell.* London: Macdonald, 1971.

Tobolka, Zdeněk. *Politické dějiny československého národa od roku 1848 až do dnešní doby.* 5 vols. Prague: Československý kompas, 1932.

Ulč, Otto. *Politics in Czechoslovakia.* San Francisco: Freeman, 1974.

Ústav dějin Komunistické strany Československa. *Dějiny Komunistické strany Československa.* Edited by Pavel Reiman. Prague: Státní nakladatelství polit. literatury, 1961.

Vávra, J.; Lvová, M.; and Vávra, I., eds. *ČSSR-SSSR. Z bojů za svobodu a socialismus.* Prague: Československá akademie věd, 1961.

Velká říjnová socialistická revoluce a naše národní svoboda. Brno: Rovnost, 1950.

Veselý, Jindřich. *O vzniku a založení KSČ.* Prague: Státní nakl. polit. literatury, 1953.

Vietor, Martin. *Slovenská sovietska republika v r. 1919.* Bratislava: Slovenské vyd. polit. literatúry, 1955.

Vnuk, František. *Slovenská otázka na západe v rokoch 1939–1940.* Cleveland, Ohio: (n.p.), 1974.

Vondracek, Felix J. *The Foreign Policy of Czechoslovakia 1918–1935.* New York: Columbia University Press, 1937.

Vozka, Jaroslav. *Hrdinové domácího odboje.* Prague: Práce, 1946.

Wandycz, Piotr S. *France and Her Eastern Allies 1919–1925: French-Czechoslovak-Polish Relations from the Paris Peace Conference to Locarno.* Minneapolis, Minn.: University of Minnesota Press, 1962.

Warren, William Preston. *Masaryk's Democracy: A Philosophy of Scientific and Moral Culture.* Chapel Hill, N.C.: University of North Carolina Press, 1941.

Wellek, René. "Czech Literature and Slovak Literature." In *Columbia Dictionary of Modern European Literature,* edited by Horatio Smith. New York: Columbia University Press, 1947.

––––––. *Essays on Czech Literature.* The Hague: Mouton, 1963.

Weltsch, Felix. "A Critical Optimist." In *Edward Beneš: Essays,* edited by Jan Opočenský. London: Allen and Unwin, 1945.

Werstadt, Jaroslav. *O filosofii českých dějin: Palacký–Masaryk–Pekař.* Prague: Svaz národního osvobození, 1937.

Wheeler-Bennett, John W. *Munich: Prologue to Tragedy.* London: Macmillan, 1948.

Wiskemann, Elizabeth. *Czechs and Germans.* London: Oxford University Press, 1938.

Zacek, Josef F. *Slovakia and the National Revival: Introduction to a Case Study.* Reprint. The Hague: Mouton, 1973.

Za svobodu do nové Československé republiky: Ideový program domácího odbojového hnutí, vypracovaný v letech 1939–1941. Prague: Nová svoboda, 1945.

Zinner, Paul. *Communist Strategy and Tactics in Czechoslovakia 1918–1948.*
New York: Praeger, 1963.

Živé tradice: Kapitoly z národně osvobozeneckého a protifašistického boje naše-ho lidu. Prague: (n.p.), 1964.

Zločiny nacistů za okupace a osvobozenecký boj našeho lidu. Prague: Státní nakladateství politické literatury, 1961.

Změny v sociální struktuře Československa a dynamika sociálně politického vývoje. Prague: Svoboda, 1967.

Periodicals

Baláž, Ondrej. "Vývoj poľnohospodárstva na Slovensku v rokoch 1949–1960." *Historický časopis* 9, no. 1 (1961): 3–28.

Bartlová, Alena. "Slovensko-poľské vzťahy v rokoch 1919–1938." *Historický časopis* 20, no. 3 (1972): 363–84.

Betts, R. R. "The Influences of Realist Philosophy on John Hus and Predecessors in Bohemia." *Slavonic and East European Review* 29 (1951): 402–19.

Bouček, M. and Klimeš, M. "Národní fronta Čechů a Slováků a slovenská otázka." *Historický časopis* 21, no. 1 (1973): 1–20.

Burks, R. V. "The Decline of Communism in Czechoslovakia." *Studies in Comparative Communism* 2 (January 1969): 21–49.

"Cesta k 28. říjnu." Beseda s historiky. *Reportér* 3, no. 37 (September 26–October 2, 1968): 1–10.

Chalupný, Emanuel. "Realismus a mystika v české národní povaze." *Svědectví* 12, no. 46 (1973): 269–88.

"Čtvrtstoletí jedné neblahé události." *Svědectví* 12, no. 46: 252–68.

Dolezhal, I. and Grozienchik, I. "Mezhdunarodnaia solidarnosť v slovatskom national'nom vosstanii 1944 goda." *Voprosy istorii* No. 7 (July 1961): 70–80.

Ducháček, Ivo. "Záznam rozhovoru s šéfem zpravodajské služby českoslo-vesnké vlády v Londýně s plukovníkem Moravcem 5.4.1941." *Svědectví* 13, no. 49 (1975): 83–84.

Firt, Julius. "Cestou k únoru: Počátky byly v Londýně." *Svědectví* 12, no. 46 (1973): 211–51.

Gajanová, Alena. "K charakteru první republiky." *Historie a vojenství* No. 5 (1968): 797–823.

Galandauer, Jan. "T. G. Masaryk a československý stát." *Život strany* No. 17 (August 1968): 29–31.

Golan, Galia. "The Short-lived Liberal Experiment in Czechoslovak Socialism." *Orbis* 13, no. 4 (Winter 1970): 1096–1116.

Gosiorovský, Miloš. "K niektorým otázkam vzťahu Čechov a Slovákov v politike Komunistickej strany Československa." *Historický časopis* 16, no. 3 (1968): 354–406.

Hanák, Jiří. "Malá dohoda—Zdravá myšlenka." *Reportér* 3, no. 13 (March 27–April 3, 1968) and no. 30 (July 24–31, 1968).

Hauner, Milan. "Září 1938: kapitulovat či bojovat?" *Svědectví* 13, no. 49 (1975): 151–68.

Holotík, L. "Vznik Československa a jeho význam pre slovenský národ." *Historický časopis* 6, no. 4 (1958): 487–502.

Hunt, Richard. "The Denigration of Masaryk." *Yale Review* 43, no. 3 (1954): 414–26.

Janáček, František. "O čechoslovakismu a československství (1918–1938–1968)." *Reportér* 4, no. 7 (1968): 5–8.

Janáček, Oldřich. "Tomáš G. Masaryk." *Nová mysl* 22, no. 6 (1968): 680–89.

Jelinek, Jeshayahu. "Nationalism in Slovakia and the Communists, 1918–1929." *Slavic Review* 34, no. 1 (March 1975): 65–85.

Klimeš, Miloš and Zachoval, Marcel. "Příspěvek k problematice únorových událostí v Československu v únoru 1948." *Československý časopis historický* 6, no. 2 (1958): 186–233.

Kořalka, Jiří. "Cesta k 28 říjnu," *Reportér* 3, no. 41 (1968).

Král, Václav. "Československo a Mnichov." *Československý časopis historický* 7, no. 1 (1959): 25–48.

————. "Historická literatura o Mnichovu 1938." *Československý časopis historický* 22, no. 1 (1974): 31–56.

Křen, Jan. "Dr. Beneš za války." *Československý časopis historický* 13, no. 6 (1965): 797–826.

Kural, Václav. "Ke stykům mezi československým odbojem a SSSR v letech 1939–1941." *Historie a vojenství* No. 3 (1967): 437–71 (part I); No. 5, pp. 731–71 (part II).

Křížek, Jaroslav. "Ještě jednou k otázce ruského Října a vzniku ČSR." *Historie a vojenství* No. 5 (1968): 691–748.

————. "Říjnová revoluce a vznik Československa." *Politika* No. 8 (October 17, 1968): 9–12.

Kulíšek, Vladimír. "Úloha čechoslovakismu ve vztazích Čechů a Slováků (1918–1938)." *Historický časopis* 12, no. 1 (1964): 50–74.

Kvaček, Robert. "K bezprostřední diplomatické přípravě Mnichova." *Československý časopis historický* 6, no. 3 (1958): 409–46.

Laštovička, Bohuslav. "Vznik a význam košického vládního programu." *Československý časopis historický* 8, no. 4 (1960): 449–71.

Lederer, Jiří. "O politice zcela otevřeně" [Interview with Václav Slavík]. *Reportér* 3, no. 7 (February 14–21, 1968).

Liehm, Antonín J. [AJL]. "Two Days with Novomesky." *Kulturný život* (April 22, 1966). *Research Departments of Radio Free Europe* 1771–1811 (May 2, 1966).

Lipták, Ján. "Československo v evropské rezistenci za druhé světové války." *Historie a vojenství* No. 1 (1974): 86–97.

Lukeš, František. "Poznámky k čs.-sovětským stykům v září 1938." *Československý časopis historický* 16, no. 5 (1968): 703–32.

Luza, Radomir. "The Communist Party of Czechoslovakia and the Czech Resistance, 1939–1945." *Slavic Review* 28, no. 4 (December 1969): 561–76.

Lvová, Míla. "K otázce tzv. objednaného ultimata." *Československý časopis historický* 13, no. 3 (1965): 333–49.

Machovec, Milan. "Je naše vědecko-ateistická výchova správně orientována?" *Filosofický časopis* 13, no. 3 (1964): 354–61.

Magocsi, Paul R. "The Ruthenian Decision to Unite with Czechoslovakia." *Slavic Review* 34, no. 2 (June 1975): 360–81.

Mastný, Vojtěch. "Benešovy rozhovory se Stalinem a Molotovem." *Svědectví* 12, no. 47 (1974); 467–98.

Melichar, Václav. "Některé otázky obrany Československa v roce 1938." *Československý časopis historický* 22, no. 3: 321–26.

Mlynárik, J. "Vznik československého státu." *Reportér* 3, no. 41 (October 23–30, 1968).

Molok, F. "O traditsiakh proletarskogo internatsionalizma i antifashistskoi bor'by narodov Chekhoslovakii." *Voennoistoricheskii zhurnal* No. 5 (1967): 76–79.

Nedorezov, A. I. "Chekhoslovakiia v gody revoliutsii i stroitel'stva sotsializma." *Voprosy istorii* No. 5 (May 1970): 721–85.

———. "Narodnye massy Chekhoslovakii v bor'be za revoliutsionnye preobrazovaniia (1945–1948 g.)." *Voprosy istorii* No. 5 (May 1955): 66–78.

———. "Vydaiushcheesia sobytie v antifashistskom dvizhenii narodov Chekhoslovakii." *Voprosy istorii* No. 5 (May 1965): 65–76.

Nový, Lubomír. "T.G. Masaryk v českém myšlení." *Filosofický časopis* 14, no. 1 (1966): 22–44.

Olivová, Věra. "Československo-sovětská smlouva z roku 1935." *Československý časopis historický* 13, no. 4 (1965): 477–500.

Ort, Alexander. "Konstanty a kontinuita zahraniční politiky." *Reportér* 3, no. 22 (May 29–June 4, 1968).

Oschlies, Wolf. "Die kommunistische Partei der Tschechoslovakei in der ersten Tschechoslowakischen Republik (1918–1938)." Köln: *Berichte des Bundesinstituts für Ostwissenschaftliche und internationale Studien* No. 61 (1974).

Pfaff, Ivan. "Masaryk a dějiny." *Proměny* 12, no. 1 (January 1975): 1–10.

Pichlík, Karel. "Cesta k 28 říjnu," *Reportér* 3, no. 37 (1968).

Průcha, Václav. "Hospodářský profil předmnichovské republiky." *Nová mysl* 22, no. 3 (1968): 296–306.

Šik, Ota. "O straně včera a dnes." *Život strany* No. 17 (August 1968): 9–12.

Skilling, H. Gordon. "Communism and Czechoslovak Traditions." *Journal of International Affairs* 20, no. 1 (1966): 118–36.

Špičák, Milan and Lipták, Ján. "Únor 1948 a československé ozbrojené síly." *Československý časopis historický* 21, no. 3 (1973): 309–34.

Strhan, Milan. "K niektorým otázkam hospodárského vývinu Slovenska v rokoch 1918–1938." Historický časopis 9, no. 2 (1961): 201–28.

Táborský, Edward. "Beneš and the Soviets." Foreign Affairs 27, no. 2 (January 1949): 302–14.

———. "Beneš and Stalin—Moscow 1943 and 1945." Journal of Central European Affairs 13 (1953–54): 154–81.

Taborsky, Edward. "Triumph and Disaster of Eduard Beneš." Foreign Affairs 36 (July 1958): 669–84.

Tigrid, Pavel. "Jací jsme, když je zle." Svědectví 12, no. 46 (1973): pp. 303–20.

Tomáš, Petr. "Kapitoly z české geopolitiky." Svědectví 12, no. 45 (1973): 21–38.

Turchan, Pavel. "Sotsialisticheskaia industrializatsiia Slovakii." Voprosy istorii No. 5 (May 1959): 123–40.

Valenta, Jiri. "Soviet Decisionmaking and the 1968 Czechoslovak Crisis." Studies in Comparative Communism 8, nos. 1 and 2 (Spring/Summer 1975): 147–73.

Vesely, Indrzhikh. "O prichinakh vozniknoveniia i gibeli burzhuaznogo chekhoslovatskogo gosudarstva." Voprosy istorii No. 11 (November 1958): 107–25.

"Vznik československého státu." Beseda s historiky. Reportér. 3, no. 41 (October 23–30, 1968): 1–11.

Wellek, René. "The Cultural Situation in Czechoslovakia." Slavonic Review 14, (1936): 622–38.

———. "The Philosophical Basis of Masaryk's Political Ideals." Ethics 55, no. 4 (1945): 298–304.

Werstadt, Jaroslav. "The Philosophy of Czech History." The Slavonic Review 3, no. 9 (March 1925): 533–46.

Willars, Christian. "Znovu: Smysl českých dějin." Svědectví 12, no. 46 (1973): pp. 289–301.

Zacek, Joseph F. "Palacký's Politics: The Second Phase." Canadian Slavic Studies 5, no. 1 (Spring 1971): 51–69.

Index